AF147539

Managing Emotions in Journalism

Maja Šimunjak

Managing Emotions in Journalism

A Guide to Enhancing Resilience

Maja Šimunjak
Department of Media
Middlesex University London
London, UK

ISBN 978-3-031-38630-5   ISBN 978-3-031-38631-2   (eBook)
https://doi.org/10.1007/978-3-031-38631-2

© The Editor(s) (if applicable) and The Author(s), under exclusive licence to Springer Nature Switzerland AG 2023

This work is subject to copyright. All rights are solely and exclusively licensed by the Publisher, whether the whole or part of the material is concerned, specifically the rights of translation, reprinting, reuse of illustrations, recitation, broadcasting, reproduction on microfilms or in any other physical way, and transmission or information storage and retrieval, electronic adaptation, computer software, or by similar or dissimilar methodology now known or hereafter developed.
The use of general descriptive names, registered names, trademarks, service marks, etc. in this publication does not imply, even in the absence of a specific statement, that such names are exempt from the relevant protective laws and regulations and therefore free for general use.
The publisher, the authors, and the editors are safe to assume that the advice and informa-tion in this book are believed to be true and accurate at the date of publication. Neither the publisher nor the authors or the editors give a warranty, expressed or implied, with respect to the material contained herein or for any errors or omissions that may have been made. The publisher remains neutral with regard to jurisdictional claims in published maps and institutional affiliations.

Cover illustration: © Kamila Bay/shutterstock

This Palgrave Macmillan imprint is published by the registered company Springer Nature Switzerland AG
The registered company address is: Gewerbestrasse 11, 6330 Cham, Switzerland

ACKNOWLEDGEMENTS

I didn't think I'd ever write a textbook. Yet, here it is—inspired and made possible by dozens of journalists who shared with me their experiences of everyday work, talking frankly about their highs and lows. This book is about them and for them. A special thank you goes to journalists who share their stories of working in this thrilling, yet often challenging profession in the book's vignettes—Aubrey Allegretti, Kurt Barling, Alden Bentley, Rachael Dexter, Sian Elvin, Leona O'Neill, Maja Sever, Haroon Siddique and Sarah Taillier.

My gratitude also goes to colleagues in the Media Department, especially Anna Charalambidou, James Graham, Sophie Knowles and Giannina Warren, who were wonderful advisers and cheerleaders. Throughout writing this book I reminisced about my newsroom life, so it's only fair to thank my fellow journalists and editors too, as they made newsroom life exciting and worth writing about. I owe much to family and friends as well. Above all, happiness.

Finally, the support received from the Arts and Humanities Research Council and Middlesex University's Faculty of Arts and Creative Industries in data gathering, analysis and writing of this textbook has been much appreciated. Also, I acknowledge that some sections of the Introduction chapter have been previously published by Sage journals in: Šimunjak, M. (2023). Teaching Emotional Intelligence for Enhancing Resilience in Journalism. *Journalism & Mass Communication Educator*, 78(2), 127–141.

CONTENTS

LIST OF TABLES

CHAPTER 1

Introduction: Emotional Intelligence & Resilience in Journalism

Frustration would come about often in the early stages. So, a story breaks and you can't find the right person to interview, or you can't get to where you need to be quickly enough, so there can be a lot of, kind of, frustration in the early stages.

And then maybe as the story develops, the day develops, you might have a bit of excitement, you get something really great, you get the interviewee you've been striving for. Or, equally, anxiety begins to set in, maybe about the deadline looming and you haven't got what you need, and you start worrying, or something's gone wrong.

And then there's normally kind of the nervousness of the last half an hour because you're rushing to get the report out where you're going live. And then often after the program there's, like, elation... There's, like, kind of, like the adrenaline rush and the endorphins of having hopefully had a successful day.

—Mid-career broadcast editor

Journalism textbooks often describe journalism as 'exciting.' There are occasionally other references to journalists' emotions too—mainly about the thrill of chasing a story or making a discovery, and sometimes about the nervousness and anxiety of working with sources and doing interviews. However, it is uncommon to see detailed accounts of emotions that the broadcast editor, quoted above, speaks of, or how to manage these while doing the job. This may not be surprising given that the

© The Author(s), under exclusive license to Springer Nature Switzerland AG 2023
M. Šimunjak, *Managing Emotions in Journalism*, https://doi.org/10.1007/978-3-031-38631-2_1

1

acknowledgement and discussions of emotions in journalists' practice has been seen at odds with the ideas, or indeed ideals, of journalists' rationality, objectivity and detachment (Kotisova, 2019; Wahl-Jorgensen & Pantti, 2021). And yet, my own experience of working in journalism, and working with journalism trainees, tells a somewhat different story about journalists' work. I found it to be quite an emotional experience, with emotions making themselves known in most parts of the process, very much in line with how the broadcast editor describes it above. The emotional journey that is journalism seems also quite evident to my journalism students, who often reference their emotions in producing journalistic work, say in their reflective essays. They speak of being frustrated with finding stories, nervous about approaching sources, anxious ahead of interviews and worried whether their copy will meet the standards of journalism. Add in a microphone or a camera, as well as quick turnaround and short deadlines that they work to on Newsdays, in which we simulate daily news programming, and the fear and anxiety often translate to strong physical reactions. These sometimes include 'freeze,' meaning they have trouble completing the work, and sometimes 'flight,' which in a training environment usually means not showing up for class due to being terrified of everything that needs to be done. The conventional wisdom in the industry, perpetuated even by some textbooks, is that if you can't 'handle it,' you should reconsider your career choice. I disagree. Yes, journalism may not be for everyone, but if journalists are not trained in how to 'handle it,' then why do we expect them to? In other words, while there are set procedures and routines in journalism that journalists are inducted into to become members of the profession, then why don't we also train them in how to manage the various emotions that arise in the process, given they can have significant impact on their well-being and the quality of work they produce? This book is aimed at precisely that—raising awareness of different emotional situations that practitioners are likely to encounter on the job, and offering guidance on emotion management strategies they can use in order to be able to do quality work while also feeling good about themselves and their work. As such, it does not substitute journalism textbooks that outline key skills, routines and expectations of the profession—it complements them by focusing on the skill that has been mainly overlooked in journalism education and training—emotion management.

EMOTIONAL LABOUR[1]

The skill of emotion management is increasingly being recognised in journalism as research in the past decade repeatedly found it to be a high emotional labour job—that in which practitioners face a range of stressors in everyday work and have to manage the emotions that arise in the process in order to be able to continue doing their jobs (Gascón et al., 2021; Pearson & Seglins, 2022; Thomson, 2021). The stressors and emotional situations range from reporting about trauma and conflict, over anxiety about approaching sources and presenting live broadcasts, to worry about posting content on social media due to perceived hostility of these spaces (Šimunjak & Menke, 2022). The persistent stressors in everyday work of journalists arguably contribute to a range of ill-effects of work, impacting journalists' well-being, job satisfaction and commitment and consequently also the quality of work they produce (Monteiro et al., 2016; Thomson, 2021). It, hence, does not surprise that many studies looking at journalists' labour and its effects find concerning levels of stress, anxiety and burnout among this group of professionals (Gascón et al., 2021; Pantoja Lima et al., 2022; Pearson & Seglins, 2022; Posetti et al., 2021). Yet, in an industry that has long perpetuated the myth of its labourers 'handling it' by having 'thick skin' (Chen et al., 2020; McCaffrey, 2019; Posetti et al., 2021), the recognition of the need to develop support systems for journalists' well-being has only recently started gaining ground.

The social and organisational behaviour literature argues that a worker's well-being can be supported through three key systems: workers' personal resources, social support from peers and supervisors, and organisational support, based on employers implementing fair and transparent systems, offering developmental training and so on (Aldamman et al., 2019; Roodbari et al., 2021; Shanock et al., 2019). The focus of this book is on the first pillar, i.e., the personal resources that labourers can employ in managing emotional challenges and stressors in order for these not to have a negative impact on their well-being and work. Specifically, the

---

[1] Some of the content presented in this chapter has been previously published in: Šimunjak, M. (2023). Teaching Emotional Intelligence for Enhancing Resilience in Journalism. *Journalism & Mass Communication Educator, 78*(2), 127–141. https://doi.org/10.1177/10776958231165103 (published by SAGE journals in April 2023).

book deals with the issue of developing one of the key personal resources in labour—resilience (Luthans et al., 2006).

Consequently, the book introduces a tailored approach to enhancing resilience among practising journalists, as well as emerging professionals, such as journalism students, which can assist them in dealing with emotional situations and stressors they are likely to experience on the job.

RESILIENCE

Resilience is considered to be the ability to cope with a difficulty and bounce back from it (Rajan-Rankin, 2014; Tucker, 2021). The body of work on 'psychological capital' (PsyCap) provides a useful framework for understanding its importance in labour. PsyCap is defined as 'an individual's positive psychological state of development that is characterized by the following:

(a) having confidence (self-efficacy) to take on and put in the necessary effort to succeed at challenging tasks;
(b) making a positive attribution (optimism) about succeeding now and in the future;
(c) persevering toward goals and, when necessary, redirecting paths to goals (hope) in order to succeed; and
(d) when beset by problems and adversity, sustaining and bouncing back and even beyond (resiliency) to attain success' (Luthans et al., 2007).

Hence, resilience is understood as one of workers' personal resources—alongside efficacy, optimism and hope—that enables them to feel and perform well in work life (Youssef-Morgan & Dahms, 2017). Importantly, there is evidence to suggest that each of these characteristics are developable and measurable (Luthans et al., 2008; Youssef-Morgan & Dahms, 2017), and that increase in this psychological capital can contribute to lower stress levels, increased job satisfaction and work commitment (Avey et al., 2009, 2011; Paek et al., 2015) and improved job performance (Luthans et al., 2010; Paterson et al., 2014).

There has been much scholarly attention devoted to the study of resilience in the workplace setting in the past decade (Hartmann et al., 2020; King et al., 2016; Robertson et al., 2015). The research has been focused on the analysis of resilience among professionals in occupations characterised with high levels of stress and burnout (Vanhove et al., 2016), giving evidence about, for example, resilience among Australian nurses (Delgado et al., 2021), Chinese bankers (Cooke et al., 2019) and American police officers (McCraty & Atkinson, 2012). However, there are warnings that resilience also matters in work settings where there may not be severe and intense stressors, yet there are everyday stressors whose effects accrue (Vanhove et al., 2016).

Journalists as labourers are at risk of both types of these work experiences that require resilience. On the one hand, journalists covering trauma and conflict are regularly faced with acute stressors while performing work (Barnes, 2016; Buchanan & Keats, 2011; Feinstein et al., 2002). On the other hand, the workings of the industry, which involve, but are not limited to, long and irregular working hours, requirement of constant availability, multiplatform production in limited timeframes, social media abuse and precarious working conditions, can be seen as everyday stressors which can over time lead to chronic stress and burnout (Miret, 2021; Pearson & Seglins, 2022). And while research into resilience in journalism is underdeveloped, existing rare studies provide some insight into this personal resource in the industry. With regard to trauma reporting, the report from Dart Centre based on a survey of journalists across the world found that the majority of trauma and conflict reporters undergo safety training, with rare useful training offered in building resilience and self-care (Slaughter et al., 2017). Consequently, Murphy and colleagues (2020) trialled a more holistic training that heavily focused on the development of resilience alongside safety skills and found evidence of its effectiveness in preparing journalists for trauma reporting. Similarly, it has been suggested that induction into and regular practice of 'mindfulness-based meditation' could help trauma and conflict journalists build resilience for coping with the demands of their beats (Pearson et al., 2021), as can regular debriefs with peers and colleagues which allow emotional release and support (Barnes, 2016). An interesting perspective on journalists' resilience is also that from neuroscience as reported in Swart's (2017) study which examined journalists' lifestyle, health and behaviour, as well as blood and heart rate. She found that journalists' resilience was impacted by poor sleep which contributes to stress and impedes stress recovery, suggesting this could be partly mitigated with better hydration and reduction in intake of alcohol and caffeine. What this short overview illustrates is that the importance of resilience as a personal resource in journalists' work is gaining recognition, yet there is limited insight into its levels and development, particularly beyond trauma reporting.

In sum, resilience is considered as one of the key personal resources that workers need to effectively cope with difficulties they face in work, and there is increasing recognition of its importance in journalism. Yet, little attention has been paid to development of this resource among journalists who are not perceived to be regularly faced with acute stress deriving from coverage of trauma and conflict but can experience chronic stress and burnout.

Emotional Intelligence: Stop, Think, Choose

Useful and transferable practices for enhancing resilience that is needed for managing everyday stressors could be adopted from related disciplines. Notably, studies from work sociology and psychology suggest that work-related stress can be mitigated with emotional intelligence, which enables workers to effectively manage their emotions, which in turn contributes to development of emotional resilience (Durán et al., 2004; Extremera et al., 2018; Sarrionandia et al., 2018). Emotional intelligence is, as resilience, considered a developable skill—one that enables a person to recognise, understand and manage own and others' emotions in a way which leads to positive outcomes (e.g., relieves stress, enables effective communication etc.) (Pérez-González et al., 2020). The logic of the argument is that by developing emotional intelligence, that is, being able to recognise and effectively manage work-related emotions, labourers are better able to cope with emotional situations they face in the job and bounce back more easily after experiencing these challenges. Importantly, based on the suggestions for development of other elements of PsyCap (Luthans et al., 2007; Youssef-Morgan & Dahms, 2017), growth in emotional intelligence has also the potential to increase other factors of PsyCap.

A useful model of emotional intelligence is based on the 'Stop, think, choose' practice. As the name suggests, the model is based on a three-step process of emotion management: its recognition (stop), understanding (think) and management (choose) (Mapes, 2000). In other words, it suggests that a person in an emotional situation should stop and consider what they are feeling and why they feel like this, and then think about options for going forward and choosing the one they feel most comfortable with. In this way, even if the outcome is not as positive as one would expect or hope for, there is evident agency over choices and emotions. Importantly, applying the 'stop, think, choose' model must be 'active and experiential, not just verbal and cognitive' meaning that the process should be practised over time in order for the skill to be developed and internalised (Matthews et al., 2012: 181).

The 'stop' step requires the recognition that one is in an emotion-inducing situation. One of the simplest ways to understand the rise of emotions is through the ABC model in which A stands for an activating event, B for the belief about what is happening, or what the outcomes might be, and C for consequences—emotions and behaviours—triggered by beliefs about the activating event. Sometimes these consequences, particularly emotions, are quite clear. If we perceive a threat, in any shape or form it might be, our bodies have a physical reaction to it that includes the release of adrenaline and cortisol, increased blood pressure and heart rate, tensing of muscles and so on. So, if our bodies are telling us that we're dealing with a high-pressure situation, through shaking hands, sweating and pounding hearts, we are usually aware that we are in a situation of heightened emotions. Yet, we can be experiencing emotional situations even if we're not fully aware of them. We can feel sad, angry, frustrated or anxious, without being able to put our finger on it. This might be evident in feeling less motivated to do work, having less energy to complete tasks, getting easily annoyed and/or lashing out at others, particularly if it's out of character. Hence, recognising an emotional situation and being able to identify the emotions we are feeling in that moment is a process that is not always easy nor straightforward. It requires practice and skill. So, the first step is to 'stop' to acknowledge and recognise the emotions that are being experienced.

The next step is 'think' which enables us to understand why we are feeling what we're feeling. A long time ago, Greek philosopher Epictetus has been noted as saying that people are not disturbed by things, but by the views they take of them. And this is at the heart of the 'think' stage—identifying what it is that is driving emotions in regard to the activating event. In line with Epictetus' observation, research from psychology is telling us that it is usually our beliefs, values, expectations and experiences that are influencing our perceptions of the activating event and driving the emotions associated with it. It is important here to distinguish between beliefs and values. In simple terms, beliefs are the assumptions we are making about the world around us and the events we expect or live through. So, belief is what we think/believe is happening and what the potential outcomes might be in any given situation. Importantly, these views on an event can be reframed and changed. Values are the standards on which we evaluate the world, its objects, subjects and events. They are tied to the worth we assign to objects and behaviours. Values are also enduring, yet subject to change throughout different stages of life; hierarchical, meaning that some will be more important than others; and individualistic, as each person has their own set of values that drive their emotions and actions. Hence, if we experience a situation we believe will lead to good outcomes, or is in line with our values, we're likely to experience positive emotions. Equally, if we think that an activating event is not in line with our values, and/or we believe that it poses a threat of some sort, negative emotions arise. As with the first step, identifying the drivers of our emotions is sometimes quite straightforward, while at other times there is a need to think through the beliefs and values that one associates with an event in order to understand emotions that are being experienced. This can often be quite challenging, particularly in the early days of employing this practice, but it is a skill that can be trained and mastered.

This brings us to the last step—'choose'. Only when we've realised why we feel what we feel can we make a conscious decision of how to respond to the situation, rather than simply react to it. The 'freeze, flight or fight' reactions have been well documented and researched in psychology. The freeze meaning a person is unable to move or act, flight referring to running away from the perceived threat and fight indicating a usually aggressive facing of the threat. These are considered to be subconscious reactions of human bodies to situations of perceived threats. The 'stop, think and choose' model of emotional intelligence enables us to consciously respond to the stressor, instead of engaging in these subconscious reactions. The response options will vary between situations and individual circumstances, as will the decisions of the best way forward in order to achieve the best possible outcome. Sometimes finding the best option to respond is a process of trial and error while the response that leads to the preferred outcome is identified. Yet, by making a conscious choice about the way to manage a situation and our own behaviour we are likely to feel better even if we did not fully achieve our desired outcome simply by taking control of the situation, and not feeling like things are happening to us without having a say in them.

ENHANCING RESILIENCE IN JOURNALISM

Based on interviews with more than 30 British journalists, and personal reflections on working as a reporter, presenter and editor, as well as teaching journalism, this book offers a practical guide to managing stressors and emotions in everyday journalism work. Specifically, the data about the common emotional situations in journalism, and the strategies that can be used to manage these, are derived from interviews with British journalists from 15 different organisations. Interviewed journalists vary in terms of gender, levels of seniority, years of experience in the industry and their medium's geographical reach. Journalists' responses to questions about emotional situations they face in everyday work and strategies they use to deal with them have been explored with thematic analysis following the procedure from Ayres (2008). The analysis revealed that emotional situations faced in daily work routines of reporters can be grouped under seven key themes:

(1) **finding stories and pitching**—there can be excitement, as well as anxiety and the pressure of responsibility that can be induced by finding scoops or being assigned to cover a 'big story'; anxiety, fear and/or worry in situations in which a journalist does not have a story; as well as emotions of hopefulness and often anxiety about pitch's reception by editor; and frustration with a rejected pitch.

(2) **working with sources and interviewing**—there can be nervousness of contacting sources; frustration with non-responsive sources or those who appear to be withholding information; feelings of responsibility towards telling their stories and protecting them from harm; excitement and satisfaction, as well as anxiety related to conducting interviews; worry about displaying inappropriate emotions (particularly in trauma-related interviews), and difficulties in dealing with vicarious emotions.

(3) **research and writing**—there can be excitement with uncovering an important piece of information; frustration with time-consuming or challenging research; worry about story's accuracy; and anxiety about writing in a detached and balanced manner.

(4) **live broadcasting and presenting**—there can be fear and/or excitement that leads to adrenaline surge and cause some to thrive off this pressure and enter 'tunnel vision' and others to experience adrenaline anxiety; as well as nervousness related to performing;

and fears about issues that might arise when reporting from environments that cannot be fully controlled or require many technical elements to operate as planned.

(5) **reflection and feedback**—there can be feelings of pride and satisfaction when positively evaluating your work, as well as receiving positive feedback within and outside the newsroom; the anxiety and frustration that come with the lack of feedback from editors and/ or audiences; and the anxiety, frustration, anger and sadness when the feedback is critical and/or negative.

(6) **working with social media**—there can be frustration arising from the pressure to do work with social media; the anxiety and nervousness about posting content given the perceived negativity of social media spaces; and the frustration, sadness, anxiety and anger with received abuse and harassment on these platforms.

(7) **speed of process & 24/7 journalism**—there can be anxiety related to meeting deadlines; exhaustion caused by the need to be 'always on;' and frustration with work-life conflict caused by overwork.

The analysis showed that journalists most commonly apply four key emotion management strategies to deal with these emotional situations:

(1) **Verbal processing**, which entails speaking about their experiences with peers, personal networks, but also counselling in some cases.

(2) **Internal processing**, that is, thinking about situations that trigger emotions and reframing the beliefs and expectations that are leading to upsetting emotions.

(3) **Boundary setting**, often applied to the use of digital technologies, which refers to setting boundaries which can help prevent emotional labour or give space to process and manage emotions.

(4) **Attentional deployment**, that is, refocusing attention, which comes in two key forms: focusing on professional routines (including breaking down a stress-inducing activity into manageable steps—'stepping') and focusing attention to non-work-related activities that induce happiness, to balance negative with positive emotions.

The book is organised around the above outlined key themes of journalists' work, describing in relation to each the key emotional situations
journalists may face, followed by advice from practitioners suggesting
strategies for effective management of these emotions. The potential
emotional situations, and common strategies for managing emotions in
these, are mapped against the 'stop, think, choose' model of emotional
intelligence in each chapter. Specifically, the list of emotional situations
speaks directly to the 'stop' phase, as gaining awareness of them can
increase journalists' ability to recognise an emotional situation. The
common emotion management strategies are related to the 'choose'
phase, given they represent assets from which to choose from to manage
stressors.

It is important to emphasise here that, in line with the concept of
emotional intelligence, interviews showed that emotions are subjective,
meaning that different individuals may experience different emotions and
choose different strategies for managing them, when faced with the same
situation. For example, the prospect of being tasked with covering the
story of the day may induce feelings of happiness in one person, and
of fear in another. In the latter case, one journalist may wish to relieve
that fear by consulting with peers or editor (verbal processing), while
another may apply 'stepping' (attentional deployment) to make the task
appear more manageable through the process of following procedures and
routines.

Given this, it is important to recognise that the emotional situations and strategies discussed in the book are neither prescriptive nor
comprehensive. Rather, the aim of the book is to raise awareness about
potential emotional situations that might be expected in the job, so journalists are better prepared to face them; provide suggestions of practical
emotion management strategies that can serve as assets in the process; and
equip practitioners with the knowledge of a useful process of emotion
management (i.e., 'stop, think, choose') that they can apply in critical
reflection on their work, which can enhance their emotional intelligence
and resilience and consequently, enable them to feel and perform better
in the workplace.

It is worth mentioning also what the book does not do. The data is
derived primarily from accounts of staff journalists, so it does not speak to
some of the specific circumstances that may be emotion-inducing to freelancers in the industry, such as the issues of precarious labour. Also, while
trauma reporting is mentioned in some chapters, the book focuses on

journalists' everyday work, rather than these specific contexts. In addition, the book deals with experiences of British journalists which may not be transferable to other contexts. That said, there is evidence to suggest that many of their experiences are common to those in some other journalistic cultures. Where this may be the case, there are references to evidence from these other contexts. Several journalists' vignettes from other countries, including the US, Australia and Croatia, that can be found across the book, attest to it as well.

Finally, while the book is focused on journalists' personal resource of resilience, it needs emphasising that it is not arguing that personal resources are the answer to all issues in journalists' labour. Rather, as mentioned earlier in this chapter, they are one pillar of support for journalists' well-being. As such, they are not a substitute for, but are complementary to, systems of social and organisational support that should also be in place to safeguard journalists' well-being and the quality of journalism.

EXERCISES: RESILIENCE LEVEL AND VALUES

As mentioned, emotions are often driven by values and response to stressors will partly depend on an individual's resilience levels. Before learning more about potential stressors and emotional situations in different aspects of journalists' everyday work, as well as possible responses to these, it might be useful to establish your starting points in terms of resilience levels and key values you hold that may impact on the way you perceive and interpret challenging situations. Hence, the following two practical exercises are aimed at raising self-awareness about personal values, as well as individual resilience levels.

Resilience Level

Step 1: This is Brief Resilience scale.[2] Indicate to what degree you agree with each statement. For each statement, circle the corresponding number or make a note of it.

---

[2] Brief resilience scale according to Smith et al. (2008).

	Strongly disagree	Disagree	Neutral	Agree	Strongly agree
I tend to bounce back quickly after hard times	1	2	3	4	5
I have a hard time making it through stressful events	5	4	3	2	1
It does not take me long to recover from a stressful event	1	2	3	4	5
It is hard for me to snap back when something bad happens	5	4	3	2	1
I usually come through difficult times with little trouble	1	2	3	4	5
I tend to take a long time to get over setbacks in my life	5	4	3	2	1

Step 2: Add the numbers you've chosen for all statements and divide the sum by 6. This is your Brief resilience scale score.

BRS score	Interpretation
1.00–2.99	Low resilience
3.00–4.30	Normal resilience
4.31–5.00	High resilience

Values

Step 1: From the list of basic human values,[3] choose 5 that are most important to you. Then put them in a hierarchical order.

Ambition	Daring	Obedience
Authority	Friendship	Pleasure
Adventure	Freedom	Politeness
Broadminded	Health	Respect for tradition
Capable	Helpfulness	Self-discipline
Choosing own goals	Humble	Sense of belonging
Cleanliness	Independence	Social recognition
Creativity	Influence	Tolerance
Enjoying life	Loyal	Varied life
Equality	Moderate	Wealth

Step 2: Record the five values on the Values map (Fig. 1.1). Is there a category that is most important to you?

[3] Basic human values according to Schwartz et al. (2006).

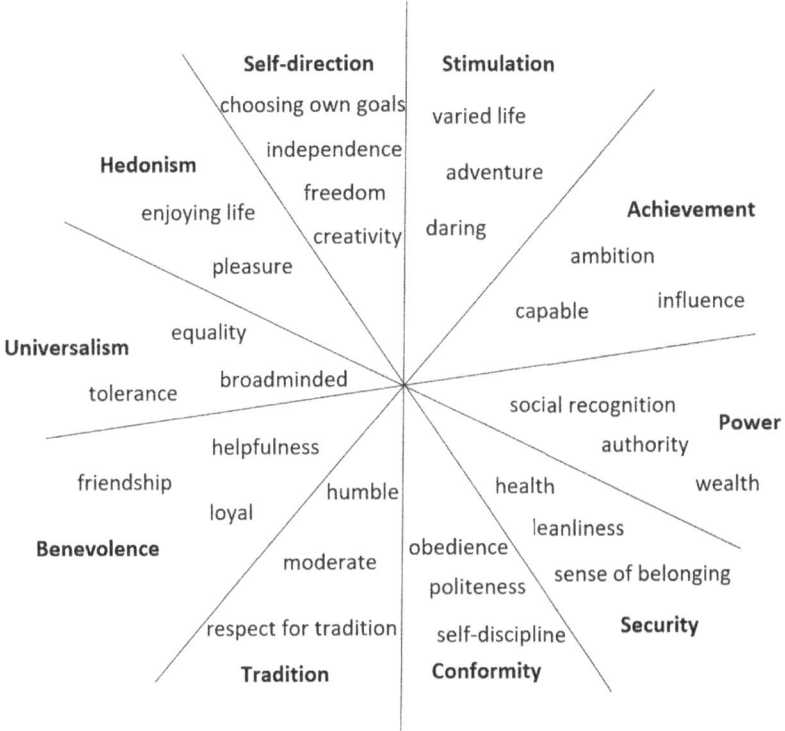

Fig. 1.1 Values map (based on Schwartz et al., 2006)

References

Aldamman, K., Tamrakar, T., Dinesen, C., Wiedemann, N., Murphy, J., Hansen, M., Elsiddig Badr, E., Reid, T., & Vallières, F. (2019). Caring for the mental health of humanitarian volunteers in traumatic contexts: The importance of organisational support. *European Journal of Psychotraumatology, 10*(1), 1–12.

Avey, J. B., Luthans, F., & Jensen, S. M. (2009). Psychological capital: A positive resource for combating employee stress and turnover. *Human Resource Management, 48*(5), 677–693.

Avey, J. B., Reichard, R. J., Luthans, F., & Mhatre, K. H. (2011). Meta-analysis of the impact of positive psychological capital on employee attitudes, behaviors, and performance. *Human Resource Development Quarterly, 22*(2), 127–152.

Ayres, L. (2008). Thematic coding and analysis. In L. M. Given (Ed.), *The SAGE encyclopedia of qualitative research methods* (pp. 867–868). Sage publications.

Barnes, L. (2016). *Journalism and everyday trauma: A grounded theory of the impact from death-knocks and court reporting.* Auckland University of Technology.

Buchanan, M., & Keats, P. (2011). Coping with traumatic stress in journalism: A critical ethnographic study. *International Journal of Psychology, 46*(2), 127–135.

Chen, G. M., Pain, P., Chen, V. Y., Mekelburg, M., Springer, N., & Troger, F. (2020). 'You really have to have a thick skin': A cross-cultural perspective on how online harassment influences female journalists. *Journalism, 21*(7), 877–895.

Cooke, F. L., Cooper, B., Bartram, T., Wang, J., & Mei, H. (2019). Mapping the relationships between high-performance work systems, employee resilience and engagement: A study of the banking industry in China. *International Journal of Human Resource Management, 30*(8), 1239–1260.

Delgado, C., Roche, M., Fethney, J., & Foster, K. (2021). Mental health nurses' psychological well-being, mental distress, and workplace resilience: A cross-sectional survey. *International Journal of Mental Health Nursing, 30*(5), 1234–1247.

Durán, A., Extremera, N., & Rey, L. (2004). Self-reported emotional intelligence, burnout and engagement among staff in services for people with intellectual disabilities. *Psychological Reports, 95*(2), 386–390.

Extremera, N., Mérida-López, S., Sánchez-álvarez, N., & Quintana-Orts, C. (2018). How does emotional intelligence make one feel better at work? The mediational role of work engagement. *International Journal of Environmental Research and Public Health, 15*(9), 1–13.

Feinstein, A., Owen, J., & Blair, N. (2002). A hazardous profession: War, journalists, and psychopathology. *American Journal of Psychiatry, 159*(9), 1570–1575.

Gascón, S., Fueyo-Díaz, R., Borao, L., Leiter, M. P., Fanlo-Zarazaga, Á., Oliván-Blázquez, B., & Aguilar-Latorre, A. (2021). Value conflict, lack of rewards, and sense of community as psychosocial risk factors of burnout in communication professionals (Press, radio, and television). *International Journal of Environmental Research and Public Health, 18*(2), 1–12.

Hartmann, S., Weiss, M., Newman, A., & Hoegl, M. (2020). Resilience in the workplace: A multilevel review and synthesis. *Applied Psychology, 69*(3), 913–959.

King, D. D., Newman, A., & Luthans, F. (2016). Not if, but when we need resilience in the workplace. *Journal of Organizational Behavior, 37*(5), 782–786.

Kotisova, J. (2019). The elephant in the newsroom: Current research on journalism and emotion. *Sociology Compass, 13*(5), 1–11.

Luthans, F., Avey, J. B., Avolio, B. J., & Peterson, S. J. (2010). The development and resulting performance impact of positive psychological capital. *Human Resource Development Quarterly, 21*(1), 41–67.

Luthans, F., Avey, J. B., & Patera, J. L. (2008). Experimental analysis of a web-based training intervention to develop positive psychological capital. *Academy of Management Learning and Education, 7*(2), 209–221. https://doi.org/10.5465/AMLE.2008.32712618

Luthans, F., Vogelgesang, G. R., & Lester, P. B. (2006). Developing the psychological capital of resiliency. *Human Resource Development Review, 5*(1), 25–44.

Luthans, F., Youssef, C. M., & Avolio, B. J. (2007). *Psychological capital: Developing the human competitive edge*. Oxford University Press.

Mapes, K. (2000). *Stop! Think! Choose!: Building emotional intelligence in young people*. Zephyr Press.

Matthews, G., Zeidner, M., & Roberts, R. D. (2012). *Emotional intelligence 101*. Springer.

McCaffrey, R. (2019). Stoicism and courage as journalistic values: What early journalism textbooks taught about newsroom ethos. *American Journalism, 36*(2), 220–241.

McCraty, R., & Atkinson, M. (2012). Resilience training program reduces physiological and psychological stress in police officers. *Global Advances in Health and Medicine, 1*(5), 44–66.

Miret, M. (2021). *Journalism has a health condition and it is not COVID*. Empower Project. https://empower-project.eu/empowered-while-working/journalism-has-a-health-condition-and-it-is-not-covid/%0ANews

Monteiro, S., Marques-Pinto, A., & Roberto, M. S. (2016). Job demands, coping, and impacts of occupational stress among journalists: A systematic review. *European Journal of Work and Organizational Psychology, 25*(5), 751–772.

Murphy, C., Deeny, P., & Taylor, N. (2020). A new pedagogy to enhance the safety and resilience of journalists in dangerous environments globally. *Education Sciences, 10*(310), 1–15.

Paek, S., Schuckert, M., Kim, T. T., & Lee, G. (2015). Why is hospitality employees' psychological capital important? The effects of psychological capital on work engagement and employee morale. *International Journal of Hospitality Management, 50*(1), 9–26.

Pantoja Lima, S., Mick, J., Nicoletti, J., Barros, J. V., Henriques, R. P., Moliani, J. A., Patrício, E., Pereira, F. H., & Zacariotti, M. (2022). *Perfil do Jornalista Brasileiro*.

Paterson, T. A., Luthans, F., & Jeung, W. (2014). Thriving at work: Impact of psychological capital and supervisor support. *Journal of Organizational Behavior, 35*(1), 434–446.

Pearson, M., McMahon, C., O'Donovan, A., & O'Shannessy, D. (2021). Building journalists' resilience through mindfulness strategies. *Journalism, 22*(7), 1647–1664.

Pearson, M., & Seglins, D. (2022). *Taking care.*

Pérez-González, J.-C., Saklofske, D. H., & Mavroveli, S. (Eds.). (2020). *Trait emotional intelligence: Foundations, assessment, and education.* Frontiers Media SA.

Posetti, J., Shabbir, N., Maynard, D., Bontcheva, K., & Aboulez, N. (2021). *The Chilling: Global trends in online violence against women journalists.*

Rajan-Rankin, S. (2014). Self-Identity, Embodiment and the development of emotional resilience. *British Journal of Social Work, 44*(8), 2426–2442.

Robertson, I., Cooper, C., Sarkar, M., & Curran, T. (2015). Resilience training in the workplace from 2003–2014: A systematic review. *Journal of Occupational and Organizational Psychology, 88*(3), 533–562.

Roodbari, H., Axtell, C., Nielsen, K., & Sorensen, G. (2021). Organisational interventions to improve employees' health and wellbeing: A realist synthesis. *Applied Psychology.* https://doi.org/10.1111/apps.12346

Sarrionandia, A., Ramos-Díaz, E., & Fernández-Lasarte, O. (2018). Resilience as a mediator of emotional intelligence and perceived stress: A cross- country study. *Frontiers in Psychology.* https://doi.org/10.3389/fpsyg.2018.02653

Schwartz, S. H., Hammer, B., & Wach, M. (2006). Les valeurs de base de la personne: Théorie, mesures et applications. *Revue Française De Sociologie, 47*(4), 929–968.

Shanock, L. R., Eisenberger, R., Heggestad, E. D., Malone, G., Clark, L., Dunn, A. M., Kirkland, J., & Woznyj, H. (2019). Treating employees well: The value of organizational support theory in human resource management. *Psychologist-Manager Journal, 22*(3–4), 168–191.

Šimunjak, M., & Menke, M. (2022). Workplace well-being and support systems in journalism: Comparative analysis of Germany and the United Kingdom. *Journalism.* https://doi.org/10.1177/14648849221115205

Slaughter, A., Brummel, B., Drevo, S., & Newman, E. (2017). *Journalists and safety training: Experiences and opinions.* DART Center. https://dartcenter. org/sites/default/files/journalists_and_safety_training_-_experiences_and_ opinions_.pdf

Smith, B. W., Dalen, J., Wiggins, K., Tooley, E., Christopher, P., & Bernard, J. (2008). The brief resilience scale: Assessing the ability to bounce back. *International Journal of Behavioral Medicine, 15*(3), 194–200.

Swart, T. (2017). *Study into the mental resilience of journalists.* https://www.tar aswart.com/mental-resilience-of-journalists/

Thomson, T. J. (2021). Mapping the emotional labor and work of visual journalism. *Journalism, 22*(4), 956–973.

Tucker, P. (2021). What is resilience? *Psychiatric times, 38*(7), 9–10.

Vanhove, A. J., Herian, M. N., Perez, A. L. U., Harms, P. D., & Lester, P. B. (2016). Can resilience be developed at work? A meta-analytic review of resilience-building programme effectiveness. *Journal of Occupational and Organizational Psychology, 89*(2), 278–307.

Wahl-Jorgensen, K., & Pantti, M. (2021). Introduction: The emotional turn in journalism. *Journalism, 22*(5), 1147–1154.

Youssef-Morgan, C. M., & Dahms, J. P. (2017). Developing psychological capital to boost work performance and well-being. In R. J. Burke & K. M. Page (Eds.), *Research handbook on work and well-being* (pp. 332–350). Edward Elgar.

CHAPTER 2

Finding Stories & Pitching

My first foreign assignment was to cover handball qualifications for 2008 Beijing Olympic games that were held in Leipzig, Germany. The daily newspaper I worked for at the time sent me, and quite unexpectedly too, as I was only a junior sports reporter at the time. I was told I'm going only the day before, and with little time to prepare, the thrill of going on a foreign and covering a major event immediately mixed with anxiety and nervousness associated with the responsibility I've been given. I was confident I could cover the tournament, having done similar reporting before, but surely they expected more of me given I'll be on the ground? What stories that others don't have could I tell? What if I can't find them? The three tournament days felt like an emotional jigsaw. The excitement of working on a big story, and satisfaction that comes with filing a decent copy, was regularly and quickly followed by the worry about what story I'll file come tomorrow. In the end, the scoop materialised only on the way home when I got the tip-off that the manager was on the way out given that the team did not qualify for the Olympic games. I've made a few calls once I've arrived back and confirmed that there is indeed talk about the change in leadership among the association's officials. My story was the first to break this news. And while this would normally call for a bout of happiness, I remember seeing the story go out on the website, but just feeling physically and emotionally exhausted from the intense few

© The Author(s), under exclusive license to Springer Nature Switzerland AG 2023
M. Šimunjak, *Managing Emotions in Journalism*,
https://doi.org/10.1007/978-3-031-38631-2_2

days. I didn't go to celebrate. I went to bed. The manager was voted out at the next board meeting.

On reflection, I don't think I have handled the mentioned rollercoaster particularly well. On the one hand, I work well with adrenaline that comes from the pressure to file a copy within minutes of the game being finished, and I knew I could do it having done it before, which relieved some of the anxiety. In post-match interviews I would fall back on my training and knew to prepare a few questions, so I'd come to the mix zone and press conference prepared and, in the end, have quotes to work with. On the other hand, the constant worry about being able to offer extra value in terms of finding scoops and securing exclusive interviews kept me up at night and prevented recovery that good quality sleep offers. It meant that I had to rely on running on adrenaline assisted with caffeine most days, which inevitably leads to exhaustion once it wears off. I've learned from it, though. The strategies of internal processing that include perspective-taking and acceptance, which will be discussed in this chapter, have personally been very helpful.

This chapter deals with emotional situations that can arise in the stages of finding stories and pitching and examines them through the 'stop, think, choose' model of emotional intelligence. The 'stop' section discusses emotional situations related to finding stories and pitching, namely: excitement, as well as anxiety and the pressure of responsibility that can be induced by finding scoops or being assigned to cover a 'big story'; anxiety, fear and/or worry in situations in which a journalist does not have a story; as well as emotions of hopefulness and often anxiety about pitch's reception by editor; and frustration with a rejected pitch. In the 'think' section, some beliefs and thoughts which may be driving mentioned emotions are outlined. The 'choose' section suggests emotion management strategies informed by interviews with practising journalists. These include attentional deployment in the form of following professional practice and training; verbal processing with colleagues and editor; and internal processing practices of perspective-taking and acceptance.

STOP: EMOTIONAL SITUATIONS

Finding stories is what it all starts with. It's the first phase in the journalistic production process, and one that distinguishes journalists as 'gatekeepers' of news—we decide which stories are going to be told on our platforms (Vos, 2019). And while this role has come under question with the rise of social media and other user generated content (Bro & Wallberg, 2015), the data tells us that audiences still get the majority of their news through media (Newman et al., 2022)—with journalists and their editors deciding which stories will get the media limelight. Yes, stories are all around us, but not all of them qualify to be told by media. In making this decision, journalists rely on established news values, among which prominently feature the proximity of the story to the audience (geographical, but also cultural, religious, etc.), the potential impact of the information on the society, involvement of elite people and/or elite places, conflict or negativity, as well as positivity that might bring a smile or a sense of hope to audiences (Harcup, 2020). And while it might seem straightforward enough, it isn't. Finding a story is a skill, and an important one, which gets much attention in journalism textbooks. Many of them detail the different ways in which journalists can find a story, mentioning the importance of the news agencies and press releases, social media statements and trends, reports and documents, contacts with services and institutions and perhaps most importantly, engagement with contacts and communities (Harcup, 2015; Reimold, 2013). So, in finding stories, it is partially about knowing where to look, and partially about making informed decisions about whether a piece of information or an event is newsworthy. Both require a particular look at the world which takes time to internalise. On the other hand, once it becomes second nature, journalists become notorious for seeing everything as a potential story, judging its newsworthiness and everyone as a potential source with a story to tell.

Finding Stories

The process of finding a story is commonly described as 'exciting.' For example, Hudson and Rowlands (2018: 171) write, 'Getting out of the office to cover a story—any story—is one of the joys of broadcast journalism. There's an excitement and an expectation—the thrill of not knowing exactly what might happen or how people will react to you.' Journalists interviewed for this book emphasised two key types of stories that regularly ignite excitement, yet also often come with some anxiety. In the first place, **working on a 'big story'**—a developing media event that attracts global attention—can cause excitement, exhilaration, thrill, as well as feelings of responsibility and anxiety about getting the story right. As a mid-career print correspondent puts it:

Probably around 70 to 80% of what I do, I would consider to be, you know, fairly standard, not particularly fascinating or shattering stuff, but stuff that I enjoy doing and it's fine. And then there's kind of 20% of stuff that I feel is, you know, really quite exciting. And if it involves travel or if it's some big breaking event... [...] I would say there's always some combination of, like, worry, excitement...

A senior print editor describes it in a similar way:

I suppose you feel a combination of... Exhilaration is probably too strong a word. You know, heightened interest, heightened excitement, heightened sense of involvement with things around you, the world around you. I think you... Once you start thinking about journalism, and start thinking about political journalism, your sort of pulse starts racing a bit more. Because you're inevitably thinking about your involvement with sort of people who hold power and you're thinking about the end product that you will produce... [...] So, it's a combination of raised consciousness and excitement, I think, and coupled with anxiety.

Hence, the thrill of the story is often associated with the 'thrill of being witness to history' (Hudson & Rowlands, 2018: 149), and the anxiety or worry is associated with it given the responsibility of doing the story justice and getting it right for your audience. A senior print editor describes this in the context of her role in covering several major events:

I both went and was embedded [in a war zone], but I also watch the Commons votes, which was incredibly moving at the time, and that's going way back, to the whole Brexit, the whole experience of covering Brexit and, you know, the sort of, the link between how that was debated in Parliament and how that reflected what was going on in the real world. And then, of course, the pandemic, which has, you know, on the one hand, is very much a political story, but also affects all of our lives on the ground. So, with those examples you feel, you know, a real sense of responsibility, I suppose that you are, like I said, in the front row of history and you're having to try and share what's going on with your readers.

Another story finding situation that is often described as **exciting is when a journalist secures a 'scoop'**—an exclusive story that is likely to have a significant impact. Journalists, usually those in more senior roles who have had such experiences, often describe it as a very satis-fying process, with excitement about being the first to break the story, thrill about knowing something that others don't, but also anxiety about ensuring that the story stands up and getting it right. For example, a senior print editor describes the buzz that a tip-off which might lead to a scoop generates:

> I guess that the thrill and excitement comes with the tip off because it's sort of like… It's a challenge, it's like you've got… You've been given some clues and you need to patch it all together and see if there's a story there.

Finding exclusive stories, and particularly being able to find and tell stories that someone may not want told, is considered to be one of the key roles of journalists, usually considered to serve the aim of holding powerful to account (Hanitzsch & Örnebring, 2019). Beyond delivering on this, journalists, logically, have personal benefits from finding such stories as it increases their prestige and helps them position in the industry. In the words of a senior print correspondent:

> I think the uncovering stories is one of the most intense emotional experi-ences in the sense that if I do come up with something or find a piece of information which I think would make an interesting story, a good story, then there's the thrill, it's almost quite a kind of physical, visceral thrill, like a kind of… Not quite a chill going up your spine… Kind of shimmery feeling of 'Oh, my goodness, this is actually really good.' And you know, part of it is inevitably going to be connected to self-interest because, you know, whilst I'm a staff journalist, you get judged to an extent on the stories that you create and it's just, you know, always a good thing to bring in a story that seems is an interesting one. But it's also more than that, it's just the, you know, that's basically what the distilled essence of the job is - is to try and find out interesting things.

And while major scoops are usually secured by more senior journal-ists, the importance of finding exclusive stories, both as an exciting part of the job and an opportunity to gain respect of peers, bosses and audi-ences, is not lost on emerging professionals either, as this early career print correspondent elaborates:

You know, when you have a story in the first stage of the process, there's a lot of... Yeah, I'll use the word again, like excitement. Because you've got information that other people aren't privy to. You're thinking, 'How... You know, this is really good. It's kind of, A – newsworthy and important, and B – It will, kind of, lift me up in the minds... You know, it will lift my, kind of, my value in the minds of my editors and my contemporaries, my peers...'

Encouragingly, it does not seem that the thrill of finding information others don't have loses its excitement-inducing power over a span of one's career. As this mid-career digital editor claims:

I think finding a story... Whether that's, you know, reading a long report and finding something interesting or something unheard of, or talking to someone and realising something they've said is going to be a great news line... There's always that adrenaline and excitement, I guess, that comes with that. And that never goes away, I don't think.

Yet, with the rise of digital platforms and increasing economic pressures on media, we have been witnessing decreasing numbers of journalists needing to produce an ever-increasing number of news at high speed to meet audience demand and be competitive in the market that started putting strong emphasis on 'immediacy' (Örnebring, 2010; Rom & Reich, 2020; Siapera, 2019). For many journalists, this means relinquishing the excitement of finding stories for desk reporting that to a large extent relies on churning out wire copies, press releases, and statements made on social media. 'Churnalism,' as the practice has been called, isn't particularly new to the industry. Several studies, like those in the UK (Lewis et al., 2008), Greece (Saridou et al., 2017), and South Africa (Heyl et al., 2020), have found large numbers of copied or repackaged press releases and wire copies among mainstream media's output. It is often early career journalists who do this kind of work, which can lead to frustration as the excitement-inducing aspect of the job is missing from their work life. This is how an early career digital journalist describes it:

It's a bit monotonous at times. And relatively easy, probably. I can feel like I'm coasting. But it is... It's a bit tiresome to do that, over and over again. [...] I don't want to say that I'm above that sort of work, but certainly I'm capable of doing a lot more than that. And it's quite easy for me to sit there and just... You know, rewrite it, and not necessarily get anything out of it. So, I try to get something out of it when I can. But it can be a bit boring at times.

More senior reporters, correspondents and editors, often spoke of another story finding situation that can invoke emotions—that in which **they do not have a story.** Reimold (2013: 4) mentions it in his textbook on finding stories where he writes: 'we are often stuck, staring at the world (wide web) without a plausible or publishable idea and no real clue how to even begin searching. Nervousness leads to guilt, then fear, and finally outright desperation.' Journalists interviewed for this book can be seen to share some of these fears, as they speak of anxiety about missing things and fears that competition is doing better. A senior broadcast editor describes it like this:

It's possible when you're not having a very busy period, [to] become a little bit anxious that you haven't got a story. That you ought to be out there, getting a scoop. That your competitors may either have found a better story than you or have a different angle or have managed to get an interview that you've failed to get. So, once you finish the broadcast, there's always a sense where you're looking around to see what everybody else has done with the same story, with a degree of anxiety as well.

Again, some of this anxiety is tied to concerns about one's own reputation and standing among peers and bosses. There is a worry that one's value as a reporter who delivers on exclusive stories that make a difference, and hence, attract audiences, is in question if peers are seen as better able to find and tell these. In the words of a mid-career digital reporter:

When you're sort of like looking around, when you haven't got that much to do, when you're not working on a story, or you're looking for ideas... Obviously, like, if you follow a lot of other journalists and you see that they have got stories and they have reported stuff, then it's sort of like... It can make you... Like, that can sort of stress you out a bit because you're like, 'Well, they're getting stuff, they're reporting and stuff, and I'm not. I'm missing it.' And you think, 'Well, my editors probably follow these people as well and they're seeing, you know, this happened and stuff...'

The fear of missing an important story is particularly evident among those who are seen to be solely responsible for a beat in their newsrooms, such as specialist reporters in small or local newsrooms, but also foreign correspondents. In these situations, there is a perception that finding and covering important stories is on their shoulders only, which causes anxiety because if they miss it, their media outlet will not be competitive in the news market and their audiences will be left uninformed. A mid-career print correspondent put it like this:

> So, the way that I have almost always worked has been, you know, a solo correspondent in a particular place working as a sort of one-man band. And so, I think with that there's often like a low-level anxiety that you're missing things or that, you know, you can never quite switch off. [...] I would describe it as a sort of low-level worry that, you know... Often I would feel that there's plenty of time when you're not working, but you only really know that it was time off after it's happened, because you're sort of sitting there, scrolling and freaking out that you're missing something.

Pitching

Pitching is another key skill in journalism by which journalists are trying to convince their editors that the story they found is worth pursuing. It requires journalists being able to explain not only its newsworthiness, but also how and why the story fits the media outlet and its target audience, all in a few sentences. The story also needs to be viable for editors to invest people resources in it, i.e., journalists should be able to explain how they plan to go about it, what kind of research they can use, who they can speak to on the subject and how much time they need to produce a copy. Hence, there are lots of questions to address, and given pitches should be short and to the point, very little time to deliver lots of convincing arguments.

Two emotional situations have been mentioned by British journalists when it comes to pitching. In the first place, **before the pitch, there is a feeling of hopefulness and/or anxiety about how the pitch will be received by the editor**. This emotional situation was commonly mentioned by early career journalists, who are trying to prove themselves to editors. Regarding hopefulness, an early career print correspondent described it like this:

> Pitching a story... I'd say, you know, I'm feeling sort of hopeful, maybe, because you're sort of... You're putting what you've been told sort of

down into a couple of sentences, you're distilling it, and you're hoping that your editor is going to say yes.

Another emerging professional, an early career digital journalist, spoke how anxiety is one of the key emotions induced when it comes to pitching:

> Probably anxiety is quite a big one, I guess. When pitching a story sometimes I feel a little bit anxious about how it's going to go.

The pressure to prove yourself and get the story idea accepted have been mentioned by those with a few more years of experience in the industry as well, particularly if they have previously spent much of their time working on non-original stories, such as doing desk reporting or live reporting. The move from a desk job to that of a reporter, correspondent or editor, requires finding, and pitching, original stories. So, journalists feel pressure to prove they can deliver good exclusive stories. A mid-career digital reporter put it like this:

> Pitching something... And, again, this comes back to the fact that I was a live journalist for a while, in which case you don't necessarily have to pitch stuff, because stuff just happens and you just do it. But the job that I do now is more balanced and there's lots more of kind of pitching longer term features and stuff, you know, that will take a few weeks. And I guess that... There's sort of pressure there, because they have to be pretty good, they have to be self-generated, and so there is a pressure that you pitch something that's good.

Even some senior journalists spoke of the anxiety related to pitching, often invoked by previous negative experiences with getting the green light for stories. While it is unlikely that stories lack newsworthiness or viability given they're pitched by senior journalists, successful pitches sometimes require jumping through more hoops. For example, some editors may have their own priorities in topic coverage or must represent those imposed by higher ups. Then, there are also staffing and other financial implications to consider. A good story may not pass the pitch if there are other story priorities meaning the editor can't spare staff to cover it, or there are other costs to covering the story, such as travel expenses, which are not available. A senior broadcast correspondent describes their personal struggle with pitching in this way:

Pitching tends to be fraught with anxiety because I've never been very good at it and the organisation I work in can be somewhat… Difficult to get stuff off the ground. It's a large, complicated organisation and you don't always know where the interest is, where the money is. And so that is an anxiety-inducing part of the job.

And while a successful pitch is often followed by joy and excitement (Reimold, 2013: 305), **an unsuccessful pitch can invoke feelings of frustration**. On the one hand, this frustration can be the result of differing views on the type or quality of a story between a journalist and an editor, as this mid-career broadcast journalist explains:

You can feel really, really frustrated if those ideas aren't taken on or if your older colleagues disagree that you're, you know… That your story idea isn't what they want to hear.

On the other hand, frustration can be borne out of inability to get the story idea running due to other story priorities, particularly if there is another major story in the news at the time. For example, a senior print correspondent describes the frustration with getting the green light to cover some political stories during the COVID-19 pandemic:

[There is] frustration that you can't get… Can't get your story right up to the, you know, the top of the agenda. Your news editor doesn't feel the same way as you do about a story, but your news editor is looking at a, you know, a wide waterfront of stories every day and in the present environment with COVID, that's dominated by COVID, it's more difficult to get attention for stories that are outside that. Even though you know they are, you know, fantastic - can be fantastically important and significant.

For early career journalists, an unsuccessful pitch can cause frustration with the quality of work they do, increasing doubts in their skills and impacting self-confidence. In the words of an early career print correspondent:

Obviously, sometimes out of that [rejection] comes frustration, because you realise that actually the story's not quite as good as you were kind of getting, you know, wrapped up in your mind about. Or your editor says, 'Actually, I don't think this is as good as you think it is.'

British author Neil Gaiman has given succinct advice on how to deal with a pitch rejection, saying, 'Swear, shrug, write the next thing.' What else can you do? Continue reading.

THINK

As explained in the Introduction chapter, emotional and physical responses to a situation are driven by our beliefs and thoughts through which we interpret that situation. If we are interpreting a situation with negative thoughts, it's more likely that we will perceive it as an inevitable occurrence which we have little or no control over. This can then lead to increased stress. Thinking of the emotional situations discussed above, Table 2.1 outlines several beliefs and thoughts that might be driving negative emotions.

If you are experiencing negative emotions which you feel you need or want to manage, you can check the beliefs and values, as well as thoughts and expectations that are driving these. In other words, think about what is driving your emotions, how can you update and reframe these with a more positive outlook, and what options you have moving forward. For example, if you're worried that you won't be able to stand up a story, consider if you've done it before? If so, what makes you think that you

Table 2.1 Potential beliefs and thoughts that might be driving a negative emotional response to emotional situations associated with finding stories and pitching

Anxiety about getting a big story right	*Fear of not having a story*	*Frustration with unsuccessful pitches*
I don't have the skills to cover this story	I'm incompetent	I lack skill in finding good stories
I will not be able to stand it up	Everyone else is better at this than me	I am not good at pitching
Sources will not want to speak to me about it	My editors will think less of me	Editor does not realise the quality of pitched story
Others will do better than me in covering it	My peers will respect me less	
Colleagues, editors, audiences will be disappointed with my story treatment	I will not be able to progress in my career	

won't this time? If you weren't able to get the story off the ground previ-ously, were the consequences dire? Don't many stories don't pan out or there is not enough evidence to make them stand up? Similarly, if you don't have a story and are anxious about what your peers will think of you, consider if this situation is that unusual? Does everyone always have an original story to pitch? If they don't, what happens? If your pitch was not successful and you're concerned that you don't have the skills to find good quality stories, consider if this has happened before? Have you had successful pitches before? Is it that unusual that a pitch gets rejected? Reimold (2013: 309) has an interesting take on pitching—he says, 'expect rejection.' Why do you think that is? How often are all the stories a journalist wants to do given a green light?

The beliefs and values that drive these emotional situations will differ from journalist to journalist, so it's important you try to unpack what exactly is inducing your own emotions in this context. Are they rational? Logical? What evidence do you have to believe what you believe is happening? And while, similarly, journalists may decide to manage their emotions in diverse ways, there are some common emotion management strategies that journalists apply when faced with emotional situations tied to finding stories and pitching, that the chapter now turns to.

Choose: Emotion Management Strategies

The most commonly mentioned emotion management strategies by British journalists when dealing with emotional situations outlined above are attentional deployment in the form of focusing on practice and routine; internal processing by perspective-taking and acceptance; and verbal processing with peers and editors.

Attentional Deployment

As story finding and pitching are some of the key journalistic skills, heavily addressed in journalism textbooks and in training, one of the key emotion management strategies that can be used in emotional situations tied to these is attentional deployment in terms of following practice and training, and especially applying the 'stepping' technique. As explained in the Introduction chapter, the 'stepping' technique relies on breaking down a task into smaller steps, which makes the process seem more manageable, alleviating some of the anxiety and stress that comes with it. In terms of finding stories and pitching, there are clear protocols and routines to observe, which can be considered steps towards the overall goal—finding a good original story and/or delivering a successful pitch. This approach can be useful in managing the anxiety that arises when faced with coverage of a big story, as well as that induced by not having an original story, or preparing to pitch one. For example, worry and anxiety before pitching might be managed by outlining (in writing if it helps) the elements a good pitch should have and checking that you have all the key information that the editor needs to make a decision. If any information is missing, and/or you know from previous experience of pitching to a particular editor what kind of questions they are likely to pose about the newsworthiness or viability of the story, you have time to prepare this additional information so you can be reassured that you are going into a pitch as ready as you can be.

However, following routines and stepping your way to a goal might be an important emotion management strategy in a positive emotional state too—that filled with thrill and excitement related to covering a big story or a scoop—as positive emotions might contribute to negative outcomes (An et al., 2017), hence, they might need to be managed. For example, Hudson and Rowlands (2018: 151) quote Helen Boaden, then the Director of BBC News who worked in a range of radio and television roles, saying:

> The worst thing I ever did, I was so excited about a story I drove off in my car and only halfway to the story did I realise I'd left the tape recorder behind, which, given the fact that it was radio, was a bit of a problem.

Hence, the feeling of excitement that comes with finding a good story might lead to making impulsive, rash decisions and not considering the implications of your actions or choices. Harcup makes a similar point in outlining the potential dangers of giving yourself up to the thrill of being tasked to cover an exciting story. He writes:

> Despite the thrill of the chase – or perhaps precisely because, as a reporter, it's so easy to get caught up in the excitement of a pursuit – it is vital to question your own expectations and assumptions during any investigation. Then, once you have gathered your material from a range of sources, you must decide whether the story still has potential. (2015: 106)

So, in order to try to manage the excitement in a way that leads to positive outcomes, you can choose to stop and consciously consider the routines and protocols that need to be observed to successfully cover a story, and then follow the routine step by step to ensure that the story is covered in line with journalistic standards and practice. It may dampen your excitement a bit, but it should be worth it if the management of excitement contributes to a successful story production process.

Internal Processing

The second strategy commonly mentioned in relation to managing emotions that arise in the story finding and pitching process is internal processing, particularly through perspective-taking and acceptance. In the first place, journalists say that the anxiety about not having original stories can be alleviated by taking the perspective that this situation happens to everyone, and it should be accepted there are periods when you're more productive than in others. A senior print correspondent describes it like this:

> I try and think about it in the longer-term context. You know, because there are some journalists who get really very, very anxious if they haven't brought anything in like a few days, or they haven't had anything particularly exciting for a while. I'm probably on average better than most in terms of being able to think, you know, 'I've been in this paper really long time, you know, I'm valued for what I do, this is just one of those kinds of periods.

Perspective-taking is also useful when rationally considering the negative consequences of not having a story that might be driving your anxiety, fear or worry. Journalists often say that this perspective is developed based on experience, when you witness first hand that not having a story is not really a career-ending situation, or one that will have a serious impact on your standing in a newsroom. A mid-career print correspondent put it in this way:

> You get more confident that, you know, you have that level of experience and even if you do miss something, it is not the end of the world.

Yet, while having a personal experience of this is likely to make you more comfortable in the situation, it is worth considering that you can learn from this attitude even if you are still in the early stages of your career and trying very hard to make a name for yourself.

Similarly, more experienced journalists talked about developing a perspective on unsuccessful pitches by drawing on their developed understanding of how story commissioning works, which emerging professionals can benefit from too. These journalists, in trying to manage their frustration with a rejected pitch, take the perspective that not all stories can be covered, even if they're newsworthy, particularly in news saturated markets. Indeed, the 2022 Digital News Report revealed that in a range of countries the number of people who avoid the news has increased (e.g., in the UK from 24% in 2017 to 46% in 2022; in Australia and Ireland from 30 to 41%), with around a third of people who avoid news saying this is because they are worn out by the sheer amount of stories on offer (Newman et al., 2022). A senior print correspondent describes their reasoning like this:

> There isn't room... There isn't room in people's heads to consume all the news, you know the thousands and tens of thousands of journalists are generating across the piece that, you know, we in Europe in the western world are interested in. You know, if you consider the last year, we've had COVID, American election and we've had Brexit. That's three massive stories. And, you know, don't tell me that people, even journalists, are reading all of those. They're not, there isn't the capacity.

Arguably, it's a perspective that can assist emerging professionals too in trying to accept the fact that some pitches will be unsuccessful even if their stories are newsworthy and viable.

Verbal Processing

Finally, verbal processing, that is, talking to peers and editors to gain emotional release and support, has also been mentioned by journalists as an effective strategy to relieve both the anxiety about not having stories and the frustration with rejected pitches. Regarding the former, a senior print correspondent says:

I chat about it with colleagues because that's something journalists are actually quite good at, you know, whining to each other.

Indeed, as is evident throughout this book, discussing issues with colleagues can be beneficial in sharing your emotions and through this gaining emotional release, but also normalising and legitimising these emotions and emotional situations as something that regularly occurs in the industry. Through sharing and talking, it is likely that you will learn that others have faced similar situations, which can help in alleviating some of the worry and anxiety as it evidences that many go through similar experiences and that the outcomes are rarely as negative and drastic as you may be thinking them to be.

Similar reasoning has been offered by journalists who talk to their colleagues to manage their frustration with unsuccessful pitches. In the words of a mid-career broadcast journalist:

> Talking to friends, talking to other colleagues... Yeah, it's all about sharing the frustration, really. Yeah, speaking to other colleagues about it, and, I guess, you know, you're looking for...You're kind of looking for validation from your colleagues when you're talking about those kinds of things... Particularly sort of commissioning stories. I think it's a big issue.

A senior print correspondent further describes the benefits of verbal processing with peers when feeling frustrated with a story not being given a green light due to the news desk having other story priorities:

> You talk to your colleagues. I think a default position in every newsroom is colleagues moaning about the news desk. It's common, it's part of the job, it's an occupational hazard, and it's fun to.

Of course, by speaking to colleagues, you might also learn from them other useful strategies to manage your emotions, as well as actionable steps that you can take to make your next pitch more successful. For example, they can provide insight into how you might approach the pitch next time or offer advice on how to cover a major event, and common mistakes that occur in the field that you might want to avoid. Similarly, you may wish to speak to the editor who rejected the pitch to learn more about the reasoning behind it and what you can do to be more successful next time.

In sum, this chapter has covered several emotional situations that are likely to arise in the story finding and pitching process, namely: excitement, as well as anxiety and the pressure of responsibility that can be induced by finding scoops or being assigned to cover a 'big story'; anxiety, fear and/or worry in situations in which a journalist does not have a story; as well as emotions of hopefulness and often anxiety about pitch's reception by editor; and frustration with a rejected pitch. It has been suggested that key strategies to manage these emotions include attentional deployment in terms of following practice and training; verbal processing with colleagues and editors; and internal processing practices of perspective-taking and acceptance.

The UK: Haroon Siddique on Pitching

Haroon Siddique is legal affairs correspondent for the Guardian and is also journalist director of the Scott Trust, which owns the Guardian. He has worked at the Guardian for over 15 years, having begun his career in journalism with the Ham&High (Hampstead and Highgate Express) group of local newspapers.

It is an old adage in newsrooms that 'you're only as good as your last story.' It can be a healthy attitude to prevent you resting on your laurels but not if it makes you anxious. Journalism is not a competition but can feel like one. Many journalists (myself among them) worry about how they are perceived (a friend who works in mental health told me journalists are among the most self-critical people he's come across), which can create anxiety around pitching and finding stories. It's all too easy to get bogged down by what peers, editors, readers and even friends think, given what a public-facing role it is. I've also felt responsibility to people who have provided a tip-off, particularly when they have shared a personal story/injustice.

Experience can help, whether it's knowing you have got good stories in the past to understanding that a knockback to a pitch is not a reflection on you personally or even the strength of the story but is often a reflection of the prevailing news agenda/mix of stories required. Hopefully just hearing this from an experienced journalist helps but I would also encourage you to talk to those you know, they'll have been through the same emotions. I have had rookie journalists express concerns to me that they are not highly thought of by editors because they have not received feedback on a pitch, when it is just a function—albeit an annoying one—of busy newsrooms, and happens to all of us on occasion.

Another anxiety of the pitch can be what happens if it gets accepted—will I be able to deliver it? Again, experience lends itself to having more confidence in being able to deliver based on past work, although I still get doubts. But I also find that refining the pitch (e.g., pinning down what the intro/first paragraph will be) before you send it can actually give you the core of the story if it is commissioned as well as improving the chances of it being commissioned in the first place. It's also a useful process for clarifying in your own mind whether it is worth pitching.

Other ways I deal with the anxieties that the job can bring are more generic. I don't always practise what I preach but breaking up the day through any kind of exercise, meditation, positive affirmations (look it up but essentially saying/repeating things like 'I'm calm, I'm confident,' etc.) are some of the things I do. And, remember, at the end of the day, it is untrue that you're only as good as your last story. No matter how good a journalist is, they will probably have a recent story in their portfolio that they wouldn't like to be judged on and so they won't make the mistake of doing the same to others.

Top Tips

- Be aware of the routines and procedures needed to find a story and pitch it
- Be aware of editorial priorities, the type of stories your outlet covers and the interests of the outlet's target audience
- Be aware of diary events in your beat so you can pitch these if you have no original stories to offer
- Grow your contact list and nurture relationships with sources and communities to improve your chances of finding original stories

- Consider that getting the green light for a story does not depend solely on its newsworthiness and your competence in delivering it
- Consider that most journalists don't have brilliant exclusive stories on the go every day of their career
- Break down the processes into smaller steps to make them more manageable
- Speak to your colleagues to gain emotional release, get practical advice on how you can move forward and have some fun in the process

READ, WATCH, AND LISTEN

- Read Cristiana Bedeis' article 'What to do when pitching articles takes a toll' published by International Journalists' Network—https://ijnet.org/en/story/what-do-when-pitching-articles-takes-toll
- Read Monica Guzman's article 'Fear of screwing up' published by Columbia Journalism Review – https://www.cjr.org/first_person/fear_of_screwing_up.php
- Watch Pulitzer Center's tutorial 'How To Find Under-Reported Stories' - https://www.youtube.com/watch?v=5Fez7XtjFOQ
- Listen to Backstory Media Freedom podcast episode 'Reporting on Africa's dangerous beats' in which journalists from Cameroon, Kenya and Uganda explain how they find big stories while considering their and their sources safety—https://wan-ifra.org/2022/05/podcast-reporting-on-africas-dangerous-beats/
- Listen to The Tip Off podcast episode 'Beyond the Horizon' featuring BBC journalist Nick Wallis who broke 'The Great Post Office Scandal'—https://thetipoffpodcast.com/podcast/ep-61-beyond-the-horizon/

SCENARIO EXERCISES

Scenario 1

You have been working as a desk journalist for a digital lifestyle magazine for a few years, covering topics such as fitness and wellness, travel and fashion. Your work has mostly consisted of repackaging press releases, as well as following social media and writing stories from posts of celebrities and opinion makers. You have covered only a handful of original stories in this period, including one about the relationship between slow fashion and environment.

Your editor calls you in and notifies you that you will be covering the upcoming London Fashion Week. They expect daily news reports, insightful reviews and analysis, as well as interviews with designers and celebrities attending the event. You have never covered such a big story.

- How does this make you feel?
- What are you going to do? Why?

Scenario 2

You work for a regional broadcaster as a video journalist, meaning that you are regularly sent out to cover diary events. You're skilled in multi-media production, and you do research, interviewing, recording and editing, all on your own. You're good at it, and your editor considers you reliable and competent.

You've started growing tired of doing daily news and want to branch out in covering more feature-like original stories. You pitched a few original stories in the past, with varying success. Your editor seems to give the green light for stories that can be reasonably done within a short time frame, usually a day, but any bigger ideas, although there are no questions about their newsworthiness, are usually shot down.

While covering an opening of a new city council building, you noticed a small group of protestors with banners such as 'Money for nursery workers not politicians,' 'Build nurseries, not politicians' temples,' etc. You spoke to some of them. Protesters claim that money for the new nursery was repurposed to complete the council building whose costs have spiralled since the start of the build. You check the budget reports, and it appears that there might be some truth to this—there was supposed to be a new nursery opened last year, yet the construction hasn't even started. You pitch a story about the misappropriation of city council funds to the detriment of citizens who struggle to get children into the existing overcrowded nursery. You're convinced this is an important story that addresses citizens' concerns and holds power to account. The editor says 'no.'

- How does this make you feel?
- What are you going to do? Why?

References

An, S., Ji, L. J., Marks, M., & Zhang, Z. (2017). Two sides of emotion: Exploring positivity and negativity in six basic emotions across cultures. *Frontiers in Psychology, 8*(April), 1–14. https://doi.org/10.3389/fpsyg.2017.00610

Bro, P., & Wallberg, F. (2015). Gatekeeping in a digital era: Principles, practices and technological platforms. *Journalism Practice, 9*(1), 92–105. https://doi.org/10.1080/17512786.2014.928468

Hanitzsch, T., & Örnebring, H. (2019). Professionalism, professional identity, and journalistic roles. In K. Wahl-Jorgensen & T. Hanitzsch (Eds.), *The handbook of journalism studies* (pp. 105–122). Taylor & Francis Group.

Harcup, T. (2015). *Journalism principles and practice* (3rd ed.). SAGE.

Harcup, T. (2020). *What's the point of news? A study in ethical journalism.* Springer International Publishing.

Heyl, A., Joubert, M., & Guenther, L. (2020). Churnalism and hype in science communication: Comparing university press releases and journalistic articles in South Africa. *Communication, 46*(2), 126–145. https://doi.org/10.1080/02500167.2020.1789184

Hudson, G., & Rowlands, S. (2018). *The broadcast journalism handbook* (7th ed.). Routledge.

Lewis, J., Williams, A., & Franklin, B. (2008). A compromised fourth estate?: UK news journalism, public relations and news sources. *Journalism Studies, 9*(1), 1–20. https://doi.org/10.1080/14616700701767974

Newman, N., Fletcher, R., Robertson, C., Eddy, K., & Nielsen, R. (2022, July 23). *Digital News Report 2022.* https://reutersinstitute.politics.ox.ac.uk/sites/default/files/2022-06/Digital_News-Report_2022.pdf. Consultadoi em, 16, 29.

Örnebring, H. (2010). Technology and journalism-as-labour: Historical perspectives. *Journalism, 11*(1), 57–74. https://doi.org/10.1177/1464884909350644

Reimold, D. (2013). *Journalism of ideas: Brainstorming, developing, and selling stories in the digital age.* Routledge.

Rom, S., & Reich, Z. (2020). Between the technological hare and the journalistic tortoise: Minimization of knowledge claims in online news flashes. *Journalism, 21*(1), 54–72. https://doi.org/10.1177/1464884917740050

Saridou, T., Spyridou, L. P., & Veglis, A. (2017). Churnalism on the rise?: Assessing convergence effects on editorial practices. *Digital Journalism, 5*(8), 1006–1024. https://doi.org/10.1080/21670811.2017.1342209

Siapera, E. (2019, May). Affective labour and media work. In M. Deuze & M. Prenger (Eds.), *Making media* (pp. 275–286). Amsterdam University Press.

Vos, T. P. (2019). Journalists as gatekeepers. In K. Wahl-Jorgensen & T. Hanitzsch (Eds.), *The handbook of journalism studies* (pp. 90–104). Taylor & Francis Group.

CHAPTER 3

Sources & Interviewing

We had a live broadcast interview each day following the evening news at the national sports channel I worked for. Interviewees were sportspeople who were in the news that day, someone whose story our audiences wanted to hear beyond a short soundbite in the news section. We rarely knew who would be coming in, as they had to be topical and relevant on the day. The news would also frequently come in late in the day, usually just a few hours before going live. One day, while I was on 'interview' duty, that is, tasked with conducting the interview, the editor managed to book a gymnast who represented the country at the just finished European Championship. I had a few years of experience in sports journalism at the time. Yet, I knew little to nothing about gymnastics. With a live interview just a few hours away, my first reaction was panic. I don't have enough time for proper prep! What am I going to ask? How will I know they have answered the question? I'll look like an idiot.

I did two things then. First, I took our gymnast specialist aside and asked him to give me a briefing about the interviewee and the Championship, as I didn't have time to do the research on my own. Then, we wrote the interview questions together. Well, to be honest, the colleague did most of the work. He even briefed me on how the interviewee might respond to each of these, and what keywords to pay attention to (there is lots of jargon in sports!) and how to progress with the questions if I hear these. In the end, I had the interview questions list on paper with a

© The Author(s), under exclusive license to Springer Nature
Switzerland AG 2023
M. Šimunjak, *Managing Emotions in Journalism*,
https://doi.org/10.1007/978-3-031-38631-2_3

little diagram that should lead me through them depending on the interviewee's answers. I knew I'd sit far enough from the interviewee in the studio for them not to be able to see it. All this did wonders for my anxiety, although the issue of the interview going live kept a sense of nervousness about it. I remember the interview, and that I felt a sense of control over it. Yet, I couldn't really tell how well it went as I still didn't know enough about gymnastics to be able to properly evaluate interviewee's answers. The smile of the editor once I came out of the studio put me at ease momentarily. 'Watching that, people might assume you're some sort of expert in gymnastics,' he said. And—breathe. Here's to wonderful colleagues!

This chapter focuses on the original newsgathering phase of the journalism workflow and investigates emotional situations that might arise while working with sources and interviewing them, examining these through the 'stop, think, choose' model of emotional intelligence. The 'stop' section discusses emotional situations related to sources and interviewing, namely: nervousness of contacting sources; frustration with non-responsive sources or those who appear to be withholding information; feelings of responsibility towards telling their stories and protecting them from harm; excitement and satisfaction, as well as anxiety related to conducting interviews; worry about displaying inappropriate emotions (particularly in trauma-related interviews) and difficulties in dealing with vicarious emotions. In the 'think' section, some beliefs and thoughts which may be driving mentioned emotions are outlined. The 'choose' section suggests emotion management strategies informed by interviews with practising journalists. These include verbal processing with colleagues; internal processing practices of positive reappraisal and perspective-taking; as well as attentional deployment techniques of following routines and engaging in diversionary activities.

STOP: EMOTIONAL SITUATIONS

Working with sources and interviewing them is another key skill and practice in journalism, which gets much attention in journalism textbooks. As Pape and Featherstone (2005: 139) rightly claim, 'the best sources are people—someone, somewhere knows someone who knows something that you want to know more about.' Naturally, textbooks regularly provide guidance on who might be considered key sources, that is, information holders, in a society, writing about officials, experts, press officers, victims, witnesses and members of the public, among others (see, e.g., Harcup, 2015; Hudson & Rowlands, 2018; Pape & Featherstone, 2005). On the other hand, to get information from these sources, journalists need to ask them questions, that is, interview them. After all, it is what journalists do. As Hudson and Rowlands (2018: 79) note: 'Journalism is all about asking questions. Lots of them. And the right ones.' Yet, this is often easier said than done. As many journalism trainees will tell you, even getting people to speak to you is a high task. As journalists, we may have the right to ask questions, but sources, in most cases, have the right not to answer them. The relationship between journalists and sources is often complex and dynamic, described as symbiotic and pragmatic—as journalists need sources to get information, and sources often need, or could benefit from, speaking to journalists to get their point of view on the agenda (Berkowitz, 2019). There is also a power dynamic to it, as journalists aim to uncover information and sources try to control it. Which party can be seen as having more power in any relationship depends on a variety of factors. For example, journalists' power can derive from their media affiliation, track record and/or experience in the industry, while sources' power can also come from their affiliation with an institution or movement as well as their position in its hierarchy, but also their knowledge and autonomy to speak about it (Berkowitz, 2019). Given all this, as well as newsworthiness of elite people and institutions that yield power, it perhaps does not surprise that one of the studies of sources in British media found these are most often political parties and politicians, government and its officials, representatives of police and courts, as well as businesses (Lewis et al., 2008).

Sources

As journalists often need information from people who they perceive as having more 'power' than them, it is little wonder that there is sometimes **nervousness and anxiety about contacting sources**. Importantly, this isn't the case only with early career journalists. For example, a mid-career print reporter says:

> I sometimes get nervous speaking to people if it's kind of big-name person or something or when you, kind of, you're not quite sure whether they're going to... um I guess, how amenable they're going to be; whether they're

going to speak on the record; those kinds of things. So, there's a bit of anxiety there.

Similarly, some reporting contexts and sources are deemed more difficult than others and can make journalists less comfortable, even scared for their safety. For instance, a senior print reporter described working with sources from a court context in this way:

> Approaching people directly can induce both excitement and nervousness. I've been in situations where I've had to tackle some, you know, very difficult subjects... I mean, court reporting, for instance... That can induce fear. You can be worried about your personal safety. You know, I've done many court reports, a lot of court reports in the past, and, you know... [...] I've received, you know, threats and things like that... So, there's always a certain amount of trepidation and when you're dealing with certain individuals there's a visceral fear of some things.

Nervousness and anxiety are also frequently mentioned when contacting sources who may be in difficult situations, for example, those who have experienced any sort of trauma. Studies that have explored journalists' perceptions and experiences of 'death knocks,' such as those in the UK and Australia, report that journalists find these stressful and intrusive, often feeling anxious about approaching sources who experienced trauma and guilt about imposing on their grief (Barnes, 2016; Duncan & Newton, 2010). Importantly, while these are often carried out by early career journalists, it does not appear that the sentiments of doing trauma interviews fade with experience. A senior broadcast editor describes it in this way:

> When you're talking to sources outside, and that could be anybody... [...] Ordinary people in extraordinary circumstances... So, you might wish to talk to somebody whose benefits have been stopped or somebody who has a drug problem, or it's some kind of, you know... Somebody who has lost a loved one in some circumstances where you have to be sensitive and caring, but at the same time persuasive to get them to talk to you. I definitely find that more... There's more anxiety...

Also, there seem to be gender and racial elements at play in this context. For example, female journalists in the UK and Australia have raised concerns about being labelled aggressive and difficult when asking challenging questions in interviews, saying male journalists would be more likely to be hailed as assertive in the same context (Knott, 2015; Women in Journalism Scotland, 2021). Arguably, working in such an environment might make some journalists more anxious about approaching sources than others. Journalist and columnist from the US, Merlene Davis, described her concerns about approaching sources due to her gender and race: 'I was scared of just walking up to people and asking them questions. It comes from years of being black, years of being a woman [...] It was aggressive, and you weren't supposed to be aggressive' (Braden, 2009: 164).

Another emotional situation that journalists speak of is the **frustration with non-responsive sources or those who are perceived as withholding or manipulating information**. Frustration with sources who do not engage, that is, do not pick up the phone or answer a message or email, is often raised by trainees who perceive their lack of power as impeding access to interviewees. Yet, it's a sentiment shared by some of those with many more years of experience in the industry. A mid-career digital editor shares her experience:

> My organisation gets missed off government briefings, or we don't get invited to certain things. Or people don't pick up the phone. Actually, that's a really, really massive impact on me. Like, because we're working from home, what you have to do all day is just ring ministers, ring advisors, ring people in government, and people don't pick up the phone at all. I had an example, this week, where I ran 13 people in a row, and nobody picked up the phone to me. And I'm sure and positive that happens to loads of other Westminster journalists, all the time. But just... That isn't a positive way of, like, working.

This impacts journalists' self-esteem and confidence, but also raises concerns about the quality of stories they produce if they do not get a response from a key source. A mid-career print reporter describes it like this:

> [There are] concerns about whether the story's going to be to the standard I hope it will be. And that's usually in terms of getting hold of the right people. And sometimes, you know, you don't know whether that person is going to get back to you in time and stuff like that.

As mentioned, there are also situations in which sources are perceived as trying to control the information by the extent or type of information they share, which is a common dynamic in relationships between journalists and sources (Berkowitz, 2019). In the words of a mid-career digital editor:

> I think there's frustration with the people we deal with. Often, they don't want to tell you the things you're asking them, and that can very much be like banging your head against a brick wall.

On the other hand, many journalists speak of the **feelings of responsibility towards their sources**—in telling their stories and protecting them from harm, particularly when a story is of a sensitive nature. A senior print reporter describes it in this way:

> Quite often, we will do a sensitive story; story that means a lot to the subject. And... And I feel.... I call it a 'moral nervousness' that we get it right for them. You know, again, there's so many things that we have to balance... One, we have to tell the truth and get things right. But, two, in some stories you've got a responsibility to represent the people involved... Well, you've always got a responsibility to do that, but I think in very emotive subjects or very personal stories, you do have a bigger responsibility, I think, to make sure that the person is represented correctly, in the way that they want to. If someone gives you a story about sexual assault and their experiences... There's a massive onus on you to represent that person's experiences correctly and in the right way and sensitively...

There are also worries about sources who are not accustomed to being in the spotlight as journalists express concerns for consequences of sources speaking out, including the potential trolling that may ensue on social media. A mid-career broadcast editor speaks of the guilt they felt after one such episode in which their sources have been abused over email and on social media following the report they published:

> They received such a huge amount of abuse in 24 hours that they had a mental breakdown, I think it's fair to say. You know, they were completely crushed the next day and in floods of tears with me, saying 'Why did I ever do this interview with you, I'm completely destroyed, I'll never work again,' and they were so badly damaged that... You know, I think that's my biggest concern now - the effect it's having on people that we interview.

[…] I felt incredibly guilty about the way that person felt, and I really analysed what I have done around that interview. Have I protected them enough? Was it my scripting around what they'd said? Did I go too strong? Did I, you know, push that point of view too hard?

In this context, journalists speak of their ethical considerations in such situations and the 'duty of care' they feel towards their sources. A senior broadcast editor describes his approach like this:

I took real care, and still take real care, to ensure that people feel comfortable about their participation in any of these things. […] So, I always take enormous care that people understand what they're doing. They're not going to be surprised by what they see on the TV. You're clear, both… If someone is talking about something which is bound to have a big impact on, say social media, that you say, 'Look, you need to be ready for what might come after this.' You know, I see that as part of my duty of care.

The friction between the feeling of responsibility to care for sources, make them feel comfortable and trusting with their story, and the nature of a journalist's job that requires verification and analysis, as well as observation of values of balance and impartiality in some media outlets, might be upsetting for some journalists. That is, journalists are aware that a source and their statements might not come off in the published story as they have wished and this might be disconcerting while working with them. In the words of a senior broadcast correspondent:

Dealing with sources is interesting because it is the one time when you are really having to deal with somebody on a personal level, and you are torn between wanting to sort of be friends with them, look after them, not upset them… But also having to sort of potentially, you know, assess their story to a destructive level. If they're lying to you, you absolutely have to get to the bottom of it. […] I do find it quite hard.

Interviewing

In connection to interviewing, journalism textbooks usually devote extensive attention to the process and practice of this aspect of a journalist's job. These usually include steps to prepare for an interview, including extensive research that should be carried out to learn about the topic, source and location, as well as preparing questions, followed by a list of do's and don'ts that are expected from journalists in this data gathering and performance act (see, e.g., Frost, 2010; Harcup, 2015; Hudson & Rowlands, 2018; Pape & Featherstone, 2005; Sissons, 2006). In the, often detailed, discussions of the process and practice of conducting interviews, it seems most likely that journalism textbooks will mention journalists' emotions. It is generally agreed that this aspect of journalists' job is 'daunting and difficult,' although the **nervousness, and sometimes fear, associated with interviews** is regularly ascribed to only early career journalists. American journalist Beth Winegarner (2012), who wrote for the likes of The New York Times, Washington Post and The Guardian, commented on how the requirement of doing interviews was anxiety-inducing at the start of her career: 'being a journalist meant talking to people. It meant picking up the phone and cold-calling strangers. It meant walking up to people on the street and asking them personal questions. It meant practically stalking politicians and public figures for a chance at a juicy quote. Each of these prospects terrified me.' My journalism trainees often express anxiety and nervousness about doing interviews, as did some emerging professionals interviewed for this book. In the words of an early career digital journalist:

> Sometimes I feel a bit nervous, I think, when I'm interviewing people, and especially if I'm ringing them up out of the blue, because… I used to be quite a socially anxious person so that was always a bit of a difficult thing when I was first starting the job - is actually talking to people.

However, it would be wrong to assume that this nervousness and anxiety necessarily evaporates with experience. For example, Carole Coleman, who was a Washington correspondent at the time, said she felt nervous for days before the 2004 broadcast interview with the then US President George W. Bush for Irish RTE (Hudson & Rowlands, 2018: 3). Similar sentiment was evident among British journalists interviewed for this book too. For example, a mid-career broadcast editor says:

> If you're interviewing the Prime Minister, then you might feel incredibly anxious about… Getting something… Because it's such a rare opportunity to interview someone like that, you will feel anxious about making the most of it and getting something interesting out of that interview that contributes to the sum total of human knowledge.

On the other hand, interviewing also often comes with feelings of **excitement and satisfaction, as well as pride**. As the following quotes testify, speaking to fascinating people who are doing interesting things, learning from them and enhancing their voices, can make interviewing a particularly satisfying and rewarding part of work.

Mid-career broadcast journalist:

It makes you feel plugged in, makes you feel fulfilled, makes you feel like this is what journalism is about... It is about finding voices.

Early career digital journalist:

It is also really enjoyable, I think, talking to people. You know, when you create a bond and a rapport with some people, and you get to talk to really interesting people as well, which is quite satisfying.

Mid-career print correspondent:

Quite often you just feel sort of lucky to be able to go and meet fascinating people who are doing fascinating things.

Mid-career broadcast editor:

One of the greatest satisfactions I get from my job is interviewing people who are vulnerable and nervous and helping them to tell their story. I don't know what... I don't know what emotion I would assign to that. I suppose probably pride and satisfaction.

When it comes to the conduct of the interview, journalists speak of **worrying about showing emotions that may be seen as inappropriate**, particularly in trauma-related interviews. Indeed, journalists are often trained to behave as objective and detached professionals who do not express emotion or emotionally react to their sources (Wahl-Jorgensen & Hanitzsch, 2019). Textbooks usually make reference to these under the 'don'ts' list, instructing journalists to not look nervous, excited or sympathetic to sources' testimonies, suggesting that otherwise they risk appearing unprofessional which can affect their credibility (Edwards, 2016; Hudson & Rowlands, 2018; Sissons, 2006). However, empathy is positioned as an important quality of interviewers (Lee-Potter & Adams, 2017) and British journalists who shared their experiences for this book mostly argued that you have to show some empathy with interviewees who are sharing traumatic experiences, but that it is a difficult balancing act of how much is appropriate. In the words of an early career broadcast journalist:

> You know, if somebody is telling me about a really awful situation then it's inhuman not to empathise with that. So, you do have to show empathy to people that you're interviewing. But I think there's a... There's a line between it. Because you still got to... You've got a job to do, and so, it's...You know, showing empathy without letting it kind of overwhelm you and what you need to do.

Another early career digital journalist reflected on the difficulty of restraining emotions while interviewing sources who have witnessed trauma:

> These people were saying that they have a lot of people dying near them. So, in their line of work, they had a lot of people they were looking after, a lot of clients, who were dying, and they thought it was quite unnecessary as well. You know, they saw a lot of unnecessary deaths and quite regularly in their line of work. Obviously, my job isn't nearly as stressful as that but, listening to that... umm... It's kind of tough. Emotionally it's kind of tough, because, you know... You just want to be able to hug them, but you can't.

Showing empathy in trauma interviews has also been described as perhaps a more effective way of putting sources at ease and in the end, getting more out of a story than you would if you kept in line with the set expectations of a professional journalistic behaviour. A mid-career print editor puts it like this:

> If you're knocking on the door of a parent... And I've probably done this hundreds of times... Whose child has died or... You know, the worst possible tragedy that could befall a parent... And then you've got to convince them to talk to you about it... You know, that can... You obviously can't, and you're trained not to really show any emotion at that time. But I'm a father myself, you know, I could... I mean, I probably wasn't a father, in fact, when I ever did do those things... But you can relate to these people in some way. And I think if you do, actually, you end up with a better story at the end of it.

Associated with the difficulties of **conducting trauma interviews are also the vicarious emotions that these can induce in journalists in the aftermath of interviews.** There has recently been more focus on 'vicarious trauma' in journalism, that which is associated with exposure to others' trauma, which journalists are likely to experience by interviewing victims and witnesses of trauma and hearing their often-distressing accounts of these experiences. For example, the Headlines Network (2022) have published a guide for journalists and newsrooms in how to manage vicarious trauma, emphasising that it can contribute to sleep problems, panic attacks, alcohol and substance abuse, among other things, if these emotions are not acknowledged and managed. Often times it is the feeling of sadness and grief that can stick with journalists after trauma interviews, as this early career digital reporter recounts:

> You know, I write about people dying all the time, so... You know, maybe I don't automatically get emotional about hearing about somebody dying, but then, if I do interview a family member, say he's lost a loved one in a really tragic way, and they get upset, then that can also have an impact on me. And I also feel sometimes I'm sharing, you know, the same emotions that they are. Particularly if I meet them in person. [...] I've been to people's houses to speak to them about things that happened. I had to go and knock on doors and talk to people about, you know, tragic things that have happened to them. And when you're faced immediately with someone and you get that kind of raw... You kind of feel their raw emotion... There's no way that that can't affect you.

Similarly, in the words of a mid-career print correspondent:

> If it's things more on the conflict reporting or whatever, I mean, I still feel a lot of, you know, vicarious emotions. I feel, like, so... You know, I do get, like, angry or worried or upset for the people that I'm talking to.

The feeling of anger induced by hearing accounts of injustice, often grounded in moral norms and facts, has been found in Stupart's (2022) study of investigative journalists in South Africa too. These journalists talked of anger as being appropriate and useful in journalism as experiencing it is 'something that "any, hopefully, human being" would feel' and the emotion is being used to motivate and drive work (Stupart, 2022: 8). A similar account is shared by an early career British print journalist:

Sometimes you speak to people about really emotive things and they might
be at their lowest level, really desperate for help. And that can affect you
as well, because then you feel sympathy and empathy and you want to do
what you can to help them. You can also maybe feel a bit angry about the
situation that they might be in, you know, if it involves other people that
are maybe doing things that are making their problem worse.

THINK

As explained in the Introduction chapter, emotional and physical
responses to a situation are driven by our beliefs and thoughts through
which we interpret that situation. If we are interpreting a situation with
negative thoughts, it's more likely that we will perceive it as an inevitable
occurrence which we have little or no control over. This can then lead to
increased stress. Thinking of the emotional situations discussed above,
Table 3.1 outlines several beliefs and thoughts that might be driving
negative emotions.

If you are experiencing negative emotions which you feel you need or
want to manage, you can check the beliefs and values, as well as thoughts

Table 3.1 Potential beliefs and thoughts that might be driving a negative emotional response to emotional situations associated with sources and
interviewing

Nervousness about contacting sources	Anxiety of conducting interviews	Worry about displaying inappropriate emotions during interviews
They will not want to talk to me	I will ask stupid or inappropriate questions	I won't be able to control my emotions
I'm incompetent if I'm scared of contacting them	I will not react in an appropriate way	I will look unprofessional if I show emotions
They will react negatively to me approaching them	I will upset the interviewee	My peers and/or bosses will think I am being unprofessional
I will make mistakes in the approach making me seen as incompetent or rude	I will forget what I wanted to ask	I will be labelled as weak and emotional
	They will say things I don't understand, and I'll look stupid	

and expectations that are driving these. In other words, think about what is driving your emotions, how can you update and reframe these with a more positive outlook and what options you have moving forward. For example, if you're nervous about contacting a source because you think they will not wish to speak to you, consider the various reasons why interviewees might be reluctant to speak to journalists. Is it necessarily about you? Or could it be because they are nervous about speaking to journalists? They might not have time for an interview? They might be dealing with some difficult things in their lives they do not wish to talk about? If you're anxious about asking stupid questions in an interview, consider if you feel prepared for it? Have you done the research? Have you learned about the topic and the interviewee? Consulted with your editor/or peers? If they think you're good to go, why wouldn't you? If you're worried that sharing emotions in an interview will make you appear unprofessional, consider if it is human to show no emotions at all? Wouldn't your interviewees like to know you empathise with what they're telling you? Would your audiences consider a lack of any kind of response from you the most professional way to behave?

The beliefs and values that drive these emotional situations will differ from journalist to journalist, so it's important you try to unpack what exactly is inducing your own emotions in this context. Are they rational? Logical? What evidence do you have to believe what you believe is happening? And while, similarly, journalists may decide to manage their emotions in diverse ways, there are some common emotion management strategies that journalists apply when faced with emotional situations tied to working with sources and interviewing, that the chapter now turns to.

CHOOSE: EMOTION MANAGEMENT STRATEGIES

The most commonly mentioned emotion management strategies by British journalists when dealing with emotional situations outlined above are internal processing in the form of positive reappraisal and perspective-taking; verbal processing with peers; and attentional deployment in both forms—following practice and routine, and engaging in diversionary activities.

Internal Processing

In relation to internal processing, Headlines Networks (2022) in their guide to managing vicarious trauma outlines the importance of taking the time before conducting trauma interviews to consider what you may expect from the interview and reminding yourself what is the purpose of the work you're doing. Similarly, in their study of journalists' perceptions on death knocks, Duncan and Newton (2010) suggest that positive reappraisal in the form of considering the positive outcomes from the action can be beneficial in relieving some of the anxiety of doing trauma interviews and guilt of imposing on those grieving loved ones. For example, some journalists will consider the fact that sometimes grieving family and friends might actually want to speak about their loved one and benefit from this verbal processing of their grief, and even perhaps get some satisfaction from seeing their story shared with the audiences. An early career print journalist tells of a story that made him consider that their actions in this regard are not as negative as they were perceiving them:

> I absolutely hated it [trauma interview]. Really, really hated it and felt terrible doing it. But then, some of them... [...] One that really stuck with me is... It was these two women, young women, like teenage, on maybe early 20s, and their dad died, and he had been perfectly fit and madly enthusiastic about football. And they were setting up a football charity foundation... And it was, like, one of the things where such a positive thing was coming out of it and they were so keen to talk about him and so thrilled to get it covered in the papers and stuff.

Another important practice of internal processing in relation to working with sources and interviewing is to consider the situation from the perspective of the source. While journalists try to manage their nerves, they will sometimes overlook the fact that sources might be quite nervous about speaking to journalists (Winegarner, 2012), particularly if there's a microphone and/or a camera involved. British television host, Jeremy Vine, said this on the topic: 'I do think that as professional broadcasters we underestimate the extent to which coming into a studio and talking to somebody and having five minutes to say your bit—and you're never going to get that five minutes again, and it's live—we underestimate how frightening that is' (Hudson & Rowlands, 2018: 84). In general, there are many reasons why sources may be reluctant to agree to an interview. They might be worried about how they will come across, what they will say, how readers and viewers will react to them, the reactions on social media, as well as the impact that any potential mistakes will have on their careers and relationships. They might be distrustful of the media in general or the media company from which the interview request is coming from. They might be dealing with difficult situations in their lives and preparing for and doing interviews might not be on the top of their agenda. The study by City University illustrates the issue well. Their research into the reasons why women experts are reluctant to speak to media revealed that 71% of respondents lack confidence to give interviews, 45% worry about feedback, 39% worry about appearance, and 10% fear that they will be seen as 'pushy' or 'arrogant' for giving interviews (Howell & Singer, 2019). This is to say that while not getting an interviewee can induce anxiety in a journalist or drive them to question their competence, it may be useful to take the perspective that sources can have any one of dozens of reasons for not wanting to speak to media, and this reason likely has little to do with the journalist in question.

Perspective-taking can be useful also in managing the nervousness about not getting the (perfect) interviewee or information from them. On the one hand, journalists with more years of experience in the industry draw on their experiences with the process and outcomes in evaluating potential consequences of not securing an interview. In the words of a mid-career print reporter:

> Experience just tells you that, you know, even if this person doesn't, you know, I guess, provide what you want, then it's not the end of the world.

On the other hand, taking the perspective that it is more important to try and get to the source than worry about whether they will answer your questions can lift some of the anxiety about contacting sources. A senior broadcast editor puts it in an interesting way:

> I'm more nervous of not getting the story right, than I am of talking to them. So, it's competitive fears. (laughs)

Verbal Processing

Next, many journalists find verbal processing with colleagues helpful in managing the emotions induced by the prospect of interviewing and in the aftermath of it. For example, speaking to colleagues about a lack of response from sources could help lift some of the frustration about not being able to get a source to speak to you. An early career digital journalist describes it like this:

> I'm probably complaining to colleagues about it. Definitely in my previous workplace I feel like it was very... We spent a lot of time complaining. That could in itself be quite funny, and we would compare anecdotes... I think journalism as a job, anyway, you spend quite a lot of time discussing things with your colleagues, because you're... So many aspects of journalism are judgement calls that you make and you're trying to understand, you know, how you should respond to certain things; whether press officers are being appropriate in a certain situation; whether this is to be expected from a press officer or from a source, or whether you should push a bit more. So, yeah, I feel like quite frequently I would be... Yeah, venting or complaining with colleagues about the situation.

Beyond getting practical advice on how the situation can be managed and emotional release from sharing your emotions, an important benefit of discussing the situation with colleagues is also the learning that others experience similar challenges. This can alleviate some of the worry about the lack of competence and increase self-confidence. In the words of a mid-career digital editor:

> Sometimes when I have those conversations and people can say, 'Oh it's not just you,' - that helps.

It has also been mentioned that discussing an approach to interview and interview questions with colleagues can be beneficial as they can offer practical advice, which in the end can reassure the interviewing journalist that they are doing the right thing. This can help manage some of the nervousness before an interview. This kind of briefing and brainstorming can be particularly important ahead of a trauma interview. A mid-career broadcast editor reflects on the practice by saying:

> Talking to colleagues is always really helpful. So, I would normally plan the interview and bounce some ideas off colleagues to kind of check I'm not missing anything that I want to ask. And often... You know, it's only a very small team... It's only a very small team, where I work, so we don't have huge meetings about these interviews but you're often working with

maybe one or two other colleagues, so you can kind of come together and have a bit of a support network when you're going into these interviews.

Support from peers in a form of debriefing following difficult interviews has been mentioned as especially valuable in managing vicarious emotions that arise from these. Yet, given the often-disturbing content, some journalists worry that they will pass on the vicarious emotions by speaking to colleagues about it. Hence, they approach the conversation with care and try to make sure that their colleagues are okay with being part of that conversation. In the words of an early career digital journalist:

> I actually found it a bit difficult when it was, sort of, really quite graphic... Because... I don't want to...How do I put this into words? If it's really difficult for me to listen to it, if it's a bit of a challenge for me to listen to it, then I don't want to put other people through that challenge as well, I don't want to make things difficult for them, you know. It's sort of... You're passing on a challenge to them, which is... Sometimes I feel bad, if it's like a really graphic traumatic thing. It's not necessary to do, I suppose, so I sort of capture it, I sort of say, 'Do you mind if I tell you about something a bit horrible?' and then they'll always say, 'No, of course, not,' and then I'll try to be sensitive about it.

In such and similar situations, it might also be worth exploring other forms of verbal processing, such as, for example, therapy. Several media organisations, particularly larger ones, such as the BBC and The Guardian in the UK, have counselling services on offer to journalists who may need them.

Finally, it has been emphasised that the challenge of managing emotions arising from trauma interviews has been exacerbated by remote working during the COVID-19 pandemic and the decision of some newsrooms to continue working in mainly remote or hybrid modes following the pandemic. Journalists say that this format of work eliminates some of the informal opportunities, usually common in newsrooms and around them, to gain emotional release and support from peers. An early career digital reporter describes it like this:

> I think there's a real issue at the moment with a lot of people home working, particularly journalists, that you can't have that kind of collective debrief, in a way. If you've had a big story or a big event happened, you can go to the pub afterwards and relax a bit, and you can discuss it, but

in a less formal way. And it can help it, you know, get off your chest. And I think there's also a certain amount of black humour in newsrooms among journalists... In a similar way you hear about people who work in like ambulance or police or have to deal with not very nice subjects a lot of the time. And I think journalists have a sort of similar coping mechanism where, you know, you'll have a joke in the office together, and those kinds of things, about something that only you all will understand. And sometimes that's lost when you're not around people.

Attentional Deployment

The third emotion management strategy that British journalists employ in emotional situations associated with working with sources and interviewing is attentional deployment. On the one hand, this means following the routines and practices of the profession to increase your confidence in your work and yourself as a professional whose job is to approach people and get information from them.

In terms of managing anxiety about approaching sources, particularly for journalism trainees and early career professionals, this might involve 'putting on a "professional persona"' (Edwards, 2016: 106). At a very basic level, this might involve identifying yourself as a journalist when approaching sources. Indeed, trainees and emerging professionals who start their career by freelancing, and hence, do not have media affiliations to signpost their legitimacy and power, sometimes struggle to self-identify as journalists. To assist with this, I often suggest to my journalism students to apply for a student membership of the National Union of Journalists. Among the many perks of the membership is also a student press card that can be used when approaching sources to signal your legitimacy as a journalist. I've found this to impact on their confidence to approach sources. There are also certain behaviours that are associated with journalists that can be practised to position yourself as a member of this community of practice. For example, having a reporter's notebook and/or a recording device signals to sources that you are a journalist, and hence, puts you in a position where you are expected to ask questions. As the US journalist Beth Winegarner (2012) advises: 'Your role as a journalist gives you special permission to be nosy. Police, legislators and everyday citizens might think it's weird if a stranger starts asking them questions, but if you whip out your reporter's notebook and give them your business card, they'll usually accept that it's your job to cross-examine them.'

Next, it is conventional wisdom when it comes to interviewing that good preparation can alleviate much of the nervousness and anxiety. This is where journalism textbooks and training are particularly useful, as there are clear processes to follow to ensure a journalist goes into an interview well prepared, which can increase confidence in pulling off the task. 'Stepping' your way towards the interview—doing the research about the topic, studying the interviewee, scouting interviewing locations, writing interview questions, etc.—breaks the task into smaller steps that a journalist can, and should, take to gain confidence before going into an interview. Many British journalists interviewed for this book, whatever their seniority, emphasised the importance of good preparation for alleviating some of the anxiety associated with conducting interviews. Some early career journalists spoke about other practical steps they take in order to ensure their nerves do not interfere with the conduct of the interview. For example, this early career digital journalist speaks of the value of writing yourself a script to follow and fall back onto if nerves get the better of you, which can be particularly useful in doing phone interviews:

> Sometimes, when it's a really nerve-wracking phone call I have to make, I'll write myself like a little script. It's maybe a bit pathetic, but I'll even say, 'Hello it's [name],' and I'll write that down, and I'll say, 'I'm a reporter from…,' and then I'll write that down. Then I'll say what the questions I want to ask them are. That really helps, I think, because it sort of shuts off your brain from thinking too much and you're just reading. And that's a bit of a more of a simple task to do.

Similarly, it is suggested that a journalist should have questions written down so they don't forget them in high-adrenaline situations. This will often be on paper or on a digital device, but an early career print correspondent shares an additional tip:

> If it's a doorstep, then the tip is normally to write it on your hand, because otherwise you sort of forget it, and the specific wording of the question can be very important. You don't want it written on your phone, because unlocking your phone in a brief… You know, two seconds when somebody walked past you is… Time lost.

In relation to the worry some journalists feel about managing sources' expectations, journalism textbooks and training emphasise that it is important to be honest and transparent with sources about what you are doing and how the gathered information will be used (see, e.g., Lee-Potter & Adams, 2017). Arguably, by briefing sources before an interview, some of the anxiety about what they might feel about their participation once the story is run can be alleviated, as a journalist can reassure themselves that the source was aware of potential consequences. A senior broadcast correspondent describes their approach:

> I do this more and more and sort of the experience of last few years has led me to do this... You say, 'Look...' And actually, I'm amazed that people accept it... But you say, 'Look, I really want to come and get to the bottom of this, but you may not like the way it comes out. You may find that I'm stressing bits of the story you don't think are right or, you know, I find that something he says is not quite right and I proved it the other way. You know, I may not do the story at all... You know, we may just... You know, it may come to nothing. But what I'm going to promise you - I'll take a professional approach to it. And the organisation I work for gives me the time and the space and the resources to do that. And also, I've got the experience to do that.' Actually, that comes across pretty well. People generally don't run away, you know, when you do that.

As mentioned, the feeling of responsibility towards sources can be particularly strong in trauma interviews. And while the practices and protocols of caring for trauma interviewees are yet to become standard in journalism schools and newsrooms, there is increasing focus on this aspect of journalists' work and growing number of resources that can be consulted in order to ensure that best practice is being followed. For example, the Dart Centre for Journalism and Trauma, Reynolds Journalism Institute, Poynter, International Journalists' Network and Jo Healey's Trauma Reporting are just some of those who offer useful practical advice and training on how to conduct trauma interviews in ways that care for both interviewees and interviewers. By ensuring that you are up to date with the best practice in the field, you can alleviate some of the anxiety associated with doing this work.

In order to manage the worry that inappropriate emotions will be shown in trauma interviews, some journalists say that alongside being briefed about what to expect and considering what their own reactions might be, they also try to focus in the interview on 'listening' as one of the key elements of any interview. They say this helps them to stay focused and maintain a 'professional' appearance, while expressing empathy through active listening. An early career print journalist puts it like this:

> I guess mostly I just try and keep the view that I'm just listening to what they're saying, I'm not... I'm not giving my opinion on their situation. I'm just listening to what they have to say, what they want to tell me. [...] Just trying not to involve myself really and focus on the details of anything that's going on.

When it comes to managing vicarious emotions induced by doing trauma interviews, journalists commonly spoke of the other form of attentional deployment—engaging in diversionary activities. This is in line with the advice from Headlines Network (2022) which outlined regular exercise, good sleep and disconnection strategies, among practices that can help in managing vicarious trauma. In the words of an early career digital reporter:

> I have to make sure I, you know, tune out, really. I have to make sure I've got some kind of distraction. I found that that has been a lot more difficult in the lockdowns. You know, the year of lockdowns. You know, normally, one of my things I'll do is I'll just go see a friend, or you know, we just go to the pub, or relax, or go for a meal, or just, you know, anything. (laughs)

Engaging in diversionary activities has been mentioned as a useful strategy in other situations too, such as dealing with the frustration from non-responsive sources. A mid-career digital editor describes their practice like this:

> It's getting out of the house. It's stopping thinking about it. It's going for a run. It's... You know, it's a way of switching off. You have to. Otherwise, you'll just sit and dwell on it for the entire evening, week, month, whatever. But yeah, that does involve doing something completely unrelated. I'm a mom, I've got friends, I go running... Any of those things are things that... Anything to forget the day you've had, really.

In general, exercise has been hailed as particularly useful in fighting the stress of the job by journalists of all levels of experience. For example, this senior print reporter says that exercise helps them manage both nervousness and excitement associated with contacting interviewees and conducting interviews:

> I do a little bit of running, as well... Physical activity... Which I found has been really beneficial, and it's lowered the stress levels.

In sum, this chapter has covered several emotional situations that are likely to arise while working with sources and interviewing them, namely: nervousness of contacting sources; frustration with non-responsive sources or those who appear to be withholding information; feelings of responsibility towards telling their stories and protecting them from harm; excitement and satisfaction, as well as anxiety related to conducting interviews; worry about displaying inappropriate emotions (particularly in trauma-related interviews) and difficulties in dealing with vicarious emotions. It has been suggested that key strategies to manage these emotions include verbal processing with colleagues; internal processing practices of positive reappraisal and perspective-taking; as well as attentional deployment techniques of following routines and engaging in diversionary activities.

The UK: Sian Elvin on Sourcing

Sian Elvin is an award-winning British journalist with a decade of experience across national, local and student media. She is currently the deputy news editor of the Metro and was previously a content editor for local news websites MyLondon and Kent Live. She has also had bylines in several other national publications and is a mental health first aider.

I remember very clearly it was in April 2022 that our news desk was flooded with some of the most horrific images I've seen in my career—the atrocities in Bucha around one month into the Ukraine war. The awful details and witness accounts of what had happened started to trickle in, and those of us working that day simply got on with our jobs by sifting through vast quantities of graphic, upsetting and potentially traumatising material. We put aside our shock to communicate a story to our readers clearly, while maintaining the dignity of those killed and respecting a grieving community.

But when I finished work that evening, I felt utterly exhausted and drained. I sat on the sofa until the sun went down, pretty much staring into space while I waited for the terrible images I'd seen to fade from my mind.

At least when I trained as a journalist almost 10 years ago, it was drilled into us how to be 'perfect' reporters. From learning the ins and outs of media law to being faced with difficult interviewees, we were prepared to ask tough questions, take down exact quotes in court and avoid being sued. What I was not ready for at the end of my course, however, was how emotionally taxing this career can be.

After a difficult and sad weekend where I slept dreadfully, I sloped back into the office the next week feeling somewhat guilty. People were dying in Ukraine, but I was living in relative safety and stability. So why was I this upset? Over the course of the day several of our team reached out to one another and started to talk it through, acknowledging we'd all had a similar reaction and offering our support. I finished work that day not feeling exactly like a problem shared was a problem solved, but feeling somewhat lighter. I went to an exercise class that evening and the endorphins were a great distraction, then I had dinner with a friend who works in a similar industry. When she asked me how I was, instead of responding 'I'm fine' I told her more about how I was feeling, and both her and my acknowledgement of my emotions was soothing and made me realise my guilt was unfounded.

My experience above is not unusual—it's something which happens to journalists all the time, and not just as a result of reporting on war. I've sat in my car and cried after a court case; I've walked out of an emotional interview with a poker face but then sobbed all the way home. We all need to talk about this more in journalism and share our coping mechanisms. Do whatever you need to process your completely understandable emotions, whether that is sitting in the dark and processing, watching trashy television or simply sharing a quiet pint at the pub with a colleague who understands.

Top Tips

- Be aware of the routines to prepare for an interview—research the topic, the source and the interviewing location, write a list of questions, consider what kind of challenges you may face and what your own reactions to interviewee's responses may be
- Practise journalistic behaviours to signpost to interviewees that you are a journalist—obtain a press card, have a reporter's notebook and/or recording device and identify yourself as a journalist from the start
- Consult with your editors and peers before the interview including the briefing about any potential challenges you may face in particularly difficult interviews (e.g., involving victims or witnesses of trauma)
- Debrief with your peers or editor following interviews, especially those that induce vicarious emotions. If you think you'd benefit from further verbal processing of your emotions, consider counselling.
- Consider why you're doing a particular interview and what may be the positive outcomes of it for the source, the audience and yourself professionally
- In interviews, be polite and honest, transparent about who you are, what you are doing, what sources can expect from the story and any potential consequences of the published story
- Take regular breaks from work—engage in non-work-related activities that make you happy—to give yourself time to process your emotions and balance the negative emotions with positive ones
- It's ok if you need more support than you can give yourself—be aware of organisational support on offer and engage with it when needed (e.g., counselling service)

Read, Watch and Listen

- Read Jo Healey's Trauma Reporting Toolkit—https://traumareport ing.com/resources/toolkit/
- Read Headlines Network's guidelines on managing vicarious trauma—https://bit.ly/HNVTdoc22

- Watch the training session on doing trauma interviews and taking care of yourself following them, delivered by Bruce Shapiro, the executive director of the Dart Center for Journalism and Trauma— https://www.youtube.com/watch?v=ytSjDpF7XtM
- Listen to Behind the Headlines podcast episode featuring ABC correspondent James Longman in which he speaks about his sense of responsibility towards sources, considering the consequences of them sharing their stories—https://podfollow.com/behind-the-hea dlines-with-headlines-network/episode/3dd44bc8ff022273d8200 dd853cd27a8e4de9a43/view
- Listen to The Tip Off podcast episode 'What a scoop!' featuring Sam McAlister telling the story of how she booked Prince Andrew for the Newsnight interview—https://thetipoffpodcast.com/podcast/ ep-66-what-a-scoop/

Scenario Exercises

Scenario 1

You work freelance as a science journalist. You have just successfully pitched a story to a national daily newspaper about new research showing that 'forever chemicals' (think non-stick fry pan and rainproof jackets) can have serious health consequences, including pregnancy complications and cancer, and the implications of this for the manufacturing industries. In the pitch, you named several scientists and industry representatives who may speak on the topic.

Yet, five calls in, and they either didn't pick up the call or said that they do not wish to comment on the issue. You've exhausted your list of top sources to consult for the story. The deadline to submit the article is fast approaching—only a few days left to file the copy.

- How does this make you feel?
- What are you going to do? Why?

Scenario 2

You work for a regional radio station as a city reporter, covering anything from council meetings to local market shenanigans. Occasionally you also report on a local scuffle, and you've once done a 'death knock' assignment following a traffic accident. News comes in from the police department that there has been a knife fight at a local college, with two young adults dead and four in hospital with life changing injuries. The story is too big for radio's crime reporter to cover it on its own, so it's all hands on deck. You are dispatched to the hospital to find relatives of students who were attacked and get background on them, as well as quotes from the family and friends.

- How does this make you feel?
- What are you going to do? Why?

REFERENCES

Barnes, L. (2016). *Journalism and everyday trauma: A grounded theory of the impact from death-knocks and court reporting.* Auckland University of Technology.

Berkowitz, D. (2019). Reporters and their sources. In K. Wahl-Jorgensen & T. Hanitzsch (Eds.), *The handbook of journalism studies* (2nd ed., pp. 165–179). Taylor & Francis Group.

Braden, M. (2009). *She said what? interviews with women newspaper columnists.* The University Press of Kentucky.

Duncan, S., & Newton, J. (2010). How do you feel? Preparing novice reporters for the death knock. *Journalism Practice, 4*(4), 439–453.

Edwards, V. (2016). *Research skills for journalists.* Taylor & Francis Group.

Frost, C. (2010). *Reporting for journalists* (2nd ed.). Taylor & Francis.

Harcup, T. (2015). *Journalism principles and practice* (3rd ed.). SAGE.

Headlines Network. (2022). *Vicarious trauma: A guide for journalists and newsrooms to recognise vicarious trauma and mitigate against it.* Headlines Network. https://img1.wsimg.com/blobby/go/6ca5410e-ac1d-4642-b85f-b717e6a71453/downloads/VicariousTrauma_final.pdf?ver=1668672882671

Howell, L., & Singer, J. B. (2019). Pushy or a princess? Women experts and UK broadcast news. *Journalism Practice, 13*(8), 1018–1023.

Hudson, G., & Rowlands, S. (2018). *The broadcast journalism handbook* (7th ed.). Routledge.

Knott, M. (2015). *Female interviewers attacked for just being tough: ABC's Emma Alberici.* The Sydney Morning Herald. https://www.smh.com.au/politics/federal/female-interviewers-attacked-for-just-being-tough-abcs-emma-alberici-20150518-gh4a3f.html

Lee-Potter, E., & Adams, S. (2017). *Interviewing for Journalists* (3rd ed.). Routledge.

Lewis, J., Williams, A., & Franklin, B. (2008). A compromised fourth estate?: UK news journalism, public relations and news sources. *Journalism Studies, 9*(1), 1–20.

Pape, S., & Featherstone, S. (2005). *Newspaper journalism: A practical introduction.* SAGE.

Sissons, H. (2006). *Practical journalism how to write news.* SAGE.

Stupart, R. (2022). Anger and the investigative journalist. *Journalism,* 1–18. https://doi.org/10.1177/14648849221125980

Wahl-Jorgensen, K., & Hanitzsch, Thomas. (Eds.). (2019). *The handbook of journalism studies* (2nd ed.). Taylor & Francis Group.

Winegarner, B. (2012). *5 ways journalists can overcome shyness during interviews.* Poynter. https://www.poynter.org/reporting-editing/2012/5-ways-journalists-can-overcome-shyness-during-interviews/

Women in Journalism Scotland. (2021). *Being challenging shouldn't be seen as aggressive - it's just doing your job properly.* Women in Journalism Scotland. https://www.wijscotland.com/tips-advice/being-fair-is-not-aggressive-its-just-doing-your-job-properly

CHAPTER 4

Research & Writing

One of my favourite jobs in journalism was writing destination profiles for a lifestyle magazine. I didn't do this often, maybe a couple of times a year, mostly by combining business and pleasure. Meaning, if I travelled somewhere for pleasure, I'd pitch the destination profile to the magazine for which I've been freelancing. The pitch was regularly successful if that destination hasn't yet been covered and so I'd proceed to produce the story. It was a classic destination profile they were after—what to do, what to see, where to eat and where to stay—those kinds of things. I would consider my trip as a sort of experience research which I thought helped me choose the relevant facts to present in the story. Yet, this was also the catch—my experience was personal and subjective. Hence, I'd often fret about which of the things I've experienced should make the story, and how should I discuss them in a neutral way.

And while I'd regularly go through this cycle of worrying about how to detach myself from my own experiences and write the profile in what I thought was an objective manner, I'd also in the end regularly resort to focusing on the professional routines in producing the story. I would do desk research to check the key attractions and experiences, as well as places to stay and restaurants to visit, paying attention to visitors' reviews of these. Of course, I would make a subjective selection of which elements to include in the profile, and this was sometimes influenced by my own experience of these. Also, after checking that my own experience was

© The Author(s), under exclusive license to Springer Nature Switzerland AG 2023
M. Šimunjak, *Managing Emotions in Journalism*, https://doi.org/10.1007/978-3-031-38631-2_4

not unusual, I'd add occasional remarks of things I've witnessed which I thought would add value to the story. For example, I'd mention that visitors can expect a long queue to get a scoop of ice-cream from a famous *gelatteria*, that seasonally there are jellyfish in the sea of a popular beach, or that the subway is packed during peak travel times. I would reflect on the choices to check my reasoning and the underlying assumptions and values and as long as I was content that I can rationally defend the choices; the worry about the subjectivity of the story would be kept at bay.

In this chapter, the emotional situations related to the stages of research and writing are examined through the 'stop, think, choose' model of emotional intelligence. The 'stop' section discusses emotional situations related to research by focusing on excitement about uncovering new and unknown information, but also signposts that research can be seen as frustrating, dull and laboursome, and putting the story together can be quite draining. In connection to news writing, the discussed issues are nervousness about the story's quality and standards, especially accuracy; and the worry about not being seen as objective, neutral, detached and impartial. In the 'think' section, some beliefs and thoughts which may be driving mentioned emotions are outlined. The 'choose' section suggests emotion management strategies informed by interviews with practising journalists. These include verbal processing with colleagues and editors; internal processing practices of perspective-taking, as well as acceptance; and attentional deployment in the form of focusing attention on professional routines and practices to ensure expected standards are met with care.

STOP: EMOTIONAL SITUATIONS

Research, as a process of gathering and verifying information, is thought to be the cornerstone of journalism as it is often seen as a boundary marker which distinguishes journalistic work and its outputs from those of other actors, particularly in the digital sphere. In other words, while nowadays anyone with an internet connection can publish content online, it is expected that content that journalists publish will have been researched and verified, and hence, has higher levels of credibility. Accordingly, journalism textbooks regularly instruct trainees in how they can do research and what types of research are common in the industry. For example, Chater (2002) describes talk, desk and experience research;

Iorio (2004) focuses on qualitative research processes and methods, such as interviews, focus groups, ethnographies, textual analysis and civic mapping; while a range of textbooks emphasise online research, including working with email alerts, social media and search engines (Bradshaw, 2018; Bull, 2016). In a specialised textbook, Edwards' (2016) Research skills for journalists, working with digital and non-digital data is described.

Research

British journalists interviewed for this book spoke of the process of research as being frustrating and laboursome, yet if the research yields interesting and important information, then the process can be seen as quite exciting and gratifying. In particular, journalists speak of the **excitement that comes with uncovering new and unknown information**. For example, a mid-career print editor describes how 'gratifying' it is to be the first to learn a new piece of information:

> You know, getting... Speaking to the right people, them saying what you want them to say, or what you expect them to say... Finding out things that other people don't know yet is a real thrill.

Some journalists speak of the 'rush' that comes with research when it leads to revealing information that is a game-changer for a story and/or they can see how important it might be to their audiences, the public, even if the process of obtaining it was difficult. In the words of a senior broadcast editor:

> Trying to get a story, trying to work your contacts, that can be quite stressful, that's quite pressurised. It can be quite wearying. But the exhilaration of getting a line or landing a piece of information is just like a massive adrenaline hit. Uncovering something that you think has a substantive difference to policy or people's lives, that's quite... That's obviously very professionally rewarding. So, you have different... You kind of have the input of the story, which is how you get it and how you put it together, and that's both pressurised and exhilarating at the same time. That's the kind of enjoyable, slightly addictive bit of the job, actually.

The excitement is also evident in accounts of journalists who do experience research by being part of big events, such as rallies or protests, but also those that bear witness to gatherings of people that are perceived as important and powerful. A senior print correspondent tells of their experience:

> You know, another really thrilling bit is actually physically, which is not something I've obviously done for that last year, but physically being amid a story which is exciting, for whatever reason. So, it can just be because of the kind of personnel there. So, for example, you know, in the job that I do now, if you're at a political event and there's a lot of people who are incredibly powerful there's this reflected kind of... I don't know, not reflected importance, but it's, kind of, reflected thrill it comes from it, which I think is quite a big part of being a journalist.

And while journalism textbooks tell us how research should be done, journalism studies reveal far less about how journalists actually do research, particularly in everyday work, as the majority of studies that look into the practice focus on that of investigative journalists, who can be broadly defined as those journalists who spend a significant amount of time uncovering and verifying information that some may prefer to be kept out of the spotlight. While investigative journalists usually have more time to research stories, same or similar methods are applied in research processes and the distinction between investigative and 'normal' journalism remains contested. Indeed, investigative journalists themselves have described their work as 'normal journalism' (Cancela et al., 2021). For example, a study of Norwegian journalists' investigative work revealed that some of the most common ways to gather information are obtaining and scrutinising public documents and datasets, and interviewing sources, while claims are being verified by, for example, cross-referencing with other sources and digital verification procedures (Bjerknes, 2022). Most of these methods have been mentioned by British journalists interviewed for this book too. In general, while successful research can lead to excitement, the **research process itself is often described as tiresome and frustrating**. For example, this senior broadcast editor describes the process of scrutinising public data in this way:

> There are less exciting things that you do, which is trawling through hours and hours and hours of parliamentary committees, for example. [...] Sometimes it makes me feel a bit bored, sometimes it makes me feel a bit frustrated because the politicians, sometimes, don't ask very good questions. And sometimes it can actually be great because you find an absolute nugget of news in it. And that can be absolutely fascinating.

Edwards (2016) describes the research process as rarely being linear and straightforward, as uncovering new information will often return the journalist to the start of the research process in trying to verify this information and/or find new perspectives on it. Hence, it doesn't surprise that many journalists describe the process of research as both tiresome and exciting. In a similar perspective to that above, a senior print editor shares their experience of news gathering:

> The business of actually fixing these things up is rather dull often, and laboursome, and tiresome, because you often don't get very far, and it takes a long time and it's not the end product. However, when you have fixed up... When you... When you can see how something is going to come together, who you've got involved in your story, who's going to respond to it and how it might work, then you do begin to again feel a raised sense of excitement / anxiety...

In the political economy of media in which less journalists are required to produce more work and resources for long-term investigations with uncertain outcomes are scarce, some newsrooms now require beat reporters to do investigative journalism within their specialisms (Cancela, 2021).This certainly holds true for interviewed British journalists, as especially the more senior ones have regularly been running longer-term investigations that resulted in big scoops. Similar experiences have been mentioned by Swiss journalists, who in this context spoke of extreme workloads and exhausting pace of work in which they tried to cover their beats' everyday news while investigating a big story (Cancela & Dubied, 2022). British journalists often described the pace of longer investigative work as time consuming and slow, causing frustration. In the words of a senior broadcast correspondent:

> There's quite a lot of frustration about just the simple difficulty of doing sort of investigative work, which I'm increasingly doing or trying to do and doing... And just kind of the amount of work and effort that has to go into getting quite small steps forward.

The importance of gathering and verifying information has been regularly mentioned by early career journalists too, who also spoke of the frustration that arises when they face obstacles in the research process. This may not be surprising given the importance that is put on publishing verified stories in this media system. According to the Worlds of Journalism study, three out of four British journalists do not approve of publishing stories with unverified information, nor do almost 90% of journalists from the US (Hanitzsch et al., 2019). 'Unhelpful press officers' and 'rejected FOI requests' have been mentioned among 'brick walls' that journalists face in the research process. An early career print correspondent describes their experience:

> Frustration is definitely a feeling you get a lot, when you are kind of trying to stand something up and you're trying to verify something or get to the bottom of something and you're facing a lot of obstacles. Or when you... When you're not sure where to take the story next or how to verify the story or how to, kind of, get it over the line, if that makes sense?

Given the barriers and setbacks, the pressure to gather and/or verify information can lead journalists to over-work, as this account of a mid-career digital reporter illustrates:

> Like, it makes you do things like... Work later than you might do, or you might start early, or you might work at the weekend, because you feel this kind of pressure to get the job done.

When working on an investigative story or a scoop, even if there is no set deadline to deliver it, journalists speak of the pressure and stress they feel in making the story stand. This seems to particularly be the case when the story is seen as in public interest and one that will hold powerful to account. British journalists' experiences seem to be comparable to those of Swiss journalists who revealed that working on investigative stories can intrude on their private lives and off-work time and can lead to fatigue and burnout (Cancela & Dubied, 2022). A senior print editor shares their experience of working on a scoop:

> That also puts a huge amount of pressure on you as well, because I've had stories where I've laid in bed at night thinking, 'How can I get this over the line? Who do I need to speak to? What bit of information do I need to find? How can I corroborate this?' And that's quite, you know, that's not as enjoyable experience, because you sort of have this constant fear that you might not be able to get it over the line. And we all have stories in our careers that we've not been able to stand up. We were pretty sure that they happened but, for whatever reason... Because we have both

moral and ethical and legal obligations before we publish anything, we've not managed to get them over the line so... You know, you're kind of driven by this desire to expose the truth, on the one hand, but on the other hand, this sort of fear that you might not manage it.

It isn't just journalists working to stand up a story that are often kept up at night by thinking about research. Journalists who are tasked with covering diary events also speak of the pressure to deliver extra value to stories they know everyone will cover through their information gathering. In the words of a senior broadcast editor:

> The story that you know is going to be coming up in a month's time and you're sort of... I mean that does... I find myself when... There are not many of them, but you do have sort of anniversaries and big stories you know are going to happen... And I do find myself thinking about them all the time. Thinking, 'How can I make...' You know, everyone's going to come up there... It's not a surprise, the story, it's not a big exclusive, it's just... I want my coverage, my explanation, my journalism, to stand out and be as helpful as it can be. And I... I do find that these stories will nag away at me. I will wake up in the middle of the night, sometimes with, 'Oh my God, how can we make this work?'

Writing

Once the newsgathering and verification processes are complete, comes the task of writing the story. Journalism textbooks devote significant attention to the process of writing stories, often making distinctions by genre, that is, offering guidance on the expected norms in writing, for example, news, features, opinion and review pieces (see, e.g., Bull, 2016; Harcup, 2015) and the specific language and structure expectations when writing for different mediums and platforms (e.g., see Bradshaw, 2018 about writing for web; Hudson & Rowlands, 2018 about writing for broadcast). And while for some stories the writing part could be quite quick and straightforward, this isn't always the case, and especially with stories that contain many, sometimes moving, pieces of information. A senior print editor explains how writing a complex or big story can be a challenging task:

The writing of it, for me... I always dread it. Because it is the moment where you have to sort of perform and it's the moment in which you really begin to think, 'Is this going to work and how well?' Well, you begin to realise is it going to be good, is it going to work, and you begin to also realise how well it's going to work.

One of the key stressors in this phase, according to British journalists, is **the worry about ensuring that the story is accurate in how it's presented to audiences.** Their experiences of emotions in this situation seem to echo Randall and Crew's (2021: 86) claim that 'a certain paranoia about getting things wrong is the hallmark of professionals' in this industry. Yet, stories often contain inaccuracies. Studies applying the Charnley method, that is, asking news sources to evaluate the accuracy of stories in which they feature, found factual inaccuracies in 60% of newspapers stories reviewed in Switzerland, 52% in Italy, and 61% in the US (Maier, 2005; Porlezza et al., 2012). In the UK, research found that broadsheets, which are considered quality papers and 'truth keepers,' tend to publish more inaccurate stories nearer elections (Wilczek & Thurman, 2022). These conditions and practices have an impact on the level of trust that the audiences have in media, journalists' reputation, as well as the willingness of sources to continuously engage with the media (Maier, 2005). The study of Canadian journalists' verification practices found that they are keen to ensure information in stories is accurate, but also that they put more focus on accuracy of names, numbers and quotes, than, for example, sources' statements (Shapiro et al., 2013). The anxiety about getting the information about sources right is shared by this British early career digital reporter:

Sometimes I get, while I'm writing up a story, especially if I feel like it's something that's quite important... It makes me quite stressed. [...] I think, most importantly, I feel a kind of responsibility to tell my sources' stories, you know, accurately and well. And I would never want to misquote them or get something wrong, so it does make me stressed when I've got a big story and I'm sort of trying to get it out.

The decisions about what to include and exclude, what angle to take, whose voices to include, can also drive anxiety as audiences might perceive a story to be inaccurate if they feel an important angle or a piece of information has been left out. For example, a study done in the US found that news sources perceived 47% of news stories containing 'subjective' errors, among which most common is information that sources deemed was important but was left out of the story (Maier, 2005). In the UK, a senior broadcast editor tells how the process of story writing in which one reflects on the many ways a story can be told, and considered inaccurate, can be anxiety-inducing:

> Generally, the whole thing about... There're so many ways to tell a story and whatever and... So, you always have that slight sense of... Particularly earlier, I think, in your career, you feel that slight sense of, 'Oh my God,' you know, confronted by... 'How do I tell this? What do I do?'

British journalists also speak of the insecurity when it comes to writing a story in which a level of uncertainty remains about key issues. Of course, journalists can and should be transparent about what they do and do not know at the moment of writing the story. Yet, anxiety remains about the story being seen as lacking or promoting rumours that might be squashed once the story is out. An early career print correspondent tells of their experience in this situation:

> Anxiety, on occasions, as well, because sometimes you are worried about effects or the implications of a story that you're writing and whether it's wrong... Because you've done as much verification and sourcing as you can, but ultimately, things sometimes are not denied until they're published.

Even if a journalist has followed all professional routines, and the story has been cleared by the editors, publisher and the legal team, a sense of anxiety can persist before publishing an investigative piece that is likely to have a big impact and/or involves holding power to account, as the way the story will play out is often hard to predict. In the words of a senior print editor:

> I have on occasion felt slightly sick before pressing the button for an online story. You know, like a big exclusive, which, you know, would have potentially big political ramifications. You know, even if you've done all your checks and all your... You know, your lawyers are fine with it, and you've gone to the individuals involved and you've spent ages on it, there's still that moment when it just... 'Is there anything I've missed?' And that's probably the most stressful it gets.

Finally, journalists working for public service media that are required by law to report in a fair and balanced way, but also news journalists more widely who value impartiality and wish to be seen as objective and unbiased, express **worry in trying to achieve their stories are written in an objective, neutral, detached and impartial manner**, and hence, seen by their audiences in the same way. This may not be surprising in the British context in which the public service media, and especially the British Broadcasting Corporation—the BBC, are one of the key players in the media market and regularly seen by audiences as the most trusted media outlet (Newman et al., 2022)—a reputation which its journalists seem keen to maintain and protect. On the other hand, the print sector is considered to be politically aligned (Hinde, 2017). However, this too seems to drive some reporters working in it to strive towards being fair and balanced in their reporting so as to maintain their personal reputation, particularly given the labour mobility. In general, the journalistic culture in the UK, similarly to those in the US and Australia, among others, puts great emphasis of the value of objectivity, as around three out of four journalists in these countries report that they primarily see their roles as those of a 'detached observer' (Hanitzsch et al., 2019). Yet, accusations of bias are common. Most often there are perceptions of media having political bias. For example, a representative survey of British audiences in 2018 found that 22% think the BBC has a left-leaning bias, while 18% thought that it is actually biased towards right-wing views (Turner & Struthers, 2018).). Questions over objectivity are raised in other beats too, such as sports, lifestyle and travel, in which there is a concern that journalists and/or media houses might be too close to sources or commercial interests they report about (Boyle, 2006; Hanusch & Fürsich, 2014; Kristensen & From, 2012).

In general, objectivity is in many journalistic cultures positioned as a key norm according to which news journalists should be neutral and detached reporters of facts (Munno et al., 2022; Schudson, 1990).). Yet, it is also one of the most controversial norms, as objectivity is often in journalism studies, and indeed by some journalists, described as an impossible ideal (Munno et al., 2022; Weber, 2016). Instead of objectivity, then, some journalistic cultures and/or media outlets promote fairness, balance and impartiality (Weber, 2016). How exactly fair, balanced and impartial reporting looks like keeps being debated although there are attempts at defining these in ethics codes and media companies' guidelines. The fluidity of these concepts, and some would say the 'impossible' standard of objectivity and detachment, causes discomfort for some journalists who feel the need to perform in this way but are reporting on stories that they find difficult to balance or emotionally detach from. For example, speaking about covering the COVID-19 pandemic, an early career digital reporter tells of the difficulty to write in an objective manner about the many problematic circumstances that arose:

> Particularly, at the moment, reporting on something like that, it can be quite difficult to write about things because you're meant to write about things fairly, objectively as a news reporter. So, it can be… It can be quite difficult to stay objective, in a way. If it's something that's a big injustice you feel like… You're writing about it, but you can't always necessarily change the outcome of what's happening. Sometimes you can.

The friction between remaining detached and neutral, and having a more active voice, particularly in stories that induce emotions of, say, anger or sadness due to wrongdoings or unfairness, seems to be experienced by news journalists of all levels of experience. Similar negotiations and considerations have been found in a study of American journalists too (Munno et al., 2022). It's a difficult negotiation which Santos (2010: 18) describes as a 'Catch-22,' summarising it like this: 'When they [journalists] don't express emotion, they're accused of being heartless exploitation artists; when they do, they're criticised for not being vigorous enough in their reporting or for faking emotions to boost ratings.' A case in point are reports from war correspondents. For example, Martin Bell, British broadcast war reporter who covered Yugoslav wars in the 1990s, reportedly felt frustrated by the need to balance his reports from the conflict and wished there is more 'freedom to report on situations where there was a clear aggressor without resorting to the formulaic balance of the "On the one hand this, on the other hand that"' (Harcup, 2015: 81). Another British journalist, previously a war correspondent, and now a senior broadcast editor, shared a similar account in which they felt the need to suppress their emotions at the killing of civilians they've witnessed and report as detached observers as this is what they considered their role requires:

> A lot of me wanted to do a big piece to camera saying, 'This is an absolute outrage! It's a war crime!' But I thought… And something in me said, 'No, no. The better way of doing it is to just say what happened. You don't

need my feelings about it. I'm not the story. The story is what happened. Because that will have much more impact.' I knew that. Because what has happened was so atrocious... So atrocious....

And while journalists find ways to write and report in a balanced or impartial way, by, for example, using neutral language, providing context for facts they use and giving accounts of all relevant sides (Thomson et al., 2008; Weber, 2016), the process of 'detachment' can take its toll in the long run, as this mid-career broadcast editor explains:

> There's a necessary separation between reporters, producers, journalists generally... Between the thing they're covering and themselves... You have to separate yourself from it. So, if it's a kind of really horrid, awful trial, on child abuse or some terrible kind of murder or something... You're covering it, but you have to, sort of, to some extent cover it dispassionately and remove yourself from it, otherwise you'd go mad.
>
> And I think there's a danger there that it's just kind of accepted... We're all like... You know, you'll be covering something terrible; you'll be standing in the countryside doing live after live, there's been some awful murder... You're doing your job. There's this awful human tragedy, but you're just doing your job, and you... [...] Sometimes people think they've become hardened to it, but after a long period of time, that, I think, sometimes catches up with people.

THINK

As explained in the Introduction chapter, emotional and physical responses to a situation are driven by our beliefs and thoughts through which we interpret that situation. If we are interpreting a situation with negative thoughts, it's more likely that we will perceive it as an inevitable occurrence which we have little or no control over. This can then lead to increased stress. Thinking of the emotional situations discussed above, Table 4.1 outlines several beliefs and thoughts that might be driving negative emotions.

If you are experiencing negative emotions which you feel you need or want to manage, you can check the beliefs and values, as well as thoughts and expectations that are driving these. In other words, think about what is driving your emotions, how can you update and reframe these with a more positive outlook and what options you have moving forward. For example, if you're facing obstacles in getting the information you need for

Table 4.1 Potential beliefs and thoughts that might be driving a negative emotional response to emotional situations associated with research and writing

Frustration with research	Anxiety about the accuracy of the story	Worry about story being seen as biased
I won't be able to stand up the story	I may have missed something important	My choice of topic, angle and/or sources will be seen as biased
I'm not doing a good job if I can't gather this information	I'll make a mistake that will upset my sources	I am failing in my job if I can't detach myself from a story
My bosses will think I'm incompetent if I can't get this information	My bosses will think I'm incompetent if I make a mistake	I will be in breach of my role if I don't give equal weight to both sides of an argument
Audiences will remain in the dark about an important issue if I don't get this info	My personal reputation will be ruined if I make a mistake	I will be seen as biased or not suited to the job if I show emotions
My story will not have any extra value	My company's reputation will be diminished if I make a mistake	I will be seen as inhuman if I don't show emotion

a story and think that your bosses will think you're incompetent for not being able to get it, consider if you have exploited all avenues of research? Can you do anything else? If not, could anyone else do anything more than you did? Is it common that journalists can always obtain all information they're after? And do your bosses know all this? Next, if you're anxious about the accuracy of the story you're writing and think that you might have missed an important piece of information or angle, consider if you've done the necessary legwork? Have you followed the professional routines and practices? Have you spoken to key sources? Have you followed up leads and explored the avenues they've opened up? If so, what could you have missed? Or, if a new piece of information arises once the story is published, couldn't you use it for a follow up story? Finally, if you're worried about the story being seen as biased because of your choice of sources, consider why you chose them and what other options you had? Have you made an effort to engage all key stakeholders? Is it feasible that you gather information from all stakeholders for this story? Have you considered how your choice of sources will impact the story? Is your editor satisfied with the sources being consulted?

The beliefs and values that drive these emotional situations will differ from journalist to journalist, so it's important you try to unpack what exactly is inducing your own emotions in this context. Are they rational? Logical? What evidence do you have to believe what you think is happening? And while, similarly, journalists may decide to manage their emotions in diverse ways, there are some common emotion management strategies that journalists apply when faced with emotional situations tied to research and writing, that the chapter now turns to.

CHOOSE: EMOTION MANAGEMENT STRATEGIES

The most commonly mentioned emotion management strategies by British journalists when dealing with emotional situations outlined above are attentional deployment in the form of focusing attention on professional routines and procedures; internal processing in forms of perspective-taking and acceptance; as well as verbal processing with peers.

Attentional Deployment

Given that research and writing are among the key practices journalists employ in everyday work and there is ample guidance and training in how these should be carried out and to what standard (see, e.g., Bradshaw, 2018; Bull, 2016; Harcup, 2015; Hudson & Rowlands, 2018), it perhaps isn't surprising that attentional deployment in the form of focusing on professional routines was commonly mentioned as a strategy for managing emotions in situations that arise in these contexts. When it comes to information gathering, one of the first stages in the process is to consider what you're trying to achieve and plan the research and writing in line with the set deadline and available resources. This can help alleviate some of the anxiety about being able to put the story together, as this mid-career digital reporter explains:

> There are different pressures along the way, because obviously once you set a sort of a deadline for it, then you sort of work backwards and work out what you've got to do by when.

Similarly, journalists worrying about getting the information right and ensuring the published copy is accurate can mitigate some of this worry by following the verifying procedures that are part of the professional routines. An early career digital reporter shares their practice to alleviate the stress of ensuring accuracy in a story:

> Getting the story right... Checking that I've, you know, got all my sources, checking that I've transcribed my notes correctly, because I take notes in shorthand so have to transcribe them, and making sure they're all correct, making sure I got all the right information...

Alongside following the routines of professional practice, and particularly, when it comes to investigative stories and scoops that can have significant ramifications, there are checks and procedures in place, such as consulting with editor, publisher and the legal team in the pre-publishing process, that can mitigate some of the anxiety around the accuracy, language and potential impact of the story once it's published. If these procedures are observed, they can reassure journalists that their stories have been produced to the highest professional standards. A senior print editor shares how observing procedures and trusting them can alleviate pre-publishing anxiety:

> You have a mental checklist of all the things and you've... I mean, it's very rare that you would put a controversial or difficult story up without having done your due diligence. So, it's about having faith in the fact that the systems and processes work but also having confidence in your own experience.

Professional routines that lead to wanted outcomes, such as good research or an impartial story presentation, can also be learned by observing peers and the way they construct and deliver their stories, as well as how these stories are perceived and received. There are opportunities here both to learn how to do research and writing, among other things, better, but also how not to do things, which may be equally important. The knowledge about how research and writing should, and should not, be done has the potential to reassure journalists that their professional practices and outputs are in line with personal aims and professional expectations. In the words of a senior broadcast editor:

> One of the things I've done in journalism is I've always watched how other journalists report stories. Particularly other journalists who are reporting similar stories to me, or even the same story as me, just to see how they do it, to see what you learn from the way they did it. Either positively or

negatively, one way or another, but I think, you know, there's always an opportunity to learn from that. And on that basis, I've always just tried to be as fair and balanced about my stories as I can be.

In doing research, it is also important to be aware of your strengths and weaknesses in applying different methods and protocols and adapt accordingly. For example, a global study of investigative journalists revealed that many worry they do not have necessary digital skills in order to gather and analyse data in investigative projects (Kunert et al., 2022). In order to mitigate the anxiety of missing important aspects of the story, they collaborate with those who do have the relevant skills and newsgather in collaborative teams (Kunert et al., 2022). Journalists may also wish to train in particular methods of research they think they'd benefit from, as well as apply practices they know will work for them in the story production process. An interesting example has been shared by a mid-career broadcast journalist who decides to forego shorthand in information gathering process, which is deemed a 'fundamental skill for all journalists' by the British National Council for the Training of Journalists, as they recognise that it does not assist them in the process of putting the story together:

> I write longhand. I don't use shorthand, generally, anyway. I had the option to study it when I was studying to be a journalist and I refused. But I tend to write in longhand regardless of what I'm doing... When I'm preparing to go on the radio or whatever else, very simply because... That helps me to memorise what I'm going to say, actually, or at least, you know, get the ideas firmer in my head. Shorthand does nothing for me. Longhand takes time and people have watched me... When I've been at a story, where there are many other journalists... People watch me writing out reams of words and they're like, you know... I'm sure one of them said, 'What are you doing?!' (laughs)

Internal Processing

The second common strategy to manage emotions that arise in the process of research and writing is internal processing, that is, thinking about the process and outputs by taking different perspectives on these or accepting them. For example, journalists who find themselves frustrated by the amount of research they need to do to make small headways with a story, could accept the fact that research is an integral part of the journalistic process and that often it takes time to get to valuable information. They could also take the perspective that while the process is laborious and tiresome, there is usually satisfaction and gratification at the end of it once a new and/or important piece of information is found.

An important part of the process of internal processing in emotional situations related to research and writing is to reflect on the choices you're making and why you are doing things in a particular way. Useful guidance is offered in Burns and Matthews's (2018) textbook Understanding journalism, which offers guided critical reflection in the processes of information gathering and writing. For example, if there's worry about the story's accuracy, it might be worth reflecting on the research you've done and why you've done it in that particular way, especially considering the assumptions with which you've started information gathering, sources you've chosen and how you've evaluated them (Burns & Matthews, 2018). Checking yourself and your data for potential bias and inaccuracies could reassure you that you have followed professional protocols and done what you should and can to ensure that your story is accurate. A senior print editor describes the reassuring reflection process leading to a positive perspective on output in this way:

> I know how stories like this work, I know what I need to check, I know what I need to have done for it to get to this point. And you need to kind of have quite a lot of faith in yourself, particularly as often you're the person that's closest to that story and there may be others in the organisation who rightly are questioning and pushing and probing to make sure that everything's been covered. They're doing their job, but then it's on you to kind of, you know, reassure them, closer you get to publication, the more so.

British journalists emphasised the importance of experience in allowing them to take a positive perspective on their research and writing. The experience allows them to put their own practice in perspective and consider the production of a story within the parameters they were given to create it. For example, the anxiety that a piece of information might have been missed in research or that the story is not as balanced as one would want, could be alleviated by rationally considering what could have been done with the resources given to produce it, and what the potential ramifications of publishing the story could be. It is primarily senior journalists, with many years of experience in the industry, who spoke of being able to rely on their experience of story research and writing to take a more positive perspective on their work, which mitigates worry and anxiety. To illustrate, a senior broadcast editor shares this account of how they manage the anxiety about the quality of stories they produce:

> I think when you get more into it and you're older and you spend a long time doing it... A bit more wisdom... A bit more of an old, you know... You're more experienced about it... You're just, kind of, little bit more phlegmatic and you think, 'Well, it's a news program. We've got to get this out. Onto the next one...' That kind of thing.

Verbal Processing

The final strategy used to manage emotions that arise while conducting research and writing stories is verbal processing, that is, discussing the frustrating or anxiety-inducing issue and/or the emotion itself with colleagues. Discussing stressors and arisen emotions with peers is an important element of social support in journalism, which enables journalists to gain emotional release from sharing their experiences and get support from colleagues. Importantly, this strategy has been emphasised as an important and useful one by journalists of all levels of seniority, from those new to industry to those who have spent decades in it. Speaking to colleagues could be useful in all mentioned emotional situations in this chapter, from sharing joy of finding a great piece of information, frustration with hitting 'brick walls' in research, worrying about accuracy of a story and/or anxiety about the way in which it's been constructed. A senior print correspondent describes the usefulness of verbal processing with peers like this:

> I think that's quite a good emotional release, to be able to do that, or just to be able to once in a while say, 'I'm really pissed off, this hasn't worked out,' or to whinge about the news desk... Just the general good-natured kind of complaining, whinging that happens in every office, I think. Probably in journalism offices more than most.

Colleagues can offer emotional support as the sole experience of being heard and emotions acknowledged and shared can assist with alleviating some of the stress and tension that has been building up. In addition, colleagues can often offer practical advice. On the one hand, on how to manage the stressor. For example, they could offer advice on new avenues of research or give feedback on a written copy. On the other hand, they could offer practical advice on how to manage the frustration or anxiety. All of these are evident in the account of an early career print correspondent who alleviates frustration with research that isn't panning out in this way:

> I think, usually, sort of moaning to colleagues, and, you know, that can usually be quite a productive and cathartic exercise. Not just because you are sort of releasing the emotion in some way, and therefore kind of not bottling it up, but also, you know, they become a sounding board and they can give me advice on how to manage that frustration or manage whatever is causing the frustration. Primarily the latter, really, not the former.

In sum, this chapter has covered several emotional situations that are likely to arise in the process of research and writing, namely: excitement with uncovering an important piece of information; frustration with time-consuming or challenging research; worry about story's accuracy; and anxiety about writing in a detached and balanced manner. It has been suggested that key strategies to manage these emotions include attentional deployment in the form of concentrating on professional routines; internal processing by perspective-taking and acceptance; and verbal processing with peers to gain emotional release and emotional and practical support from colleagues.

Croatia: Maja Sever on Newsgathering

Maja Sever is a journalist for Croatian Radio Television (HRT) and president of the Union of Croatian Journalists and the European Federation of Journalists. She participated in numerous news programme projects and reported on the wars in Croatia, Bosnia and Herzegovina. She received the Journalist of the Year Award from the Journalists' Association, the Pride of Croatia Award for humanitarian work and the Terrible Women Award for contributions to gender equality and social justice.

I have been working in TV news all my life. Speed, actuality and good sources are part of our stressful job. When my daily show was cancelled, after 13 years, my journalistic work was significantly limited. I experienced it as a blow to my professional integrity, but I started working on another important HRT show. That show is broadcast only once weekly, and my journalistic nerve was taught to the daily rhythm. I needed some daily action!

The move to working on a weekly show did not mean I stopped daily newsgathering. I kept finding new and important information and people continued reaching out to me with their stories. Given my work and roles, these were often underrepresented stories from people who live in areas that we call media deserts. It was frustrating not to be able to investigate and share these via the media organisation I work for.

The development of social networks offered enormous opportunities and I grabbed the chance. I use social networks as a platform for free journalistic work, with lots of positive dynamic and to great professional effect. It keeps me on the journalistic scene, even enables better visibility in journalistic work, despite persistent attempts by editors for some stories to be pushed to the side.

Over the last decade, I often used social networks to publish stories of social importance about people who live in media deserts, and whose problems the public is unaware of. By publishing these stories, I often face criticism and attacks, mainly from politicians responsible for such a situation, but it only strengthens my resilience and determination. As a result, many short stories (tweets) I posted on social media have found their way into the mainstream media.

For example, when an earthquake hit the region at the end of 2020, our small 'People for People' editorial office, which was born out of a story I did about difficult living conditions in the villages around Glina (a town 60 kilometres south from Zagreb where mostly live Serbian minority), proved extremely important. Already on the first day of the quake, we published the Facebook testimony of a colleague who was in the most severely affected villages; the information was shared in all mainstream media, and on the same evening, we collected enormous amounts of aid for the people who suffered in the earthquake.

And while this aspect of my work is not part of my job, it can be described as journalism and involves investigative work. Before publishing a story or video on our page, I need to research the background and context of the problem because our stories are usually reported in the mainstream media. When you talk to people who are struggling, you want to help them with your work, yet need to remain objective to do your job. This is sometimes challenging because you must balance emotions, the desire to help and the fact-based presentation of a situation.

From the perspective of a journalist whose free work at public service media is limited due to various pressures, there are positive implications of the work of journalists in the era of social networks. There are new pressures, such as experiencing hate speech that causes emotional stress. However, during my career, social networks enabled me to keep delivering the primary journalistic service—stories in public interest. Despite the additional pressure and exposure, I continued to tell stories about people, their destinies and the failures of political authorities. Thus, I got out of the frustration of limited work in my media company and continued to be a journalist.

Top Tips

- Be aware of professional routines and standards you should aim to achieve in terms of research and story writing
- Consider the resources, including time, you have to conduct research and produce a story
- Observe how peers research and construct their stories and learn from good practice you identify, as well as mistakes others have made
- Reflect on your assumptions and values, as well as practices and choices you've made in researching a story and constructing it
- Consult with colleagues, and if needed, editor, publisher and the legal team, to ensure that the produced story meets professional standards

- Share your experiences with colleagues to gain emotional release and emotional and practical support in dealing with challenges and related emotions

READ, WATCH AND LISTEN

- Read 'She Said: Breaking the Sexual Harassment Story That Helped Ignite a Movement,' a 2019 book written by New York Times investigative reporters Jodi Kantor and Megan Twohey, in which they detail the investigative process that went into uncovering sexual harassment and sexual abuse by high-profile men, including Hollywood film producer Harvey Weinstein
- Watch 'Tips from Bob Woodward on Investigative Journalism,' published by The Washington Post, in which Woodward, investigative reporter who broke the Watergate story alongside Carl Bernstein, shares top 3 ways for researching any story—https://www.youtube.com/watch?v=VVKGUctuoXE
- Watch the recording of panel 'Accuracy and Verification Across Disciplines' held as part of the 2022 Truth in Journalism conference, discussing research and accuracy in journalism production process—https://www.youtube.com/watch?v=F5DwkOEYR5s
- Listen to podcast episode 'Impartiality unpacked: a study of four countries' by the Reuters Institute for the Study of Journalism—https://podcasts.ox.ac.uk/digital-news-report-2021-episode-6-imp artiality-unpacked-study-four-countries
- Listen to Journalism.co.uk's podcast episode featuring Leona O'Neill, a journalist from Northern Ireland, on experiencing trauma when covering stories and ways how journalists can deal with it—https://soundcloud.com/journalismnews/leona-oneill

SCENARIO EXERCISES

Scenario 1

You work as a technology reporter for a public service broadcaster. You've been covering the beat for a few years, and you enjoy testing out and reviewing new technology and covering the newest trends in the digital technology sector. A senior tech correspondent in the team gets a tip off from a government insider who claims they have seen internal documents that outline plans to incorporate a spyware software within an application that the government is shortly launching. You are called onto the team to assist with information gathering.

You manage to gather perspectives from tech specialists, civil society organisations and opposition parties. Yet, you can't get anyone from the government on the record, and even after spending a week trying to verify the documents that were shared by the whistle-blower, you have no success in confirming their authenticity. The bosses are not allowing the story to run until the document is verified and the story is balanced with perspectives from all relevant parties.

- How does this make you feel?
- What are you going to do? Why?

Scenario 2

You are a travel writer who has been freelancing for the past few years. You just got back from a week-long press trip to an island country in the South Pacific organised and paid for by its national tourist board. They have openly said they are looking to increase their tourist numbers and are particularly aiming to attract high spending visitors who are interested in quality tourism. During your stay, you have witnessed outstanding natural beauty and top-quality resorts and services. You have also learned that many tourist workers receive pay that is below the country's living wage, and that the development of resorts has impacted on the island's flora and fauna.

You have pitched a travel feature to a quality paper whose audiences might be interested to travel to this destination. Now, writing the piece, you are considering two key things. Firstly, you are aware that travel journalism is often looked at as lacking independence and serving commercial interests. You are wondering how to write about the destination in an objective way, while acknowledging that you have been a guest of its government. Secondly, you know that travel journalism is traditionally focused on positivity, and that a travel feature should be an uplifting piece that sparks audiences' imagination and perhaps motivates their future travel plans. Yet, you're conscious of the negative sides of tourism you've witnessed during your visit and are wondering if you should mention them—how will you and the story be seen if you do, and how if you don't?

- How does this make you feel?
- What are you going to do? Why?

REFERENCES

Bjerknes, F. (2022). Inventive factfinders: Investigative journalism as professional self-representation, marker of identity and boundary work. *Journalism Practice, 16*(6), 1037–1056.

Boyle, R. (2006). *Sports journalism context and issues.* SAGE.

Bradshaw, P. (2018). *The online journalism handbook: Skills to survive and thrive in the digital age* (2nd ed.). Routledge.

Bull, A. (2016). *Multimedia journalism: A practical guide* (2nd ed.). Routledge.

Burns, L. S., & Matthews, B. J. (2018). *Understanding journalism.* SAGE.

Cancela, P. (2021). Between structures and identities: Newsroom policies, division of labor and journalists' commitment to investigative reporting. *Journalism Practice, 15*(9), 1361–1382.

Cancela, P., & Dubied, A. (2022). Stay strong, get perspective, or give up: Role negotiation in small-scale investigative journalism. *Journalism Studies, 23*(9), 1056–1076.

Cancela, P., Gerber, D., & Dubied, A. (2021). "To me, it's normal journalism" professional perceptions of investigative journalism and evaluations of personal commitment. *Journalism Practice, 15*(6), 878–893.

Chater, K. (2002). *Research for media production* (2nd ed.). Focal Press.

Edwards, V. (2016). *Research skills for journalists.* Taylor & Francis Group.

Hanitzsch, T., Hanusch, F., Ramaprasad, J., & De Beer, A. S. (Eds.). (2019). *Worlds of journalism: Journalistic cultures around the globe.* Columbia University Press.

Hanusch, F., & Fürsich, E. (2014). *Travel journalism: Exploring production, impact and culture.* Palgrave Macmillan.

Harcup, T. (2015). *Journalism principles and practice* (3rd ed.). SAGE.

Hinde, S. (2017). Brexit and the media. *Hermès, La Revue, 77*(1), 80–86.

Hudson, G., & Rowlands, S. (2018). *The broadcast journalism handbook* (7th ed.). Routledge.

Iorio, S. H. (2004). *Qualitative research in journalism taking it to the streets.* Lawrence Erlbaum Associates.

Kristensen, N. N., & From, U. (2012). Lifestyle journalism: Blurring boundaries. *Journalism Practice, 6*(1), 26–41.

Kunert, J., Frech, J., Brüggemann, M., Lilienthal, V., & Loosen, W. (2022). How investigative journalists around the world adopt innovative digital practices. *Journalism Studies, 23*(7), 761–780.

Maier, S. R. (2005). Accuracy matters: A cross-market assessment of newspaper error and credibility. *Journalism and Mass Communication Quarterly, 82*(3), 533–551.

Munno, G., Craig, M., Farrish, K., & Richards, A. (2022). Two mindsets among U.S. journalists: Neutral & activist. *Journalism Studies, 23*(14), 1779–1801.

Newman, N., Fletcher, R., Robertson, C., Eddy, K., & Nielsen, R. (2022). *Digital News Report 2022.* Oxford University.

Porlezza, C., Maier, S. R., & Russ-Mohl, S. (2012). News accuracy in switzerland and italy: A transatlantic comparison with the US press. *Journalism Practice, 6*(4), 530–546.

Randall, D., & Crew, J. (2021). *The universal journalist* (6th ed.). Pluto Press.

Santos, J. (2010). *Daring to feel: Violence, the news media, and their emotions.* Lexington.

Schudson, M. (1990). *Origins of the ideal of objectivity in the professions.* Garland Publishing.

Shapiro, I., Brin, C., Bédard-Brûlé, I., & Mychajlowycz, K. (2013). Verification as a strategic ritual how journalists retrospectively describe processes for ensuring accuracy. *Journalism Practice, 7*(6), 657–673.

Thomson, E. A., White, P. R. R., & Kitley, P. (2008). "Objectivity" and "hard news" reporting across cultures: Comparing the news report in English, French, Japanese and Indonesian journalism. *Journalism Studies, 9*(2), 212–228.

Turner, M., & Struthers, R. (2018). *Is the BBC biased? BMG reveals public perceptions of broadcaster impartiality in the UK.* BMG Research. https://www.bmgresearch.co.uk/is-the-bbc-biased-bmg-reveals-public-perceptions-of-broadcaster-impartiality-in-the-uk/

Weber, J. (2016). Teaching fairness in journalism: A challenging task. *Journalism and Mass Communication Educator, 71*(2), 163–175.

Wilczek, B., & Thurman, N. (2022). Contagious accuracy norm violation in political journalism: A cross-national investigation of how news media publish inaccurate political information. *Journalism, 23*(11), 2271–2288.

CHAPTER 5

Live Broadcasting

I was not prepared for my first live television presenting task. It entailed presenting News at 5 in a first-ever broadcast of a new national television channel. We were a team of early career journalists with a few years of experience in the job, but with little to no experience on television. I did live broadcasting before though, having presented a live programme and reported live from events on a local radio station for a few years. So, I was familiar with the practice, and trained in doing television packages. But not being in front of the camera. Going live in front of a camera. I was told I'll be the first presenter of news the day before the broadcast. To say I was terrified is probably an understatement. At that point, I haven't spent more than an hour in a studio. I remember thinking that I have nothing to wear. Worrying about how I'll look and sound. Our voice trainer has often told me that I speak too fast. Will I be able to control my voice when the adrenaline kicks in? I barely remember the day itself given I was so strung up on adrenaline. The team was lovely and supportive, cheering me on. But I was so tense when I sat in the presenter's chair that I could barely move. And it showed. I remember an audience comment online saying something along the lines of only my lips moving. That was probably a fair description. I felt relieved when the red light went off, but not happy with my performance.

Today, I feel proud that the bosses chose me and trusted me with this task. And I can think back on the day and be kinder to myself than I

© The Author(s), under exclusive license to Springer Nature   97
Switzerland AG 2023
M. Šimunjak, *Managing Emotions in Journalism*,
https://doi.org/10.1007/978-3-031-38631-2_5

was at the time. I did the best I could. I prepared the programme and practised my lines, controlled my voice. Beyond me looking like a robot, the broadcast went well. We did it! We launched a new television channel! Perspective is a wonderful thing. But if I had to do it all again, I'd try to make sure that I'm better prepared for the hot seat. I needed to practise live broadcasting and watch myself on camera—to be aware of how I look, how I sound, what my ticks are, what works for me, and manage all of these elements. A few months on, I still felt a buzz when going into the studio, but it was a positive buzz, one that fosters concentration and focus. I was aware of where my hands should be, the ideal font size of text on papers in front of me, how to control my eye-brow raising tick, how many deep breaths I need to compose myself before the red light goes on and what to do with myself during end credits. And I'd remind myself of this if nervousness kicked in—'You know what to do. You've got this.'

This chapter focuses on the stages of the journalistic process that entail live broadcast elements, such as live radio or television reporting or presenting, through the 'stop, think, choose' model of emotional intelligence. The 'stop' section discusses emotional situations related to live broadcasting, including the fear and/or excitement that leads to adrenaline surge and causes some to thrive off this pressure and enter 'tunnel vision'; as well as nervousness related to performing; and fears about issues that might arise when reporting from environments that cannot be fully controlled or require many technical elements to operate as planned. In the 'think' section, some beliefs and thoughts which may be driving mentioned emotions are outlined. The 'choose' section suggests emotion management strategies informed by interviews with practising journalists. These include attentional deployment in forms of focusing attention on professional protocols, but also engaging in diversionary activities, with focus on physical exercise, which enables the body to effectively deal with adrenaline surges and can foster relaxation following stressful event by reducing levels of stress hormones in the body; internal processing, such as acceptance and perspective-taking; as well as situation modification, such as removing oneself from stress inducing situations (e.g., a hectic newsroom, loud location) before a live performance to reduce the stressors ahead of it.

STOP: EMOTIONAL SITUATIONS

Broadcast journalism requires extra skills to those discussed in previous chapters, and in particular, the skill to report or present in live programming. On the one hand, live reporting, that is, unscripted reporting from location, is nowadays a requirement for any broadcast journalist as it is a standard part of programming, and on 24/7 news channels in particular given it represents a cheap and efficient way to fill in the programming with regular updates from locations at which there are developing news (Tuggle & Huffman, 1999). This usually comes in the form of a 'two-way'—in which the journalist on location answers anchor's question from the studio, and 'throw'—where the journalist reports live from location instead of, or in addition to, a package that covers the story (Hudson & Rowlands, 2018). On the other hand, live broadcasting also includes anchors or presenters who host news programming from the studio (or location in case of special events). There are specialised textbooks for broadcast journalists which cover in much detail what is expected of them and how they should perform. For example, Reardon and Flynn (2014) outline that a good anchor is also an excellent interviewer and reporter, well prepared and knowledgeable about stories in their bulletin, showcasing they are in control through focus and concentration, while appearing relaxed in their delivery of content, and remaining calm and composed even when things go wrong. If it sounds like it's quite an undertaking, that's because it is. Most journalism textbooks will mention the adrenaline that is released in this process, and the related **excitement of performing live in broadcast** (e.g., Bull, 2016; Hudson & Rowlands, 2018). It perhaps then does not surprise that a study of journalism students in the US found that broadcast trainees value excitement as a value and perceive themselves as more extroverted and conscientious than their peers training for print journalism (Carpenter et al., 2018). The feeling of excitement of going live has been shared by many British broadcast journalists interviewed for this book.[1] A mid-career broadcast editor describes it like this:

---

[1] Unlike other chapters in this book, this chapter reports only the experiences of interviewed broadcast journalists, meaning that experiences of 14 broadcasters are presented, seven of which held positions of senior editors at the time of interview.

Partly why I love the job and partly why I do it, is because I'm a 'red light junkie.' So, I love doing live TV, I always have since I was a young reporter, that's what I like doing. So, I am a bit odd, I think, but I don't get particularly nervous or amped up anymore. Not that I'm not in it, not that I'm not, 'Yeah, yeah, I want to do this,' because you have to do that to have the energy.

Broadcast journalists often talk about the 'rush' of live reporting, a feeling induced by adrenaline running through their system, which seems particularly evident in covering big and important stories that are likely to have a large audience. In the words of a senior broadcast editor:

> I would say that the most exciting thing is obviously when you have a big story and you're going live with it. Or you're doing a big interview and you're doing it... Particularly if you're doing it live. Obviously, if you're live, it's inevitably more exciting, because there is a bit of an adrenaline rush. Simply because you know you're doing it live, and you know that there are an awful lot of people watching.

Alongside the professional satisfaction of being in the middle of a big story and creating impact with their coverage, broadcast journalists often also find this part of their work fulfilling on a personal level too. Another senior broadcast editor puts it like this:

> You are very front and centre. And if you're a journalist, or you want to be impactful, it's... And you're making an impact in how you're asking a question or how you're talking on air and people are listening to you and feel that you're adding to the debate or you're enhancing the debate, and you're making a difference... [...] It's very professionally and personally rewarding.

In addition, while the adrenaline of the live broadcast situation can contribute to excitement, it can also, if under control, enable the journalist to focus and concentrate, which is of essence in live reporting. As Stewart and Alexander (2022: 357) note: 'For the reporter on location, that story is the only thing in the world that matters at that moment.' In the words of a senior broadcast editor:

> You go into a kind of zone where nothing else matters. Somebody could be trying to tell you your dog's just died or, you know, there's a heavy

piece of machinery that might come and take your foot off, and you would not care about any of that information until you have done what you can to digest the material you've got and delivered it on air. And at that point, after that, tell me that, you know, I'm minutes away from a life-threatening accident or that there's some kind of, you know, terrible or joyous family news that I might want to share in... I just got no headspace to consider that. So, I'm just in a tunnel vision of concentration.

Adrenaline Anxiety

However, adrenaline can also be a problem in live broadcasting, particularly when it's coupled with **anxiety, nervousness and/or fear ahead of broadcast** (Stewart & Alexander, 2022). Arya's (1999: 4) textbook on live television reporting is one of the rare training materials that puts emphasis on anxiety in this form of journalism, going as far as to say that 'one of the biggest obstacles to success in live television reporting is fear.' Specifically, Arya (1999) notes that fear of failure, as well as fear of losing peers' and audiences' respect, contributes to high levels of anxiety among live broadcasters. The stress of the situation is often tied to the many challenges of delivering an effective live broadcast, and considering the many things that can go wrong, as this senior broadcast editor elaborates:

> So, what is stressful is trying to assimilate a large amount or complex and detailed information, make sure that you understand it and have it correct, and then attempt to transmit it in ordinary, everyday language that people can understand, which is often not the form the information has been delivered in, and condense it into really quite a short amount of time without losing the... Without losing any accuracy, correctly conveying the sense of the story you're trying to tell, make it interesting and accessible to anybody who's going to consume it, whilst at the same time taking great care that you're not missing any important facts or getting anything wrong.

While these fears may arise in any journalist, in live broadcasting they can be seen as exacerbated by two things—deadlines and spotlight (Stewart & Alexander, 2022). Regarding the former, the often very short turnaround times leave little time to gather, process and prepare the information in a broadcast form. In the words of a senior broadcast editor:

Going on air at short notice, where information has only just been released, and you've kind of skim read it, but are worried that you haven't had the chance to digest it, highlight it, all of that kind of thing, before you take it to air... It definitely makes me more nervous.

The pressure of time is particularly anxiety-inducing if a journalist works for a broadcasting company that produces both television and radio, as they might be required to cover the story in both mediums, often in package and live—alongside the now inevitable digital and social media. This requires journalists to multi-task, adapt stories for different mediums and formats, and sometimes change locations during story production process and/or preparations for live reporting, while, of course, remaining calm and composed when on air. A senior broadcast editor described the stress of this process by using the 'swan' analogy:

If you're doing a combination thing as well, it can be really... I think, you know, you can get really... Because you're racing the deadline... And then you are also trying to get one element, your piece, edited... But then you've got to be thinking, 'Oh my God I'm going to be asked...' There's going to be this live element afterwards. [...] We'd all like to think we were like sort of, you know... Swans. You know, beautiful, all really moving fantastically on the surface... And underneath you're kind of... You know, your legs are going like mad. And it is often like that because you just... Sometimes we'll get to a position we haven't really thought through your... Haven't really had much time to assemble those thoughts. And you're going, 'Oh my God...' You know... And that's definitely a sense of anxiety. And nerves, and adrenaline.

Broadcast is in many countries, including the UK and most of Europe, also more heavily regulated than other parts of the industry, often requiring from journalists to report in an impartial and balanced way offering fair representation of different actors, particularly from the political sphere (Bleyer-Simon et al., 2022). The pressure to perform in such a way while hosting political programming creates additional anxiety to those working in this context, and especially to public service media journalists who are often judged on this aspect of their live performance. For example, Twitter users often come out in force following BBC's debate show Question Time, to accuse the host Fiona Bruce of bias of all sorts, both left and right (Grünewald, 2022). A senior broadcast editor working for a public service broadcaster describes how the fear of appearing impartial can cause anxiety ahead of and during a live broadcast:

> There's always at the back of your mind that duty of impartiality, something being pulled out of context, or something you say may be wrong, or in the course of a debate that you might be perceived as being harder on one person than another, failing to pick up on, you know, something for somebody, but then jumping on... You know, they're all aspects that social media, we know, can be brutal about and could jump on. So, I would have a certain amount of anxiety about that, on the programming.

Indeed, in unscripted live broadcasting the possibilities to make mistakes are seemingly endless, and the audience is usually quick to point out what they think about a slip of the tongue, tone of voice or facial expressions, among other things. Hence, even veterans in the field—senior broadcasters with over 20 years of experience behind them, feel frustrated when they think their live did not meet their own, and maybe industry, standards. A senior broadcast editor puts it like this:

> Obviously it doesn't always go right, yeah, so sometimes, you know, you feel frustration in yourself that something didn't quite work out or it didn't quite... Particularly when you're doing a lot of live broadcasting, you know, particularly when you... It didn't quite come out the way that you intended it to, you know, just in a kind of logistic, practical point of view, like, broadcasting can be very exhilarating and great fun, but it can also be quite like, 'Oh God, that came out wrong,' you know.

Performance

Another element of live broadcasting that adds to nervousness and anxiety is being under the spotlight, which Stewart and Alexander (2022: 223) describe as 'the point where the business of information and the game of showbusiness meet.' Hence, broadcasters may **feel anxious about the performance of live broadcasting,** as in this situation it isn't just about what is being said, but how a journalist sounds and looks like doing it. Journalists describe live broadcasting as an 'exposing' job—one in which they are judged on many elements, not just the story they're reporting, but basically everything they do on air and often on a very personal level.

As with several other situations described in this book, journalism textbooks may be more inclined to ascribe the nervousness and anxiety tied to it to early career journalists who lack experience in this performance, but the interviews with British journalists show that the pressure is felt at all levels of seniority. In the words of a senior broadcast editor:

> It's a performance. Yeah? I mean this is a difference between... Say when you're a print journalist, you write the story, you get the exhilaration, you get the splash on the front page... There's nothing better than feeling that. Nothing better than beating your competitors. It is a very satisfying experience. In television, it's a performance. So, it's not just the content, it's the performance of how you present the story, how do you sell self, how do you look, how do you sound, how authoritative are you... It's more than just journalism, you're performing. And that's quite... That's both hugely enjoyable but quite stressful.

The considerations of the use of voice and appearance are high on the agenda of broadcast journalists going on air, as they have only one chance at getting it right, which usually means that their tone of voice or appearance is not even noticed by the audiences who remain focused on the story. This is in contrast to recording pieces to camera or voiceovers for packages, where if something is off, you can usually just do another take to make it right. A mid-career broadcast journalist describes it in this way:

> The pressure of broadcasting is... You haven't got time to worry about this, that, and the other. If you're on TV... 'Is my tie straight and is my hair okay?' Because nine times out of 10 people notice that more than anything you say! And when I'm doing other things, when I'm on the radio, for example, it's, 'Am I going to be able to get things said clearly and carefully?' And that's the stress that I feel more than anything else.

Some of this pressure comes from expected standards of live broadcasting. Indeed, journalism textbooks and training will often highlight that a live broadcaster shouldn't look nervous, but relaxed, calm and unruffled by his surroundings and things going wrong (e.g., Hudson & Rowlands, 2018; Sissons, 2006; Stewart & Alexander, 2022). Considering all the things that can go wrong can induce a feeling of threat in the mind of a reporter, which leads to release of adrenaline and induces adrenaline anxiety. This can cause physical reactions such as hyperventilation, shaking and excessive sweating. So, arguably, not something a journalist would like to display live on air, which can cause further anxiety about performing live. In these situations, a journalist can feel particularly tense, which causes other physical reactions that can affect performance, such as raised shoulders—creating a nervous look; tightening of throat—making a voice higher; and dry mouth—which makes it more difficult to speak (Stewart & Alexander, 2022). British journalists report that the fear of failing in performing on air is further exacerbated when they are required to report live from surroundings they're unfamiliar with, or given an on-air task that they do not regularly perform. For example, a senior broadcast editor who regularly reports live from location described the stress of hosting a long form live programming, which is not something they commonly do:

> You know, I've done something quite recently, which I would have been absolutely terrified about, and nauseous about for two days or more. In fact, it was more time than I would have liked… Because it was a long live session, and it was live TV, for a fairly long time. […] You know, on the morning of that if someone had told me… Maybe if I suspected of having COVID, I might have preferred… I would have liked to have an excuse… If someone could have taken that away from me and told me… I would have accepted that. And in the previous years when I've done live TV like that, I've had similar things.

Finally, broadcast journalists also speak of **fears about issues that might arise when reporting from environments that cannot be fully controlled or require many technical elements to operate as planned.** Indeed, live broadcasting is a complex operation that demands a lot of personnel and equipment to work in sync and without glitch, or at least with enough time to make things work so the audience is none the wiser of the issues that the broadcasting team faced in getting on air. As any experienced broadcaster will tell you, issues arise regularly, and there are occasions when several things go wrong that causes significant stress even for those with many years of experience on the job. For example, following one such event, ITV's political editor Robert Peston, a veteran broadcaster, tweeted in December 2020: 'Stressful live for @itvnews's News at Ten. Line went down. So tried to do on smart phone. Then phone mic didn't work. Then realised I wasn't wearing shirt.

Then was too late to turn on lights. Then had to hold phone and talk without being able to hear @julieetchitv. Never again!' A senior broadcast editor describes another such situation and the toll it takes on a journalist needing to put together a package and prepare for a live with minutes to spare before evening news:

> We went to three edit suites [in the building] and we couldn't get any of them to work. It was like one of those... It was like one of those nightmares, you know, anxiety nightmares. Literally, you know, I had still not written my live... [...] We couldn't get the bloody script to print, the printers wouldn't... I mean, it was just honestly... That sort of 15 minutes that probably aged me by 15 years. But um it's just a reminder of, you know, what the expectations... What actually goes on. Even somebody who is as experienced as me... I mean the levels of stress that are going on are really intense sometimes.

Even if things are going as planned, the complexities of producing live broadcasting and reporting from location that journalists have to be aware of to do their jobs can cause stress as there are many moving parts in the operation and often a lack of control over issues and outcomes. A senior broadcast editor talks about the intensity of this process that involves working the story, paying attention to their performance and surroundings, as well as technical side of things, while in communication with a range of people involved in the production:

> You know that lots of people are watching you. You know that you'll be judged on everything you say. You have huge amounts of technical things going on behind the scenes. Is it raining on your head? Did your sound drop out? Is there talk-back? So, there's lots of technical things. You are dependent on other people. You are not entirely in control because putting things on TV depends on the journalists, the producer, the output editor, the person in your ear, the technology working, the camera man. So, it's a very intense activity.

Also, some fieldworks are more challenging than others. For example, political journalists who regularly report live from Westminster or White House, or sports journalists who go on air from stadiums' press boxes or press areas, are usually familiar with their environments and/or can exert some level of control over them. However, other locations may be less straightforward and come with additional challenges, which can cause anxiety about the environment potentially causing problems during the live. In the words of a senior broadcast editor:

> You can be in physical circumstances where you're anxious that something will go wrong. So, if you are doing a broadcast from a busy political rally or outside of football match where fans are streaming out, or any kind of busy, and potentially volatile public situation... There's a degree of anxiety around whether or not somebody is going to try and disrupt your broadcast. So, a part of your mind is kind of watching what's going on around you.

Overall, live broadcasting is an intense activity that is often characterised by adrenaline rush, which can, on the one hand, induce feelings of excitement and enable focus and concentration, and on the other hand, heighten the feelings of anxiety and nervousness, with potential physical reactions that might further impede effective performance in live broadcasting. Importantly, even when it comes to experienced broadcast journalists who are able to keep the adrenaline under control, there are circumstances which can cause anxiety and nervousness, resulting in stress, in the context of live broadcasting.

THINK

As explained in the Introduction chapter, emotional and physical responses to a situation are driven by our beliefs and thoughts through which we interpret that situation. If we are interpreting a situation with negative thoughts, it's more likely that we will perceive it as an inevitable occurrence which we have little or no control over. This can then lead to increased stress. Thinking of the emotional situations discussed above, Table 5.1 outlines several beliefs and thoughts that might be driving negative emotions.

If you are experiencing negative emotions which you feel you need or want to manage, you can check the beliefs and values, as well as thoughts and expectations that are driving these. In other words, think about what is driving your emotions, how can you update and reframe these with a more positive outlook and what options you have moving forward. For example, if the thought that you'll mess up a live is driving your anxiety, consider how often does this happen to you? What do you think could go wrong? And what are you doing to make sure things go as smoothly as

Table 5.1 Potential beliefs and thoughts that might be driving a negative emotional response to emotional situations associated with going live and presenting

Adrenaline induced fear ahead of live broadcasting	Nervousness related to performing live	Worry about things going wrong
I will mess it up	I won't be able to control my nerves	I can't control this environment
My peers will think less of me if I make mistakes	My anxiety will be evident to all	The live will be interrupted by passersby
Bosses will think less of me if I make mistakes	I will look or sound silly or unprofessional	Technology will fail
I don't have enough time to prepare a good live	The audiences will not respect me if I don't perform perfectly	I will not be able to control my anxiety if things go wrong
I might say something that will appear biased or rude	I will freeze and embarrass myself	Bosses will lose faith in my ability to perform in complex environments

they can? And if you do mess up, what are the reasonable consequences? What happened to any of your colleagues that delivered less than a perfect live? Next, if you're nervous about looking nervous (yes, I've said it) during live, how did you come across on air before? Are you aware of your posture, breathing, non-verbal communication and appearance and are working to control them? How do you usually react to adrenaline rush—does it help you focus, or does it enhance your anxiety? If your editors trust you to deliver a live, chances are they've seen your screen test and believe that you are one of those that strives off adrenaline. Finally, if you are worried that technology will fail and wreak havoc on your live, consider what you can and cannot control in this situation. Also, what makes you think it will fail? If there are reasons to doubt, have necessary checks been made? If it does fail, what is the contingency plan? In case you don't go live as planned, is this so very unusual? Can't the live be rescheduled for another slot within the bulletin or if the tech fails completely, the host might just do a reader of the story? In the end, it's about getting the information to the audience. So, if everything else fails, the presenter can arguably still deliver the information.

   The beliefs and values that drive these emotional situations will differ from journalist to journalist, so it's important you try to unpack what exactly is inducing your own emotions in this context. Are they rational?

Logical? What evidence do you have to believe what you think is happening? And while, similarly, journalists may decide to manage their emotions in diverse ways, there are some common emotion management strategies that journalists apply when faced with emotional situations tied to going live and presenting, that the chapter now turns to.

CHOOSE: EMOTION MANAGEMENT STRATEGIES

The most commonly mentioned emotion management strategies by British journalists when dealing with emotional situations outlined above are attentional deployment in both forms—focusing on practice and routine, and directing the focus on activities that will divert attention to something else; situation modification that includes removing yourself for a while from stressful situation to regain control over your emotions; and internal processing in the form of acceptance and perspective-taking.

Attentional Deployment

Attentional deployment in the form of focusing attention on professional routines and practices is among the most commonly applied strategies as it allows the journalist to gain confidence through reassurance that everything that needs to be done in the process has been done to ensure a professional outcome. Reardon and Flynn (2014) suggest that feeling relaxed ahead of going on air comes with being confident in your work and capabilities, which in turn depends on your experience with the task. In case of emerging professionals in the field, Arya (1999) claims that good preparation can compensate for a lack of experience in making broadcasters going live more confident, and hence relaxed. British journalists interviewed for this book agree that being prepared significantly relieves the pressure of the task. A senior broadcast editor describes it like this:

> Sometimes you feel real, you know... I think trepidation is probably the word, not so much kind of stage fright, it's like kind of trepidation. But it's, but it's also... I mean, it's just about being a professional and being prepared for what you do and taking it seriously and, you know, knowing what you're going to say, having researched the story properly, and if you feel secure about what you do, you know, you feel secure in the work that you've done. Well, then it's okay, right. I mean if you're flying by the seat

of your pants, you don't know what you're talking about, like, people are going to pick up on that pretty quickly.

The worry that things may go wrong in the live can arguably be mitigated by being prepared for key potential challenges—considering what these may be and how they can be mitigated (Arya, 1999). Some you may be able to avoid altogether through diligent planning and preparation. For example, this senior broadcast editor describes how they relieved some of the anxiety of going on air with little time to prepare by ensuring that the most important risks are mitigated—a few notes at hand to ensure focus, and a rewrite of presenter's questions seemed to have done the trick in this case:

> In the end I knew what I needed. What I needed was a piece of paper with the thoughts that I wanted to get across, that I can have on the desk in front of me, so that as the presenter turns to me... And I had to rewrite his question - he was going to ask me completely different questions, which I would not have been able to answer... So, I managed to dodge that bullet... (laughs)

If the situation cannot be controlled, then preparation entails preparing for different eventualities. As Stewart and Alexander (2022: 226) argue: 'The art of the accomplished recovery is to prepare for every contingency.' This might include different elements in different situations, from, say, checking the surroundings for potential hazards when reporting from a rally and choosing the spot for broadcast accordingly, to considering what you may do if you aren't able to get to the location from which you are expecting to broadcast in time. Having options and thinking them through in advance should relieve some of the worry and anxiety ahead of going live, as this account of a mid-career broadcast journalist illustrates:

> Preparation, preparation, preparation. So, even if I know that I may get asked a question I don't know the answer to - what am I going to say instead? And as long as I've got something, you know, I've got all that in my head ready to go...

Internal Processing

Sometimes the feeling of being prepared might be enough to signal to body and mind that they can relax. Other times, when anxiety is high and the body is flushed with stress hormones, it is beneficial to apply another emotion management strategy—internal processing in forms of acceptance and/or perspective-taking, as Arya (1999) also suggests in his textbook on live broadcasting. On a basic level, this entails consciously accepting that everything that could have been done to prepare for a live has been done. In the words of a senior broadcast editor:

> I always imagined what could go wrong and tense up to it, instead of taking a view... Which I think I do now bit more, which is... You know, 'What can I do? Hopefully it will... I'm sure it'll go okay. Will it be my fault...? I can only do as well as I can...'

In complex broadcasting environments, it is useful to consider what you as a presenter or live reporter can and cannot control, as well as where your responsibilities lie. For example, if you're presenting a programme and a package has not come in, is this in your control? If you're on location and the microphone isn't working, is it your responsibility to fix it or find an alternative? Working with team members to find solutions and create contingency plans is constructive and appreciated, but—and as hard as it sometimes might be—you might benefit from accepting that not everything can be controlled, and it might not be your responsibility to manage the situation anyway. Yet, it is useful to consider what a potential issue means for you, your performance and the story/programme, and plan contingencies. With alternatives in mind, some of the worries might be alleviated.

A useful perspective-taking practice when worrying about the performance and all the things that might go wrong during a live is to remind yourself that you've been there before and you have the experience to handle the situation. A mid-career broadcast editor puts it like this:

> Really, it's just the experience knowing what to expect, and also with live broadcasting, you know, often unexpected things will happen, so... You know, when you're very new reporter, you can be made very nervous by the fact that you're doing a live maybe somewhere public and someone might jump up behind you or shout a swear word or something. But the more experience you have and the more times you've dealt with that, the

more you understand how to kind of overcome it and get around it, so I think you're less... You're less nervous of the unexpected.

It is important to acknowledge that taking this perspective need not rely solely on personal experience. For example, emerging professionals who have less on-air experience can shadow their more experienced colleagues, particularly on challenging fieldworks, to learn from their practice. Observing how others manage unexpected or just challenging circumstances, and learning from these, can assist them in applying similar perspectives.

Situation Modification

The environment in which broadcast journalists about to go live apply emotion management strategies is often not conducive to quiet contemplation and processing. If this represents an issue in managing anxiety or getting the stress hormones under control, another strategy that can be applied is situation modification, which entails removing yourself from the stress inducing physical environment to change its emotional impact (Gross, 2018). In other words, if a hectic newsroom is full of stressors that increase your levels of anxiety ahead of a live broadcast, or the team on location is dealing with faulty equipment and tensions are running high, it is worth trying to remove yourself from the stress inducing environment to reduce the exposure to stressors ahead of going live (Stewart & Alexander, 2022). Two senior broadcast editors describe their approach to managing stress ahead of going on air:

> You can wander around, and go get bit of fresh air, and speak out loud... It's quite complicated sometimes, or quite a long one, or there's quite a complicated analysis to get in, or there are figures... You just maybe go out to a park somewhere and try and say it out loud a couple of times. So, you've kind of released it and rehearsed it.
> I sometimes just remove myself... If it's getting really... So, you just remove yourself from the situation and just take time out. And be that going to the toilet and sitting there for five minutes (laughs) or going for a walk.

As the above quotes illustrate, the change of physical environment can serve to provide a calm space in which a journalist can gain focus ahead of going live. However, the modified situation can also be used for direct management of stress hormones with an aim of relaxing the body. Sometimes all it's needed are a few minutes. For example, two relaxation strategies, deemed effective in relieving anxiety and managing stress hormones, can be applied in a very short time period—deep breathing exercise and progressive muscle relaxation. Deep breathing (also called diaphragmatic or abdominal breathing as the abdomen should rise and fall with each breath) can in a short period reduce the heart rate, relax muscles, lower the levels of stress hormones in the body and even improve cognitive functions and attention levels (Ma et al., 2017). The tension of the muscles, which could make the journalist appear nervous and impede their performance, can be quickly relieved through a short progressive muscle relaxation—a two-step practice involving first tensing and then relaxing each muscle. For journalists short on time, covering face, shoulders, neck, arms and abdomen muscles might be enough to relieve key tensions that affect the state of mind and performance ahead of live broadcast.

Diversionary Activities

Finally, a useful emotion management strategy to manage the stressors related to live broadcasting is attentional deployment in the form of diverting the focus on non-work activities that induce happy hormones, such as endorphins and serotonin. Ahead of a live broadcast that is causing nervousness or anxiety, this strategy could be coupled with situation modification and would entail removing yourself from a work environment and spending some time focusing on non-work activities. A senior broadcast editor shares an example of how this strategy helped them relax prior to a stressful presenting task:

> I think what I've learned... I hope I've learned... I tried to do it this time with the help of a really good colleague, actually, who I just happened to see on the afternoon, and I was able to spend a bit of time sitting there, chatting to him... I tried to forget all about it. Forget the notes, forget the structure, forget about it. It must be in there by now. I'm sure it did make a difference.

Broadcasters also regularly emphasised the importance of physical exercise both as a means to foster relaxation following stressful live broadcasts and as a pre-emptive strategy that enables their bodies to effectively deal with adrenaline surges. A senior broadcast editor describes her strategy and its importance like this:

> The stress, the adrenaline... Because when you're performing, you produce adrenaline, right? And the adrenaline is in your body. And, especially if you're in a fast moving news environment, especially the news environment we're in now, where it's not just one news program, it's kind of 24/7, 7 days a week. You know, things land on a Friday night when you're not meant to be there... And I think the adrenaline is... I think managing the adrenaline and the stress is one of the harder points of the job. And I actually think you have to be physically pretty fit to be a broadcaster in a way that I perhaps hadn't understood. The way I personally manage it, is I do a lot of exercise.

Indeed, physical exercise can help reduce the levels of stress hormones, such as adrenaline and cortisol, in the body, fostering relaxation, reducing anxiety levels and improving the quality of sleep (Brassington et al., 2012). It can also stimulate the release of happy hormones, such as endorphin and serotonin, which can relieve worry, elevate mood and increase energy levels (Rokade, 2011). Hence, regular exercise can assist in being better prepared for the stressors of live broadcast as it helps sleep quality and energy levels, and it can assist in managing the stress post-broadcast by relieving tension and boosting the mood.

In sum, this chapter has covered several emotional situations that are likely to arise in live broadcasting, namely: fear and/or excitement that leads to adrenaline surge and causes some to thrive off this pressure and enter 'tunnel vision' and others to experience adrenaline anxiety; as well as nervousness related to performing; and fears about issues that might arise when reporting from environments that cannot be fully controlled or require many technical elements to operate as planned. It has been suggested that key strategies to manage these emotions include attentional deployment techniques of following protocols and engaging in diversionary activities, with special emphasis on the benefits of regular exercise; internal processing, such as acceptance and perspective-taking; as well as situation modification, which refers to temporarily leaving stress inducing situations before a live performance to relieve tension and gain focus.

The UK: Kurt Barling on Live Broadcasting

Kurt Barling was a BBC broadcast journalist for over 25 years. He worked on BBC News programmes, The Money Programme, Assignment, Correspondent, Newsnight, Black Britain and Money Box. In 2009, he was one of the first journalists on the scene of the Lakanal House tower block fire in South London which killed 3 adults and 3 children. A story he covered to its conclusion in a public inquest 4 years later. He is a Professor of Journalism and Theme Director for inclusive socio-economic development and enriching lives through culture at Middlesex University.

One of the highlights of being a broadcast journalist is the opportunity to be the first with a big story. No waiting for print publishing deadlines. Bringing the latest information live and direct to the audience. But this can sometimes bring hidden pressures of reporting accuracy and the reality of your words and pictures impacting on people's real lives.

On a sunny July afternoon in 2009, a call came through to the Newsroom of a fire in a tower block in South London. Ironically, the closer the reporter is to home the more pressure there is on them (unlike being on a foreign assignment) because the more exacting is the precision demanded. I became the main Correspondent reporting on the consequences of that tragic high-rise inferno that killed 3 young children and 3 adults. Needless to say, knowing that people are trapped in a building focuses the mind on accuracy. Reporters were to discover this when Grenfell Tower succumbed to its own inferno, and they were criticised for intrusive live reporting.

It became practice as the Lakanal story developed over many years for me to be dispatched to deliver my reporting live from outside the fire damaged block of flats. I would often have to broadcast live with an audience of residents looking on. If I got things wrong, I would know it instantly. If listeners on the ground felt I wasn't going far enough they might heckle me in the middle of my live spot. The reporter must develop resilience and the ability to get into a focused zone to block out external distractions.

I found it important to engage with local people before any live spot, so they knew the context of the story and why it was important to keep the story 'alive.' It gave me confidence that if interruptions occurred (which they sometimes did) local people would intervene to make sure they could hear what I was saying, and that the audience got to hear the story not the heckling. I would often call the local residents' association representative to give them warning that I would be broadcasting so local people wouldn't be surprised when a TV crew showed up. Local relationships are not only important to nurture new information but also in the aftermath of the fire and the displacement of hundreds of families it helped build trust in our coverage. It often meant on arrival new information came to light to support the news line I was reporting on.

My practice of counting to ten out loud and back down to one before tuning in to listen to the news gallery output of the bulletin and for the News director's instructions would always block out extraneous activity so I could focus on the individuals at home relying on me for accurate information.

My partner too of several decades would often watch my live performances on News bulletins and offer reassuring texts. It softened the impact of criticism that might materialise later. Getting the tone right matters so much to audiences, but so does sharing your burdens.

All that said there is little that can top the adrenalin rush of breaking a story and being first with the News. Combine that with the high of the performance and the moments of intense clarity needed to make a live broadcast work is one of the best parts of the job. Learning to manage the multiple stressors is just one element of the craft you need to master to be a top broadcaster.

Top Tips

- Consider your readiness for a live broadcast assignment—you should be aware of, and able to manage, how you look and sound on air, able to deliver unscripted content, evaluate the risks of presenting in different locations, create contingency plans and control your stress hormones

- Prepare, prepare, prepare—know what you want to say and how you want to say it, what kind of questions you're likely to be asked or ask others, have contingency plans in mind, written prompts if helpful, etc.
- Consider your level of preparedness and previous success in delivering on-air content to gain confidence and relieve anxiety
- Consider what you can and cannot control, and what is and isn't your responsibility, in any live broadcasting environment
- Try to spend a few minutes before going on air in a non-hectic space to calm your body and mind, and gain focus
- If you feel tense and anxious ahead of a live broadcast, employ a quick relaxation strategy—for example, deep breathing and/or progressive muscle relaxation
- Exercise regularly to empower your body to deal with adrenaline, and ensure you have good quality sleep to avoid tiredness which can impact on your focus and performance

READ, WATCH AND LISTEN

- Read Harvard Medical School's Mini relaxation exercises: A quick fix in stressful moments - https://www.health.harvard.edu/health beat/mini-relaxation-exercises-a-quick-fix-in-stressful-moments
- Read Forbes' article 'How to deal with stress at work' - https://www.forbes.com/health/mind/how-to-deal-with-stress-at-work/
- Watch English actor Dominic Colenso's short tutorial on breathing exercises for confident public speaking - https://www.youtube.com/watch?v=dyIoUMwD7Xw
- Watch TED talk 'How to make stress your friend' by Kelly McGonigal, health psychologist and lecturer at Stanford University - https://www.ted.com/talks/kelly_mcgonigal_how_to_make_stress_your_friend
- Listen to NHS's guided progressive muscle relaxation - https://www.youtube.com/watch?v=912eRrbes2g

SCENARIO EXERCISES

Scenario 1

You work for a national television channel covering economics. You've been with the channel for a few years, previously covering economics for a regional radio channel, and for a local paper while you were a journalism trainee. While you have a fair grasp of economics, it's a difficult field and it is often challenging to translate complex matters in a concise and clear form.

Today, you are covering a newly published report from the Office for Budget Responsibility (OBR) that analyses the state of the post-Brexit trade. You have prepared a package for evening news, and you are about to go live in a two-way format from a location in front of the OBR answering the presenter's questions on reactions to the report. You've planned what you will say and coordinated with the newsroom, but minutes before going on air you see on social media a few new reactions on the Report from opposition parties and the European Union officials. Also, the weather has turned, and it appears it might start to rain any minute.

- How does this make you feel?
- What are you going to do? Why?

Scenario 2

You are a presenter of afternoon news on a regional radio station. You're fairly new in the presenter's job but have proven yourself as competent in live broadcasting having reported live on radio for several years. Given the timing of the news, reporters can still be busy with collecting information and moving from location to location, and there is often time pressure to get the packages ready to go for broadcast.

It is 10 minutes to the start of the news and you're in the studio going over the programme. The producer notifies you that there are still two packages to be completed, one of which is first in the running order of the programme, and that one of the reporters who was supposed to be on location for a 'throw' from the studio is stuck in traffic and can't guarantee they'll be on location by the agreed time.

- How does this make you feel?
- What are you going to do? Why?

References

Arya, B. (1999). *Thirty seconds to air: A field reporter's guide to live television reporting*. Iowa State University Press.

Bleyer-Simon, K., Brogi, E., Carlini, R., Da Costa Leite Borges, D., Nenadic, I., Palmer, M., Parcu, P. L., Trevisan, M., Verza, S., Žuffová, M., & Verza, S. (2022). *Monitoring media pluralism in the digital era*. European University Institute.

Brassington, G. S., Hekler, E. B., Cohen, Z., & King, A. C. (2012). Health-enhancing physical activity. In A. Baum, T. A. Revenson, & J. E. Singer (Eds.), *Handbook of health psychology* (2nd ed., pp. 353–374). Psychology Press.

Bull, A. (2016). *Multimedia journalism: A practical guide* (2nd ed.). Routledge.

Carpenter, S., Hoag, A., & Grant, A. E. (2018). An examination of print and broadcast journalism students' personality traits. *Journalism and Mass Communication Educator, 73*(2), 147–166.

Gross, J. J. (2018). Emotion regulation. In M. Lewis, J. M. Haviland-Jones, & L. F. Barrett (Eds.), *Handbook of emotions* (pp. 497–512). The Guildford Press.

Grünewald, Z. (2022). *Is Fiona Bruce the problem, or is Question Time?* New Statesman. https://www.newstatesman.com/quickfire/2022/09/bbc-question-time-fiona-bruce-problem

Hudson, G., & Rowlands, S. (2018). *The broadcast journalism handbook* (7th ed.). Routledge.

Ma, X., Yue, Z. Q., Gong, Z. Q., Zhang, H., Duan, N. Y., Shi, Y. T., Wei, G. X., & Li, Y. F. (2017). The effect of diaphragmatic breathing on attention, negative affect and stress in healthy adults. *Frontiers in Psychology, 8*(874), 1–12.

Reardon, N., & Flynn, T. (2014). *On camera: How to report, anchor & interview* (2nd ed.). Focal Press.

Rokade, P. B. (2011). Release of Endomorphin Hormone and its effects on our body and moods: A review. *International Conference on Chemical, Biological and Environment Sciences*. http://psrcentre.org/images/extraimages/1211916.pdf

Sissons, H. (2006). *Practical journalism how to write news*. SAGE.

Stewart, P., & Alexander, R. (2022). *Broadcast journalism: Techniques of radio and television news* (8th ed.). Routledge.

Tuggle, C. A., & Huffman, S. (1999). Live news reporting: Professional judgment or technological pressure? A national survey of television news directors and senior reporters. *Journal of Broadcasting and Electronic Media, 43*(4), 492–505.

CHAPTER 6

Reflection and Feedback

Very early on in my journalistic career, I've noticed that audiences have lots to say about me and my work and they don't shy away from telling me how wrong I am in very descriptive language. It was in what I think of as my first proper job in journalism—working on a retainer for a digital media outlet. I was still in my teens, with no journalistic training, at a time when Facebook had only been established, but online audiences seemed keen to comment on everything and anything in website comments. I remember seeing comments under one of my articles for the first time. I don't know exactly what I was expecting, but the feeling of high I felt for being paid for stories published on a national level while still in high school dissipated very quickly. First, there was self-doubt. 'I'm rubbish at this,' I thought. Then, I checked my stories and found that lots of the criticism was unfounded. That came with anger at being misunderstood and my words misrepresented. Somehow, I managed the courage to speak to my editor about it, which was no easy task as I was afraid that she'll think less of me based on audiences' feedback. It was a relief to learn she did not. I got my first lesson then on who comments and how I might manage and process this feedback. It was very helpful.

It was a combination of critical reflection and perspective-taking, that the editor helped me develop, that ensured I did not run away from journalism before even properly starting. I even think it made me a better journalist. With some practice, I was able to discern the destructive

© The Author(s), under exclusive license to Springer Nature Switzerland AG 2023
M. Šimunjak, *Managing Emotions in Journalism*, https://doi.org/10.1007/978-3-031-38631-2_6

comments in which audiences seemed to vent, from those from which I can actually learn something. And yes, I've had lots to learn. I still do. Training in journalism helped immensely, as it enabled me to critically reflect on my own work, establishing what I thought went well and areas for improvement. This then helped me put audiences' comments in perspective, making distinctions between constructive criticism I can learn from on the one end, and straight-out abuse that I was better off not engaging with on the other.

This chapter deals with the part of the journalistic process that entails reflecting on and receiving, or not receiving, feedback on produced work within and outside the newsroom through the 'stop, think, choose' model of emotional intelligence. The 'stop' section discusses emotional situations related to reflection and feedback, namely: feelings of pride and satisfaction when positively evaluating your work, as well as receiving positive feedback within and outside the newsroom; the anxiety and frustration that come with the lack of feedback from editors and/or audiences; and the anxiety, frustration, anger and sadness when the feedback is critical and/or negative. In the 'think' section, some beliefs and thoughts which may be driving mentioned emotions are outlined. The 'choose' section suggests emotion management strategies informed by interviews with practising journalists. These include internal processing by perspective-taking (e.g., acknowledging that a story may have an impact even when audiences do not publicly engage with it); boundary-setting, such as deciding not to see or read negative comments; and verbal processing with peers.

Stop: Emotional Situations

The practice of reflection is often mentioned in journalism training as journalists are positioned as reflective practitioners who learn from evaluating their experiences and outputs. The value of training journalists in critical reflection has been examined in education systems across the world, from Australia, over Canada, to Philippines (Forbes, 2010; Kronstad, 2016; Opiniano et al., 2021). For journalism trainees, a useful resource is Burns and Matthews's (2018) textbook 'Understanding journalism' which is based on guided reflection with an aim to increase journalists' self-efficacy or confidence, which can help them manage anxieties related to work. As Burns and Matthews (2018: 26) put it, 'a journalist who is conscious of and understands the active decisions that make up daily practice is best prepared to negotiate the challenges involved.' On the other hand, engaging in critical reflection can also assist journalists in recognising their personal accomplishments.

Reflection

Interviews with British journalists reveal that journalists reflect on their practices, considering their choices and evaluating them, across the story production process, as Burns and Matthews (2018) suggest they should. Yet, it appears that this is made most conscious in the post-publishing period, that is, once the story is made public, when they contemplate what they have done well and what they think they should have done better, as well as consider the potential consequences and the implications of the story being published. Specifically, in this **post-publishing period, journalists report feeling anxious about their output, and/or pride in their work**. The feeling of doubt about the quality of story has been most frequently mentioned by emerging practitioners, as this early career print journalist recounts:

> So, I understand how the Internet works, I understand how readers read and interact with the Internet, I can write news stories, I can picture edit... You know, I feel like if... You know, if our newsroom was blown up with a bomb, and there was only five people left, you'd want me to be one of the five people, because I could like... [...] So, I know all that but also, I just always feel like everything I do is terrible, not quite good enough and that I'm going to be criticised for it.

Yet, some more experienced journalists spoke of this too, as they consider all the ways in which a story could have been told better. In the words of a senior broadcast editor:

> And I am like that, I think, quite critical, self-critical... You can always feel when you see your piece or hear your piece back afterwards... 'I didn't use that great expression; I didn't structure that very well; I could have done that in a different way...' There were so many permutations you could get right, and I find that quite intimidating.

On the other hand, many journalists report feeling satisfied and proud of the stories they've published, which leads to a sense of accomplishment. This emotion seems to be shared across the board, that is, by journalists across all sectors and of all levels of seniority. In other words, reflecting on the story and evaluating it as a successful piece of journalism are tied to a feeling of both professional and personal success and can be understood as a rewarding part of the job, as the following quotes illustrate:

Early career print correspondent:

> Yeah, the joy... Flip side of that is fantastic, feeling really good and accomplished, particularly if that's something that you've been potentially working on for a while, whether that's kind of several days or several weeks...

Senior print reporter:

> There is an egocentric thing to that as well. Because you want to be the one to... You know, any journalist who tells you otherwise is a liar. You know, I genuinely want to do good. That's the reason that I do my job. Primarily, is because I want to do good. But there is an egocentric thing, where I want to be seen to do good as well, and, you know, and I'll be a liar to say anything else. So... It's with high ideals, but there is a payoff for me as well.

The reflection on the published story also regularly involves considering the potential consequences of it, particularly in terms of how it will be received. In this context, journalists speak of being **curious and nervous anticipating the amount and type of feedback they are likely to receive on the story,** particularly from audiences. This feeling of nervousness has been mentioned by early career journalists who may be feeling insecure about their work. An early career digital journalist describes how publishing a story makes them feel:

> It's always interesting to read what people are writing about the story, you know, in the comments and on social media. Umm And, and then again nerves, as well because thousands of people are reading what you've written and if you made a typo or something or if they say it's not a very good story... That's a bit nerve wracking sometimes.

Yet, the nervousness does not arise only when journalists are insecure about their work. It can arise even if, upon reflection, a journalist concludes that they did a good job with the story. On some occasions, this stress can be brought about by considering the limitations of the piece—as each story is necessarily limited by the angle taken on it, research that was consulted, sources that were interviewed and the time/space it has been given in the media outlet. From experience with the field, journalists are aware that their choices might be questioned. In the words of an early career digital journalist:

> It's just... Yeah, that is just stressful. Even if you know that you have... You know, you have not guessed this. You spoke to experts, you've done this. But even then, it's still a bit like... Putting it out there and waiting for that expert that you've not spoken to, to come back and go, 'Wait a minute... What about this?'

Further, the nervousness can arise from contemplating the impact of the story on sources and the ways they will react to it, as this early career digital reporter describes:

> You're also a bit nervous that your subjects, the sources, are happy with how you, you know, what you've said. Also, you know, if it's something controversial or maybe you're, you know, criticising someone for something... You do get a bit of nerves about how it's going to be received by readers, how it's going to be received by the people that you've written the story about, particularly if there's criticism. And, you know, especially if you write something controversial, there's always a risk of a complaint.

A similar worry, considering the impact that the story will have on the relationship with sources, is shared by an early career print correspondent:

> I don't think there's been any particular cases where I have necessarily published a story that I'm really worried about being incorrect that has then turned out to be incorrect... That's never happened. But you're still worried that, you know, people will carry on talking to you, will respect you, will like you, even if what you've published isn't incorrect.

Those with more years of experience in the industry speak of anxiety anticipating the reactions to their stories too. Sometimes the emotion is induced by covering complex matters that the journalist does not feel fully confident in, exacerbated by reflection on previous reactions to similar stories. A mid-career print correspondent gives this account:

I think when you move to territory where you are a bit less confident and you're perhaps...[...] You know, there's one country that I knew that every time I write about it there's like a very active group of people on Twitter, who would pass this text for like the smallest thing, and there would probably be something in it that was wrong. And. So... There were, you know... I did have this actual feeling, you know, low level but dread, I think, that, like, 'I've got to deal with these people who are going to turn my story apart again.'

Similarly, journalists, senior ones included, may feel anxious when breaking big stories, particularly if they involve powerful people, as they anticipate potential backlash and pushback, as well as potentially more work to be done on the story depending on its reception. A senior print editor tells of their experiences:

In my case, you know, you write a piece on Friday or Saturday, it goes live on Saturday night. Saturday night is not a restful time because your piece has gone live and, you know, either people are nit-picking about it or tearing it to pieces, or praising it, in which case the broadcasters might be ringing you and say, 'God, this is an interesting story, will you appear on this and that?' So, really heightened sort of anxiety and emotional involve-ment over, sort of, for me over a Saturday night, Sunday morning, which is very difficult to escape from. So, your first technical day off is not really a day off.

Feedback

Alongside reflection on their work, journalists in the post-publishing period also need to manage feedback they receive on their stories. While 'feedback' is quite a wide term, a useful definition is offered by Kluger and DeNisi (1996: 255) who describe it as 'actions taken by (an) external agent(s) to provide information regarding some aspect(s) of one's task performance.' As such, feedback can be offered in a construc-tive or destructive way by those providing it and perceived as positive or negative by those who are receiving it (Baron, 1988; Belschak & Den Hartog, 2009). Giving and receiving feedback have received much attention in the field of psychology, and have been researched in disci-plines such as education, management and organisational behaviour. This scholarship regularly outlines constructive feedback—information on performance that acknowledges effort and offers guidance on how it can be improved—as a mechanism of growth that can improve efficiency and motivation for work. Even if this kind of feedback is critical, it can still be seen as positive by the recipient if it is recognised as a developmental mechanism. Destructive and negative feedback can impact recipient's confidence and hinder development. And while the majority of studies of feedback focus on its impact on task performance, it has been acknowledged that engaging with feedback is also an affective process (Alam & Singh, 2021). For example, receiving feedback can invoke a range of emotions in the recipient, from happiness and pride to anger, frustration and guilt (Belschak & Den Hartog, 2009).

In journalism, practitioners primarily get feedback from bosses/editors and peers within the newsroom, and beyond the workplace from audiences. Receiving and managing feedback in newsrooms are fairly under researched topics (Ivask, 2019). One of the rare studies that shed light on this was the MediaAct survey which gathered experiences from 1762 journalists from 12 European and two Arab countries. The survey revealed that receiving feedback within newsrooms is not common in examined contexts (Lauk et al., 2014). Ivask's (2019) examination of feedback practices in Estonian newsrooms that followed a few years later found similar trends—there is little feedback offered to journalists in newsrooms, and the feedback that has been shared has often been negative. British journalists interviewed for this book gave a similar account of newsrooms in the UK, with an early career print journalist noting:

> I always say with newsrooms, people are very slow to give praise and positive feedback, but you certainly know very, very fast if you've really fucked something up.

Hence, one of the emotional situations that can arise in relation to feedback **is the anxiety that comes with the lack of feedback**, which seems to be an industry-wide issue. This situation seems to be most stressful for early career journalists, who rely on feedback to gain confidence in their work. So, the lack of feedback can impact journalists' self-efficacy and make them worry about the quality of journalism they produce. In the word of an early career digital journalist:

> Unfortunately, they never really give me a lot of feedback. It would be nice if they did, but... Sometimes they do. It is quite rare to be honest. Every now and then they'll say, 'This is a really good story,' or, 'This is

quite a strong story.' And again, it's nice to get that feedback, it's quite reassuring, I think. Because there's a general lack of feedback, sometimes I feel like I'm a bit left in the dark, I don't know what's good and what's bad.

Emerging professionals see feedback also as a developmental mechanism through which they can improve their performance and learn from their mistakes. They say that they welcome constructive feedback, as they would be able to learn from it and further develop their practice. Consequently, the lack of it creates anxieties about their opportunities to become better at their jobs and develop as successful practitioners, as this early career print journalist describes:

I think when I first started it was one of the hardest things for me - there was just no feedback whatsoever. So, when I first started, I was kind of... I had a bit of imposter syndrome and I kind of felt like, 'Oh my God, I don't know if I think my stories are good or bad.' [...] You have this understanding that, you know, you just sort of welcome criticism, because then you can improve. But then you suddenly get thrown into the deep end of real life, professional working, and you don't get any feedback.

Receiving more detailed and constructive feedback from editors, as well as more senior colleagues, is seen as an opportunity to benefit from their experiences and learn from others' good practice, as well as perhaps from their mistakes. When this feedback isn't offered, emerging practitioners might feel that they are missing learning opportunities. An early career digital journalist describes the situation like this:

You know, I'm still a relatively young, relatively inexperienced journalist... And I think it would be helpful to, you know, perhaps learn some things from people that know a bit more about it than me, and, you know, have been there a bit longer and, you know, could offer some useful feedback. What tends to happen is... I might get something written to me on Slack that says, 'You've made this mistake. Can you change that?' Generally, it's very minor and it's very polite. Or if I've done, you know, a good exclusive or story that's done well, or whatever... They'll say, 'Oh, good story on x.' And that's pretty much it in terms of feedback. There's nothing detailed or... That really offers me much to change the way I'm doing things, or to learn much.

Ivask (2019) noted that in Estonian newsrooms, the feedback that was offered was often destructive and perceived as negative by journalists' receiving it. Negative feedback within newsrooms hasn't been commonly mentioned by British journalists who shared their experiences for this book, but when it has, it was evident that it can impact on journalists' confidence. Specifically, it was mentioned that **receiving negative feedback within a newsroom can be disheartening and increase anxiety about current and future work**. Importantly, this is not just the case with emerging professionals who may still be developing their sense of confidence in their work, as this account of a senior broadcast editor illustrates:

> If you feel it hasn't [gone well]... And it's something that, you know, either you feel peers might not have thought was, you know, quite up to usual standards, or if your, you know, editor, your boss or your line manager or someone, you know, felt there were missing elements... [...] It's quite possible to, you know, take that quite seriously and to feel quite despondent. [...] So, the elation and the good things don't really hang around for very long, because you're starting all over again the next day. But the... But I think criticisms... And... I think that they do. They linger and they will eat away, and they will, I think, of course, sometimes, they'll definitely factor in... They'll definitely be there in the back of your head the next time you confront similar kind of, you know, scenario. Sometimes similar kind of stories, actually.

Also, some journalists expressed **frustration when they perceived that the feedback from editors is based on audience feedback**, rather than the effort and quality of the journalism they have produced. Specifically, particularly among digital journalists in newsrooms where there is significant emphasis put on website metrics—including data about the number of unique visitors on the site, number of times a story has been viewed and the time spent engaging with it—some journalists felt frustrated that the feedback they receive is more tied to how their stories perform online than the quality of their work. Research on the role and use of website metrics in newsrooms has proliferated throughout 2010s, with data from, for example, the US, Australia, Netherlands and Sweden, showing that editors regularly track these metrics and often take them into account when making editorial decisions, especially in market-oriented organisations (Ekström et al., 2022; Ferrucci, 2020; Hanusch & Tandoc, 2019; Vu, 2014; Welbers et al., 2016). The study of editors' use of web metrics from the US has shown that editors regularly shared audience metrics with staff, making some journalists perceive that they are increasingly operating in a 'a culture that privileged popularity over quality' (Ferrucci, 2020: 252). Similarly, a study of a Swedish newsroom revealed that editors tend to evaluate the performance of journalists based on website metrics of their stories and coach them in how to create stories that would perform better online, while traditional journalists' tasks, such as research, are rarely commented on (Ekström et al., 2022). Some British journalists interviewed for the book shared similar experiences and spoke of how frustrated and disheartening they found these practices. In the words of an early career digital journalist:

> Sometimes, I think, stories that maybe you'd work quite hard on but hadn't performed very well online wouldn't really get any response from editors. I think it's... My sense is that it's quite uncommon for editors to respond to, you know, every article you've ever written. Obviously, they don't have the time or resources. But I think their interpretation of how well you're doing is quite often driven by how well your stories perform online. [...] In my previous work it definitely made me feel quite undervalued. [...] Some journalists were very good at marketing their work online and sometimes I did feel a little bit frustrated that they would then get quite a lot of good feedback from editors as a result.

While website metrics can be used by editors to evaluate a journalist's performance and feedback on it, they can also be used by journalists' themselves in evaluating the ways in which their stories are received (Duffy et al., 2018; Usher, 2013). In modern journalism, these metrics are one of the key audience feedback mechanisms that journalists' have access to, alongside website and social media comments (Hanusch & Tandoc, 2019). And if journalists often feel that they do not receive enough (constructive) feedback within newsrooms, the situation is often the opposite when it comes to audience feedback—many journalists report that it has never been as plentiful nor instantaneous as it is nowadays. The receipt of audience feedback is an emotional process for journalists of all levels of experience, and more so today than it was in the past when audience feedback was communicated via letters to the editor and/or calls to the newsroom (Reader, 2015), with a mix of emotions at play, as this senior print editor explains:

There are so many different moments down the process, further on down the process, beyond having pressed that button… So, you've finished your piece… […] But then you have the whole process of the thing going live. Now, that is a particularly key moment, because these days, because you can immediately see… You can often see within 20 minutes how that story is going to be received. And, you know, if you get lots of flack flying… Well, it can hit Twitter, it can hit say the [title] website and you can see how many comments it's getting; you can see how many hits it's getting. All that is quite sort of anxiety, excitement, depression, inspiring time! (laughs)

Indeed, journalists can experience a range of emotions, from excitement to despondency, when engaging with audience feedback, as confirmed by research from various news cultures and media systems. For example, studies in the US as well as in the Middle East found that good story metrics induce feelings of happiness, pride and joy in journalists, contributing to their confidence and a sense of accomplishment, while poor reception of a story can make them sad and disappointed, increasing anxiety levels and self-doubt in their abilities and performance (Petre, 2015; Usher, 2013). Regarding the former, British journalists too spoke of feelings of **elation and pride when they perceived their stories to be received well by the audiences**. An early career digital journalist describes the situation in this way:

When I have produced the story, and I see its success… And success can be measured in my mind by comments from bosses, it can be comments from readers, it can be retweets on social media or responses on social media, it can be page views, because we have like new ways of viewing analytics… So, when I see that I've done something that is successful and I care about, then I'm proud, the main emotion is pride. And I get a kick out of that. That's basically why I do it.

Positive feedback from audiences is often perceived as an indicator of personal success and used as a tool for personal validation, enhancing journalists' confidence and satisfaction with work, as this mid-career print correspondent elaborates:

On the printed, or the final products, I guess, there is a sense of pride, there is some kind of sense of… What's the word? Like there's something gratifying about… Well, you know, people sharing it, people reading it.

Audience feedback does not have to be publicly visible in terms of a story trending on a site or being widely shared on social media. Personal and professional satisfaction with a job well done can be induced through personal interactions via emails or direct messages too. For example, this early career print journalist recounts how audience members reached out to him to applaud his reporting on complex matters, which made him feel proud of the work they've done:

> In fact, this last year, particularly around the American election, I got so many emails from readers saying how much they appreciated the coverage we were doing or the coverage that I was doing. That it was readable, and it was funny as well as being that… But also, the fact that they were always saying about how it was explaining things and how it was easy to follow…

However, it appears that the rush of positive feedback might have its downsides. On the one hand, it might be difficult to tear yourself away from following the success of your story, such as constantly checking the views a story is getting or what's being said about it on social media, which can distract from work. On the other hand, there might be an issue of tiredness and emptiness once the happy hormones wear off. In the words of an early career digital journalist:

> I do find myself too often just mindlessly scrolling through it instead of doing work. And, as well, when I get a tweet that does quite well, when it gets quite a lot of numbers on it, I really struggle with that mentally. Like, it feels like it's like a huge rush of dopamine, but then it feels quite depleted afterwards. Like, I feel, like, fantastic for like a short amount of time, but then really rubbish and down afterwards. Which I don't really understand.

When the **audience feedback is destructive and negative, journalists report feeling anxiety, frustration, anger and sadness**. This feeling too is felt by journalists of all levels of experience, as the higher profile you have it is more likely that there will be a strong audience reaction to the story, particularly in societies with high social media use. In the words of a mid-career broadcast editor:

> In years gone by, maybe before social media, if I did a report that was a bit controversial, we might have five or six phone calls, you know, from people who sat there and really felt absolutely strongly enough that they have to

research the number of the newsroom or the number of the Ofcom and phone up. So, they'd have… I mean, they'd have to really be at the end of tether to do that and feel as though it was worthwhile. Whereas now, you know, the energy it takes to find me on Twitter, send me a bit of abuse or google the name of my interviewee and send them a bit of abuse, is literally a couple of seconds worth of effort.

Journalists perceive that certain stories, such as those that deal with controversies and/or align with the media's 'watchdog' role, are particularly likely to lead to strong and extensive negative feedback from stakeholders in the story and their supporters. It has been argued that some of the aims of this kind of campaign are to undermine journalists, impact on their confidence and in the end silence them from further reporting (Posetti et al., 2021). Being at the receiving end of this backlash takes an emotional toll even when journalists perceive there is an agenda behind it, as the following quotes evidence:

Early career digital journalist:

A lot of the time, the stuff that I'm writing people don't want me to write it. And they'll ring me up and they say, 'This isn't a story; you've made a mistake here or there,' when there's definitely a story and it's fine. But, you know, that's sort of a tactic they try sometimes to undermine me, which is a bit stressful sometimes, but part of the job I suppose. Or maybe not.

Senior print editor:

If you're really going to hold power to account, which is what our job is, it's about saying things that people won't like you saying, and those people have many supporters, and those people have a lot of power. And that power can be thrown back at you, in the most vicious and awful way. And there you are sitting in your little office in lockdown, you've written what you regarded as rather a brave story about what you've uncovered somewhere, and you find, you know… A big sea of criticism hitting you online. That's difficult to handle.

The feeling of frustration can be induced if a journalist feels that the audience reaction is based on misunderstanding the story or engaging with it with preconceptions. These situations may be particularly evident in media systems with politically aligned and partisan press, such as the

British one (Hinde, 2017), as the audience may assume bias based on their perception of the outlet a journalist works for, and any other number of reasons. This can be disheartening for journalists who consider their work has been misinterpreted or misjudged, as this mid-career print correspondent explains:

> It's more, kind of, demoralising and frustrating when you feel that, you know, people are not getting your point, or people are assuming dishonest intentions.

Criticism of stories and journalists might also be more likely in media systems with high levels of distrust of media. The case of public service media is important in this regard, as these are often based on values of impartiality and balance in reporting, so their journalists might be more likely to be criticised if audiences perceive them as biased. Some of this behaviour could be examined under the concept of the hostile media perception, which Perloff (2015: 707) defines as the 'tendency for individuals with a strong preexisting attitude on an issue to perceive that ostensibly neutral, even-handed media coverage of the topic is biased against their side and in favour of their antagonists' point of view.' For example, it is telling that the British BBC and its journalists regularly face criticism of both left and right bias (Newman et al., 2022). In general, there has been weakening of trust in public service media across the world in the period from 2018 to 2022, with the biggest drops in trust observed in the UK, Canada and Australia (Newman et al., 2022). The less trust people have in the media, the more likely they might be to assume a critical stance towards journalists and their stories. Broadcast journalists interviewed for this book in particular spoke of destructive feedback inducing feelings of disappointment, sadness and anxiety. The audience reactions from social media have often been mentioned in this context as they are perceived as more personally directed at journalists, as this account of a senior broadcast editor illustrates:

> And the immediate interaction I find can be upsetting or destabilising. Because the way I presume people who tweet at you, if you've got any kind of public profile, think it's not much different from shouting at the TV when I'm on it. But it comes to me very quickly and very personally, and, you know, it's not in a mailbag of complaints that go to a different department or something. It's on my phone in my handbag that comes,

and, you know, sits beside my bed at night. [...] I'm sure they do not see me as a human being. And it's possible if I'd ever have a face-to-face conversation with somebody and say, 'This is how it makes me feel,' they might think about it again. I don't think I'm seen as a person. I'm seen as a personality. But as a person it gets me down.

And while some of the journalists who are (regularly) criticised and/or harassed by audiences might welcome the respite from audience feedback (and some actively set these boundaries by turning off comments or notifications—more on this in Chapter 7), the other extreme—**not getting any or much reaction from audiences, could induce frustration and sadness.** This situation may be particularly evident in systems with high social media use in journalism in which journalists feel the pressure to create a public profile that is seen as a measure of professional and personal success. In the words of an early career digital journalist:

I think... Very occasionally if I get absolutely no reaction to a story that I put out... I think, sometimes I would just delete the tweets. [...] Because I think it was not a very interesting story, and so, if I'm using Twitter as a promotional tool, perhaps it doesn't look very good if there's no engagement with the story.

The lack of audience feedback can also make journalists feel disheartened and question their performance, as this senior broadcast correspondent explains:

I'm conscious that there isn't a huge amount of engagement, which on occasion makes you think, 'Well, why do you bother doing this at all?' Because you're just another random person out there tweeting things and no one's paying any attention. So, who is this for really? Is it actually just for yourself?

Think

As explained in the Introduction chapter, emotional and physical responses to a situation are driven by our beliefs and thoughts through which we interpret that situation. If we are interpreting a situation with negative thoughts, it's more likely that we will perceive it as an inevitable occurrence which we have little or no control over. This can then lead to increased stress. Thinking of the emotional situations discussed above, Table 6.1 outlines several beliefs and thoughts that might be driving negative emotions.

If you are experiencing negative emotions which you feel you need or want to manage, you can check the beliefs and values, as well as thoughts and expectations that are driving these. In other words, think about what is driving your emotions, how can you update and reframe these with a more positive outlook, and what options you have moving forward. For example, if you worry that your sources will not be happy with their representation in the story, consider if it is your job to make sources happy? Have you treated them with respect and fairness? If you have, and they knew how the information will be used, then didn't you do your job? Also, if you're anxious about the lack of feedback from editors and think you won't be able to progress without it, consider whether you can spot any signs of progress until now? Do we learn only from feedback? Have you maybe also developed by learning from observing peers and editorial decisions, or maybe from audience feedback? Can you ask for feedback? What might happen if you do? Finally, if you're frustrated with negative audience feedback because you think this will diminish you in the eyes of your peers, consider if receiving negative feedback is uncommon in journalism nowadays? Are you the only person in the newsroom receiving it?

Table 6.1 Potential beliefs and thoughts that might be driving a negative emotional response to emotional situations associated with post-publishing

Worry about the quality of story that is published	Anxiety about the lack of feedback in newsroom	Frustration with feedback from audiences
The story isn't good enough	I don't know what's good or bad	They're biased in their interpretation of the story
Sources will not be happy with their representation	I am not able to learn or progress	They assume I have dishonest intentions
Elite people will not want to speak to me again	I will continue feeling anxious about my work	Negative feedback will get me in trouble at work
Bosses will be disappointed in me		My peers & bosses will respect me less if I get negative feedback
My choices will be questioned		No one cares about the stories I do

Is the criticism valid? How have colleagues perceived negative feedback aimed at others in the newsroom before?

The beliefs and values that drive these emotional situations will differ from journalist to journalist, so it's important you try to unpack what exactly is inducing your own emotions in this context. Are they rational? Logical? What evidence do you have to believe what you think is happening? And while, similarly, journalists may decide to manage their emotions in diverse ways, there are some common emotion management strategies that journalists apply when faced with emotional situations tied to post-publishing, that the chapter now turns to.

CHOOSE: EMOTION MANAGEMENT STRATEGIES

The most commonly mentioned emotion management strategies by British journalists when dealing with emotional situations outlined above are internal processing by perspective-taking (e.g., acknowledging that a story may have an impact even when audiences do not publicly engage with it) and acceptance; boundary-setting, such as deciding not to see or read negative comments; and verbal processing with peers.

Internal Processing

It doesn't surprise that journalists commonly spoke of internal processing as a strategy to manage emotions induced by reflection and feedback, given that thinking through your actions and choices as well as feedback is one of the key ways to reflect and process comments on performance. Regarding criticism, from audiences and editors alike, it is important to process it in order to evaluate its value and if needed, learn from it. Considering (constructive) feedback to be a developmental mechanism is an important element of 'growth mindset' as it allows you to learn from what you've done and consider what you can do differently next time to achieve better outcomes (Conaway, 2022). An early career digital journalist shares their approach:

> It's always good, I think, when you get criticised to not have a knee jerk reaction and say, 'Oh this person is just an asshole.' It's always good to say, 'Have they got a point? Have I actually done something wrong? Could I have done something better?' And so, I always try and, you know, I do try and take some time to actually digest what the criticism is and think,

'Is it fair?' and, 'Could I learn from this? Could I do something better?' Sometimes, yes, sometimes, no.

It might also be useful to consciously accept the fact that journalism is a public-facing profession and one that attracts much scrutiny due to its importance in a society. Some journalists emphasise that given the usually high standards of the profession, criticism from the audience is a normal part of the job, and so one that should be expected and accepted. In the words of a senior print reporter:

> I'm in a profession in which I have to expect criticism. I'm judged every single day. Everything I write is judged. I know that maybe 50% of the people reading what I write, think I'm an idiot. And 50% think I've got it bang on. If I'm lucky. Sometimes it's 90%, sometimes it's 10%, you know... But I know I will be judged. If I make a spelling mistake... I'm an idiot if I make a spelling mistake. I am illiterate if I make an error and it's not picked up by the subs. I expect to be judged. So, you've got to be... You've got to reconcile with yourself that you are, you know... In a way, in a shop window.

Additionally, particularly for journalists who internalise roles of 'watchdogs' and perceive their work as based on holding powerful to account and informing the public of the things they not only want but also need to know, it might be important to accept that the role comes with high pressure and likely resistance from those who are at the centre of the story and their supporters. For example, comparative research which analysed audience behaviour in Denmark, Germany, Italy, Spain, United Kingdom and United States has found that citizens with high interest in news and strong political views are most likely to comment on journalistic stories (Kalogeropoulos et al., 2017), which goes some way to explain why political stories might get extensive and often negative feedback from audiences. A senior broadcast editor covering politics explains their reasoning in this way:

> You don't become a journalist to make friends or to be popular. You know, you become a journalist because you want to, at the risk of sounding pompous, you become a journalist because you believe in the power of the truth. And you believe that that endeavour is really worthwhile and that does mean, particularly in politics, you're going to open yourself up to attacks sometimes, just as, you know, anybody going into this public

life does, right? It's part of public life, journalism. And I think that the importance of that far outweighs the, you know, the fact that sometimes you might get a bit frustrated or the fact that it's actually pretty grim that people feel they can write things that are rude about you online.

Considering different ways to look at the situation than the perspective which might be driving negative emotions could also alleviate some of the anxiety and frustration. For example, for journalists' worrying that their stories are not getting much visible traction on social media, it might be worth considering that the majority of social media audiences actually do not publicly engage with social media content—one of the reasons why they've been called invisible participants, silent users and social listeners. For example, the representative survey of British citizens over the age of 16 I conducted in 2020 revealed that a high 47% of them access Twitter (now rebranded to 'X'), yet this also means that more than half of the citizens, and media audiences, don't. Their voices are not among those commenting on journalists' stories on Twitter/X. This research further focused on the ways in which those citizens who use Twitter/X engaged with one of the most controversial political topics at the time— Brexit. It found that the majority of citizens who engaged with Brexit on Twitter/X did so solely in a 'listening' capacity—meaning they only read others' tweets without retweeting, quoting or liking these, or posting their own content (for more details see Šimunjak, 2022). So, the lack of publicly visible reactions does not mean that audiences are not engaging with the content, as they can be reading it, sharing via personal messaging, thinking about it and talking about it in interpersonal conversations—the latter being the key way how audiences across the world engage with news information (Fletcher et al., 2015). In other words, lack of visible reactions to a story does not necessarily mean that the audiences do not engage with it or that it is without impact.

Another useful perspective on audiences is that concerning their reactions—how likely is it that everyone will agree with you? And if they disagree, what does this say about the quality of a story or your performance? A mid-career print editor shares this perspective-taking practice:

> One of the best bits of advice I ever got in journalism was from my first news editor and I retell it to all my young journalists, and that is... 'You'll get letters...' In those days, it was letters... 'You'll get letters from readers. And half of them will tell you you're brilliant, and half of them will tell you

you're stupid.' And he said, 'Pay no attention to either of them because they're both wrong.' And I think that is actually a really clever way of looking at it. And he was right - I'm not brilliant and I'm not stupid. I'm somewhere in the middle. And most people are. You've just got to take everything with a pinch of salt.

To help yourself reflect more positively on your work, it might also be useful to develop mechanisms through which you remind yourself of previous success and accomplishments. This can increase confidence and assist in evaluating your own work and feedback on it in a more pragmatic way. One of the ways this can be achieved is through keeping a 'smile folder' that can gather, for example, emails containing praise for your work. An early career print journalist shares his practice:

> I have a Google document which is literally called 'Nice things people have said about me,' which is when I get a tweet, or an email from a reader, or something nice from one of my bosses, or you know, someone messaged me at some point, something along the lines that they hate taking the live blog over from me because it's been so good, and you set the bar so high... And so, I've saved these into a document, and I feel like... It's even not that I go back and read the document to make myself feel great... It's like the process of copying something out and putting into that document... For me is, like, mentally the acknowledgement that someone has complimented me and it's a true thing, and I am good at my job, and I shouldn't lose confidence about things.

Boundary-Setting

The second commonly mentioned strategy to manage emotions induced by reflection or feedback is boundary-setting, particularly as it relates to the use of digital technologies and social media. On a basic level, this might include practising some disconnection strategies to manage well-being as well as job performance. For example, journalists mentioned that they might limit the time they spend on social media in order to protect themselves from the emotional toll that being faced with a barrage of negative feedback from the audience takes. A senior broadcast editor describes their approach like this:

> Sometimes I'll go for days without actually checking my responses now. I mean, there were times when, you know, you check them every time you

went on. I'm way past that now. I've learned to limit that now because, I think, for your own sense of mental wellbeing it's probably not worth, you know, being across that all the time.

Similarly, it has been mentioned that disconnecting in terms of going off social media, and limiting the time spent on monitoring web metrics or comments posted on stories on the media outlet's website, might be useful in managing the excitement following positive feedback from audiences. As mentioned, the excitement that might come with a good reaction to a story could be a distraction from work, impacting job performance, and/or it might impact work-life balance. A senior print editor tells of their experience:

> I think exhilaration does need management because you can find yourself... If you have a story that's taking off, you find yourself just sitting there all night, sort of going, 'How many hits have I got, how many clicks have I got, how's it going on Twitter?' And you might just reach three o'clock in the morning and you're still manically following something that, you know, really doesn't matter if it's going to take off or it doesn't take off, so you do need to shut yourself off from it somehow.

Given that the majority of feedback from the audience nowadays comes in via digital technologies, it doesn't surprise that journalists manage their use of technology in order to safeguard their well-being, work-life balance, and allow themselves time to reflect and process feedback. In this context, some journalists spoke about the importance of setting boundaries in the use of smartphones, which are nowadays one of the key tools of journalists' practice in societies with high and advanced use of digital technologies. A senior print reporter shares their practice:

> My company phone, when I finish work, goes on a stand and I don't look at it. And I think you have to do that for your own sanity. Cause I've done those 'staying up till 11 o'clock, replying to people...' And it's... You know, those comments will still be there in the morning and you still will be able to respond to them then... You know, when you're at work and when you're in shift time. So, I think... Giving yourself that brain space away from it, is essential.

Journalists also commonly spoke about setting boundaries in their use of social media to manage both excitement and anxieties that come with feedback from audiences, as has been observed among journalists in the US and Australia too (Bossio & Holton, 2018, 2021). In other words, they consciously sometimes disconnect from social media, even for longer periods of time, to gain respite from ceaseless feedback and prevent burnout and digital overload. A senior print correspondent describes their strategy in this way:

> You know in the past, even when I first started as a journalist, you know, the only feedback you would get would be maybe an email or, like, something in the letters page on the next day. But now it's this kind of constant feedback and that can be very exhilarating, very interesting, but it takes a toll. I think people really need to be aware of it. And need to switch off. I mean, whenever I go away, I always delete the Twitter app off my phone and just don't look at it, for, you know, however long I'm away. I think that's a really, really important thing.

In general, journalists spoke of a range of practices they use to set boundaries between their work and non-work life, these often being associated with managing their access to audiences and audiences' access to them. Practices associated with managing boundaries on social media, such as turning off notifications and/or comments, are discussed in more detail in the next chapter.

Verbal Processing

Finally, some journalists emphasise the importance of verbally processing their own reflections on their work as well as feedback from editors and audiences with their peers. This allows them to check their own evaluations of their work, gain perspective about the possible intentions, motives and positions of those giving feedback, as well as the role and type of feedback that is common in the profession. In the words of a senior broadcast editor:

> But the best possible way, I think, about this, is always trying to be able to share if you can. It's with a colleague... I mean, it's... You know, and this a colleague who feels similar to you, and who perhaps you've been able to build up a completely trustworthy relationship... Where you can kind of be a little bit black in terms of humour about it... Where you can just kind of, you know, go... You need someone who kind of knows... Who is exactly in the similar kind of positions, who knows the people you've been

dealing with, knows the circumstances of the deadline, how you are having to put through that story... And that, you know, that's... You know, often an enormous help. You can just kind of... You can unwind on an encrypted service, shall we say? (laughs)

For example, gaining knowledge that a particular editor has a curt and destructive approach to giving feedback to others and not just you, that audiences on a particular social network have reacted similarly to their stories as well, or pointing out the good aspects of the published story as well as opportunities for development, can ease some of the anxiety associated with reflection and feedback, and improve confidence.

In sum, this chapter has covered several emotional situations that are likely to arise in the process of reflection on a produced story and receiving feedback on it, namely: feelings of pride and satisfaction when positively evaluating your work, as well as receiving positive feedback within and outside the newsroom; the anxiety and frustration that come with the lack of feedback from editors and/or audiences; and the anxiety, frustration, anger and sadness when the feedback is critical and/or negative. It has been suggested that key strategies to manage these emotions include internal processing by perspective-taking (e.g., acknowledging that a story may have an impact even when audiences do not publicly engage with it); boundary-setting, such as deciding not to see or read negative comments; and verbal processing with peers.

The UK: Aubrey Allegretti on Reflection

Aubrey Allegretti is a senior political correspondent for The Guardian. He has worked for national news outlets for eight years, predominantly from parliament, and reported on three general elections, five prime ministers, the Brexit referendum, as well as the death of Queen Elizabeth II. Away from Westminster, Aubrey has worked in Brussels and Washington DC—covering the European Union and 2020 presidential election, respectively. He previously worked for Sky News and HuffPost UK.

I had just filed a story that I knew would have all rival political journalists at other organisations instantly scrambling to write themselves. I was on a day off—time I try to protect to have boundaries from work and allow my brain some downtime from the constant tick of news. But when the tip-offs came in, I knew I had to get the article out. It was March 2022. The Metropolitan Police had been investigating a series of what were said to be COVID rule breaking parties. There were plenty of witnesses who had spoken anonymously to the press, but the evidence was bitty. My sources had told me that Scotland Yard was about to issue an initial tranche of fines—confirming for the first time that lockdown laws had been broken at the heart of Downing Street. Colleagues on other papers had done the heavy lifting and revealed the details of some of these gatherings, but confirmation by the police that these events warranted fixed penalty notices being issued was surely going to be the hammer blow to the prime minister's premiership. Having filed my story, it was published quickly—within 15 minutes.

I am a stickler for checking, checking and checking again. But despite all the due diligence I'd conducted pre-publication, I still dreaded the impact when the story landed. There is meant to be a thrill when you publish such a story. Instead, there was anxiety that felt so constrictive I just wanted to turn my phone off and get back to my day off.

I spoke to the most senior editors in my team and on the news desk and was reassured the story was in good shape. I was wary of being too needy for feedback, fearing I would appear amateurish by seeking repeated reassurances from my bosses and peers. But wise words from more experienced colleagues who had experienced similar situations many times before calmed my nerves.

Next, I rang a friend—someone who works in the same industry—to unload my feelings to. They gave me a good outsiders' perspective and reminded me that no matter how angry the story might make some people given the potential political repercussions, it was simply the truth.

I knew the more I worried about what to do, the longer it would take until I could publicise the story myself. Sharing a story on social media helps its reach, and means other journalists will quickly see, credit and follow your work. In the competitive world of the Lobby, this is important. Staring at the 'compose tweet' screen on my phone felt daunting. So instead I opened my notes app and simply typed the facts of the story. Short and sharp. I re-read it at least a dozen times. Then, without having to think, I copy and pasted the text on to the Twitter screen and hit post. To decompress, I decided to put my phone off on 'do not disturb' mode, and go for a run—listening to music so my mind was not distracted by thoughts about the story or the reception. When I later turned my phone back on, I was heartened by the many messages of support and congratulation from journalists on other papers. I decided to ignore those negative comments from people who wanted to diminish the significance of the story for their own political ends and turned my phone off for the rest of the evening.

Australia: Sarah Taillier on feedback

Sarah Taillier is a journalist and journalism academic in Australia. She has a diverse media background, as an established multi-platform reporter and radio producer with the country's national broadcaster, the ABC. She has also worked in television production in London and as a commercial video journalist in regional Australia. She now teaches future journalists at Curtin University in Western Australia.

My first job as a journalist was in regional Australia, based more than 250 miles away from the nearest metropolitan city. As the only news reporter at the station, I covered an area twice the size of the UK, producing content for radio, online and TV.

One day, about halfway through my shift, news broke that a vessel carrying asylum seekers had arrived at a nearby beach—a first in that part of Australia. I grabbed my video recording kit and raced to the scene. What followed were hours of live crosses, content gathering, coordinating and interviewing. I was a relatively inexperienced reporter and I found it difficult to prioritise my responsibilities. At one point, I was scolded by an editor in a metropolitan newsroom for delivering a live cross, instead of completing another task.

After hours of reporting on a significant breaking story, this was the first piece of feedback I had received. While not a critique of my work's quality, the feedback left me feeling discouraged and frustrated. I realised I didn't know what duties to prioritise, so I asked the editor to list my tasks in order of priority. I referred to that list throughout the day and it helped immensely; I was able to focus on one task at a time and regain a sense of control.

After 12 hours of reporting, a team of metropolitan reporters arrived to continue coverage. As I started to wind down, I realised the only feedback I had received had been negative, leaving me feeling deflated. I also noticed that the metropolitan reporters' work was being featured more prominently on various platforms and they were receiving praise within the organisation.

Frustrated, I reached out to a senior journalist and debriefed on my day. They listened and validated my experience, which was a comfort. They also reviewed my work and offered specific feedback. The next day, I reflected on my work and shared it with another mentor for feedback.

Early in my career as a regional reporter, feedback from within my organisation was often scarce and limited to pointing out potential issues or errors. Working remotely can often leave you feeling isolated and exhausted. Without constructive feedback, it can exacerbate feelings of insecurity. Cultivating mentors is crucial, and you should actively seek feedback, rather than wait for it.

While feedback is crucial for growth, not all feedback is equal. I have learnt to prioritise feedback from experienced, honest mentors who are constructive. To stay motivated, I also maintained a 'success wall' of positive notes and feedback from trusted sources.

Top Tips

- Take some time to critically reflect on your published story to learn from the process and output—consider what you've done well and what could be done better next time
- Receive feedback with poise—acknowledge it from the position of neutrality and grace, and give yourself time to process it before responding to it in any way

- Ask for feedback from peers or editor if you feel you need it to develop your practice
- Consider the possible intentions, positions and motives that those providing feedback may have and the context in which feedback has been given
- Set boundaries in your access to audiences' feedback to prevent distractions in work and safeguard well-being and work-life balance
- Discuss feedback with peers to gain perspective on the feedback and feedback provider(s)

READ, WATCH AND LISTEN

- Read Liz Winston's article 'Feel the love: how to accept positive feedback at work' published by Wavelength—https://wavelength. asana.com/workstyle-positive-feedback-at-work/
- Read Tamara Littleton's article 'How to: manage reader comments as a journalist' published by Journalism.co.uk—https://www.journa lism.co.uk/skills/how-to-manage-reader-comments-as-a-journalist/ s7/a546289/
- Watch video 'How to Receive & Process Critical Feedback in the Workplace' presented by Dr Kelly Waltman who specialises in workplace communication and feedback—https://www.youtube.com/ watch?v=X7Q5M8sexYo
- Watch Jeff Orlowski's 2020 documentary 'The Social Dilemma' which deals with the design and effects of social media on its users
- Listen to podcast by CIPD (charity focusing on improving working lives) titled 'The Power of Reflection' discussing how and why spending time reflecting can improve job performance—https:// www.cipd.co.uk/podcasts/ld-reflective-practice#gref

SCENARIO EXERCISES

Scenario 1

You work as a journalist for a sports magazine focusing on football. As an emerging professional with only a few years in the industry, you've mostly been writing previews and match reports. While you enjoy doing this, your passion really lies in writing long-form features and you welcome any opportunity to explore a topic in-depth and spend a few days, if not weeks, developing a story and delivering new insights on the sport you've been following from an early age. These kinds of opportunities don't come often, so you're really excited when your feature on the issues of mental health in football, putting the spotlight on the levels and experiences of burnout and anxiety among footballers, is finally published.

On reflection, you're proud of the detailed research that the story reports, as well as the interviews with footballers you've delivered that give authenticity and a human element to the story. Yet, there is no response or reaction from the editor, and the story doesn't seem to be gaining traction on the website.

- How does this make you feel?
- What are you going to do? Why?

Scenario 2

You are a freelancer writing about gaming, working primarily with the national press and digital media outlets. You've been working on this beat for a few years, and while your followership on social media has been increasing, it's been a slow and somewhat frustrating process. Your stories on social media get some attention, but the level of engagement with audiences they get is far from what you would hope for. You think it's important that you develop a social media profile as this would help position you in the beat and increase your chances of getting well-paid commissions. The latest story you've written has been an analysis piece that looked at the use of Artificial Intelligence (AI) in gaming, in which you offered what you thought was a slightly controversial take that AI is not and is unlikely to soon become a substitute for games developers. You've filed the copy more than a week ago to a national quality paper, and you haven't been informed when it'll run.

Just as you are about to set off for an evening out with friends, you open Facebook and see hundreds of notifications—the story has been published and it has gone viral. It is being shared widely and commented on extensively.

- How does this make you feel?
- What are you going to do? Why?

REFERENCES

Alam, M., & Singh, P. (2021). Performance feedback interviews as affective events: An exploration of the impact of emotion regulation of negative performance feedback on supervisor–employee dyads. *Human Resource Management Review, 31*(2), 1–14.

Baron, R. A. (1988). Negative effects of destructive criticism: Impact on conflict, self-efficacy, and task performance. *Journal of Applied Psychology, 73*(2), 199–207.

Belschak, F. D., & Den Hartog, D. N. (2009). Consequences of positive and negative feedback: The impact on emotions and extra-role behaviors. *Applied Psychology, 58*(2), 274–303.

Bossio, D., & Holton, A. E. (2018). The identity dilemma: Identity drivers and social media fatigue among journalists. *Popular Communication, 16*(4), 248–262.

Bossio, D., & Holton, A. E. (2021). Burning out and turning off: Journalists' disconnection strategies on social media. *Journalism, 22*(10), 2475–2492.

Burns, L. S., & Matthews, B. J. (2018). *Understanding journalism.* SAGE.

Conaway, C. (2022). *The right way to process feedback.* Ascend. https://hbr.org/ 2022/06/the-right-way-to-process-feedback

Duffy, A., Ling, R., & Tandoc, E. C. (2018). The people have spoken (the bastards?): Finding a legitimate place for feedback in the journalistic field. *Journalism Practice, 12*(9), 1130–1147.

Ekström, M., Ramsälv, A., & Westlund, O. (2022). Data-driven news work culture: Reconciling tensions in epistemic values and practices of news journalism. *Journalism, 23*(4), 755–772.

Ferrucci, P. (2020). It is in the numbers: How market orientation impacts journalists' use of news metrics. *Journalism, 21*(2), 244–261.

Fletcher, R., Radcliffe, D., Levy, D. A. L., Nielsen, R. K., & Newman, N. (2015). *Reuters institute digital news report 2015: Supplementary report.*

Forbes, A. (2010). Reflecting, blogging and learning in journalism: Are journalists born or made? *Proceedings of the Australian Collaborative Education Network National Conference,* 156–164.

Hanusch, F., & Tandoc, E. C. (2019). Comments, analytics, and social media: The impact of audience feedback on journalists' market orientation. *Journalism, 20*(6), 695–713.

Hinde, S. (2017). Brexit and the media. *Hermès, La Revue, 77*(1), 80–86.

Ivask, S. (2019). Communication between editors and reporters: Feedback and coaching in Estonian dailies' newsrooms. *Kome, 7*(1), 24–41.

Kalogeropoulos, A., Negredo, S., Picone, I., & Nielsen, R. K. (2017). Who shares and comments on news?: A cross-national comparative analysis of online and social media participation. *Social Media and Society, 3*(4), 1–12.

Kluger, A. N., & DeNisi, A. (1996). The effects of feedback interventions on performance: A historical review, a meta-analysis, and a preliminary feedback intervention theory. *Psychological Bulletin, 119*(2), 254–284.

Kronstad, M. (2016). Investigating journalism students' conceptions and development of critical reflection through teacher-mediated activities. *Journalism Practice, 10*(1), 123–139.

Lauk, E., Harro-Loit, H., & Väliverronen, J. (2014). Media accountability through the eyes of journalists: Feedback, responsiveness. In S. Fengler, T. Eberwein, G. Mazzoleni, & C. Porlezza (Eds.), *Journalists and media accountability* (pp. 83–97). Peter Lang.

Newman, N., Fletcher, R., Robertson, C., Eddy, K., & Nielsen, R. (2022). *Digital news report 2022.* Oxford University.

Opiniano, J. M., Daquipil, R. A., & Romarate, P. I. R. (2021). Reflective practice in the newswork of Filipino journalists: A grounded theory study. *Journal of Applied Journalism & Media Studies, 10*(3), 3150335.

Perloff, R. M. (2015). A three-decade retrospective on the hostile media effect. *Mass Communication and Society, 18*(6), 701–729.

Petre, C. (2015). *The traffic factories: Metrics at Chartbeat, Gawker Media, and The New York Times.* Columbia Journalism Review. https://www.cjr.org/tow_center_reports/the_%0Atraffic_factories_metrics_at_chartbeat_gawker_media_and_the_new_york_times.php.

Posetti, J., Shabbir, N., Maynard, D., Bontcheva, K., & Aboulez, N. (2021). *The Chilling: Global trends in online violence against women journalists.*

Reader, B. (2015). *Audience feedback in the news media.* Taylor & Francis Group.

Šimunjak, M. (2022). *Tweeting Brexit: Social media and the aftermath of the EU Referendum.* Routledge.

Usher, N. (2013). Al Jazeera english online: Understanding web metrics and news production when a quantified audience is not a commodified audience. *Digital Journalism, 1*(3), 335–351.

Vu, H. T. (2014). The online audience as gatekeeper: The influence of reader metrics on news editorial selection. *Journalism, 15*(8), 1094–1110.

Welbers, K., Van Atteveldt, W., Kleinnijenhuis, J., Ruigrok, N., & Schaper, J. (2016). News selection criteria in the digital age: Professional norms versus online audience metrics. *Journalism, 17*(8), 1037–1053.

CHAPTER 7

Social Media

I was never really interested in writing first-person accounts, opinions and columns. Most of my time in journalism has been spent doing news and features, that is, telling other people's stories. These days I mostly do analyses. That's probably part of the reason why I was somewhat reluctant to accept an offer to do a first-person piece about the day that the UK left the EU which an editor of a political magazine from the EU was trying to commission me to do. I felt uncomfortable putting myself first, speaking about my own experiences. However, I knew the hesitation wasn't only because this isn't a form I often use. It was also influenced by the awareness that I as a person will likely be attacked, mocked and ridiculed on social media when the story is shared there. Not because I was planning to write something outrageous or unsubstantiated, but because I'm well aware that this is the treatment media stories and their writers commonly receive on social media. Especially women. And those reporting about politics. Yet, seeing the opportunity to provide an account of lived experience of an EU citizen in the UK to an EU audience, and in this way bring Brexit and its consequences closer to them, I thought the story was worth the anxiety about social media audiences' reactions and potential criticism and abuse. And indeed, social media did not disappoint.

I took only a glimpse—looked at the first few comments on Facebook. The frustration about people criticising an article they obviously haven't read, and sadness about inferences of ulterior motives I knew I didn't have

© The Author(s), under exclusive license to Springer Nature Switzerland AG 2023
M. Šimunjak, *Managing Emotions in Journalism*,
https://doi.org/10.1007/978-3-031-38631-2_7

for giving the account I did, made me stop for a moment. I read a few out loud to my partner, who was next to me. 'What are they on about? Why would they say that?' he asked. At this point, I actually laughed. 'They didn't get past the first sentence, it seems,' I answered. I didn't read any more. I didn't have to. I was confident that the facts were right and that the narrative is well developed. The positive feedback from the editor helped reassure me. As did knowing what to expect from social media audiences and being aware that these Facebook commenters are not really the article's target audience. What also probably helped was the decision not to keep scrolling—there is, maybe, such a thing as knowing too much. So, I think I left this situation mostly unscathed. Yet, it's curious how those few comments I saw quickly come back to the forefront of my mind when the topic comes up. For journalists working with social media, and it's fair to say it's the vast majority in countries such as the UK or the US in the 2020s, these kinds of emotional situations are likely to come up daily.

This chapter engages with emotional situations that may develop while doing journalistic work with social media, examining them through the 'stop, think, choose' model of emotional intelligence. The 'stop' section discusses emotional situations related to working with social media, namely: the frustration related to pressure to do work on social media; the anxiety and nervousness about posting content given the perceived negativity of social media spaces; and the frustration, sadness, anxiety and anger with received abuse and harassment on these platforms. In the 'think' section, some beliefs and thoughts which may be driving mentioned emotions are outlined. The 'choose' section suggests emotion management strategies informed by interviews with practising journalists. These include boundary-setting, such as applying disconnecting practices (e.g., not using social media outside work hours; muting/blocking abusive users/conversations, etc.); internal processing in the form of perspective-taking; verbal processing with peers and well-being professionals (e.g., some journalists may find counselling helpful when experiencing abuse); and engaging in diversionary activities to balance negative with positive emotions.

STOP: EMOTIONAL SITUATIONS

Across the world, the use of social media in journalism has become ubiq-
uitous. However, interestingly, Facebook is not the top social network
journalists use, as could be expected due to it being the most used
social network worldwide. Instead, it is actually Twitter (now 'X'), which
reaches significantly less audiences. For example, it is estimated that
over 90% of British journalists use Twitter/X (Broersma & Graham,
2016). Similarly, a global study, primarily based on data from the US,
but with input also from Europe, Asia and Africa, found that around
80% of journalists consider this social network as the most valuable one
for work (Muck Rack, 2023). The key reason for Twitter/X's importance in journalism stems from the fact that it is used by those who
journalists consider sources, particularly elite sources. Hence, following
these on Twitter/X allows journalists to gather information in a quick
and efficient way. And indeed, comparative research of journalists' use
of Twitter/X in Canada, Finland, Germany, Sweden, the Netherlands,
the United Kingdom and the United States indicates that Twitter/X is
primarily used as a tool to gather information and promote work, and
to a lesser extent for networking, verifying information and monitoring
others' content (Gulyas, 2017). And to highlight just how important
social media is to journalists' everyday routines, the same research found
that in all these countries, except Germany, more than 40% of journalists think they would not be able to do their jobs without social media.
Alongside assisting them to do work, social media can also help journalists build their personal brands. Indeed, significant networks of followers
became somewhat of an indicator of prestige and importance, signposting
to audiences, and employers, the reach and potential influence that an
individual journalist holds in a society. For example, in early 2023 CNN's
Anderson Cooper had almost 10m followers on Twitter/X, India Today's
Rajdeep Sardesai was followed by 9m users, and BBC's Laura Kuenssberg
had 1.4m followers.

Media organisations are also keen to have their journalists on social
networks, but for somewhat different reasons. In the first place, social
media has been positioned as one of the key gateways to news, though
more important in some markets than in others (Newman et al., 2022).
This means that in order to catch the attention of audiences, and consequently drive traffic to their outlets, media organisations and journalists
have to be present and active in this space. Otherwise, audiences may go

elsewhere. Similarly, it has been argued that engagement with audiences on social media can help media companies build a more loyal audience base, one that will feel connected to a particular media outlet and will consequently be coming back to it when in need of information, sharing or interaction. For media companies, this means more subscribers and/ or more advertising—in any case, more profit.

Content Production

This leads us to the first emotional situation a journalist might expect in this context—**the pressure to perform on social media**. At a basic level, the frustration might be caused by the expectation to produce content for yet another platform, with this labour not being regularly recognised, remunerated or supported. In the words of a mid-career digital editor (<10k Twitter/X followers):

> We all now have Facebook pages and Twitter pages, and these are all things that my company in particular is really big on. You know, have your personal feeds and update it. And I don't think there is necessarily a realisation that, A - to do that well, you should be doing it all the time, and where the time for that comes from during the day? And also, the support of when you do get something unpleasant on that... […] I think there's a lot of reliance on social media and not necessarily training or awareness on how to deal with it.

Journalists who are generally not comfortable with these platforms, have reservations or concerns, or are just not interested in them, express particular frustration with having to do work with the networks. Interestingly, it is both digital natives and the so-called digital immigrants, in other words, journalists of all levels of seniority and years of experience in the industry, that express frustration with this work. A senior broadcast editor (>100k Twitter/X followers) even described this element of their job as inducing 'dread,' going on to explain:

> If I didn't have to do social media, I would not do it. Because it's horrible. It's like a toxic pit of awfulness. It's awful. I only do it because I don't feel that there's an option in the job I do. I hate it.

The feeling of frustration and almost helplessness is exacerbated by the perception of importance of the social media work for career advancement, both among those just entering the profession and trying to make a name for themselves, and the veterans in the field who feel the need to retain their position in relation to peers, as the following two quotes outline.

Early career digital journalist (<10k Twitter/X followers):

There's a lot of pressure from our editors to, say, you know, 'You have to use social media.' And just now we had a meeting saying, 'You got to start using Facebook more to promote your stories.' And, so, I feel like I have to do it. I don't really want to but it's important for the job and your career as well.

Senior broadcast editor (10-100 k Twitter/X followers).

I felt quite under pressure to tweet more, to build up a social media profile, and that my employer would take that... Would think that that was an important part of my job... That it was one of the outlets that I was required to service, that I didn't really have a choice about that. And that, say, for instance, if I was to interview for a new position... Looking at my Twitter account, looking at how often I tweeted, whether it was interesting, whether there was high engagement with my tweets, whether I have a lot of followers... Would be one of the things that an employer would look at in terms of deciding whether or not to give you a promotion or a new post. So, for a while, I felt quite under pressure, even though it didn't come naturally to engage in that.

Online Abuse

Other emotional situations that journalists may face when working with social media are related to the (perceived) negativity and unpredictability of social media spaces. My own experience shared in the introduction to this chapter illustrates one of these. Twitter/X, in particular, has been described as promoting discourses that are 'simple, impulsive, and uncivil' (Ott, 2017: 59). It, then, may not be surprising that studies looking at the nature of Twitter/X discussions, and especially those on political topics, regularly find these to be uncivil and impolite (Oz et al., 2018; Rossini, 2021; Rowe, 2015; Santana, 2014). The question of the structure of a social network's audiences and their motives should be considered here.

For example, it is often claimed that Twitter/X users are younger, better educated, more liberal and politically interested than the general population (Mellon & Prosser, 2017). Hence, it can be expected that this group may be particularly willing to engage with information that the media is sharing and be critical by drawing on their knowledge to point out mistakes and flaws in arguments. However, why these interventions are often uncivil remains somewhat unknown, but several motives can be considered. For example, in the case of state and parastate actors criticising and harassing journalists, there is likely to be a strategic aim to create an environment in which journalists will not wish to participate. In this way, journalists can try to be silenced, disciplined and pushed into self-censorship (Posetti et al., 2021; Šimunjak, 2022; Waisbord, 2020). In the case of ordinary citizens, there is likely an interplay of complex motives in play. For example, social media's affordances usually allow instantaneous and simple engagement opportunities—meaning that users are likely to engage as soon as they see something that winds them up and do so in an emotional state which may not be conducive to civil discourse. Also, the cloak of anonymity that social networks allow their users is considered to drive some to say things and/or say them in a way they would probably not have done if their identities weren't hidden. Or at least they might think twice before posting an uncivil comment. And while there are various attempts at changing the uncivil nature of social media discourses (for overview see Bahador, 2021), this is still a reality for many journalists working with social media.

On the one hand, **awareness about the negativity and unpredictability of social media spaces creates anxiety about posting content**. For example, a senior broadcast editor (10–100k Twitter/X followers) described the emotional situation tied to the anticipation of negative comments from social media users in this way:

> It is my job on air as a broadcaster to take facts and provide some analysis and interpretation of them. I don't go on air and just say, 'He said this, she said that. There you go. Make your own mind up.' I mean, I'm paid to provide interpretation and analysis. I guess, I find it harder to do with a Twitter character limit and I know that you're putting it out there into... Well, A - into an environment that arguably is more poisonous, and full of people who will deliberately seek to misinterpret what you're saying, for their own ends.

Many other journalists, and particularly early career reporters, said that the anticipation of potential social media backlash causes such anxiety that it makes them try to fly under the radar. Some aim to do this by keeping their social media posts 'boring,' i.e., presenting strictly professional profiles with posts communicating facts about uncontroversial topics. In taking this stance, it is evident that journalists do not see themselves having the freedom to use social networks as regular social media users. They remain first and foremost journalists when posting content through public profiles. An early career digital journalist (<10k Twitter/X followers) explains how this motivates them to refrain from sharing personal opinions on Twitter/X:

> I think that's a huge reason why I don't tweet personal views so much or... And I think sometimes, actually, to the detriment of the reporting that you could do on Twitter. Our editors always really encouraged us to tweet out little titbits or little bits of analysis, but I was always so worried that that would be taken as personal views that could be shot down by someone on Twitter.

Several other early career journalists say that the experiences of being treated in an uncivil and abusive way have caused anxiety which led them to various forms of self-censorship, from avoiding tweeting about controversial topics they'd been covering, to avoiding covering these topics altogether. An early career digital journalist (10–100k Twitter/X followers) explains how the social media context has driven them to rethink their writing:

> Running accounts and being a named journalist covering Brexit, Scottish independence referendum, UK general elections and US general elections has exposed me to a lot of abuse and a lot of just general low-level nuisance, which I think really wears down at your self-esteem. [...] I do think it makes you self-doubt, and I think it can make you cautious about the way you write and phrase things, in a way that you're perhaps being pushed by people with a specific agenda...

Another early career digital journalist (<10k Twitter/X followers) describes how the anxiety about posting content drives them to a form of self-sabotage in social media spaces:

Sometimes I think I would deliberately... Which feels really bad to say...
But I think sometimes I would deliberately post at a time when I thought
it wouldn't be seen, really. So that it could just flow by and no one would
have to engage with it. Because I think sometimes, as a journalist, you're
not always happy with how the headlines come out or you think it's a bit
overcooked... But I also knew that I had to promote it on one level. So,
I'd always feel a bit uncomfortable putting it out there at a time when I
thought everyone will be able to read it, and then someone would write
something negative about it.

Another aspect that causes anxiety about posting on social media is the
unpredictability of these spaces. In other words, tweets you plan to go
viral may not, and those you never thought would travel the world, do so
without warning or control. A story that an early career print journalist
(<10 k Twitter/X followers) tells paints a complex picture of the consequences of such experiences, even if they appear to be very positive on
the outside:

I had a time last year... I got panic attacks and, like, nightmares, the
night before [posting]. And I had to take, yeah, anti-anxiety medications
whenever I shared something. [...] So, I had an episode where something
I wrote went very viral around the world, and it was a positive thing, like,
it went viral because people really liked it. At first, I think... [...] The first
day was amazing. Like, I felt great, I felt really excited... You know, I'd
sort of not expected this at all. And a lot of people I respected, like, were
saying nice things. And that was the first day.
    But then there was a crash on day two. I was alone, I had a cold, in
my house, I was feeling, you know, quite delicate. And you open up this
thing and things are still kicking off. And it's this disconnect between 'I'm
alone in my house sick' and 'there's all this stuff, you know, I should be
caring about.' And I think from the next few days, I became legitimately
really, really... Really, really sad, I think. Very, like, just stressed.
    And I think that episode did really kind of made me realise, like, 'Oh,
I have no control over what happens when I put something out on the
Internet.' In a way, beforehand, you know, I had about like [few hundred]
followers who I all really liked. Sort of small cultural things... We were
all interested in stuff together. And ever since then... That has made me
realise like, 'Oh, this could go anywhere, and I have no control.' And
I think... Yeah, that imprinted itself in my brain when I then, after that
episode, started publishing more things. And yeah, which led then to the
panic attacks and anxiety moments.

On the other hand, there are also emotional situations arising from the received **abuse and harassment on social media platforms**, often characterised with frustration, sadness, anxiety and anger. A senior broadcast editor (10–100 k Twitter/X followers) captures it well by saying:

> Every time I get an email from Twitter saying, you know, 'You have 120 new notifications. Why don't you check in?' I'm like, 'Are you having a laugh? If I've got hundreds of new notifications, there is no way that's good news.'

Indeed, the available data does not paint a nice picture. According to the survey of British journalists, every other has experienced online abuse (Lezard, 2020). Findings from other studies around the world point to the fact that online abuse of journalists has become a wide-spread and global issue (Dubois et al., 2021; Löfgren Nilsson & Örnebring, 2016; Orgeret & Tayeebwa, 2020; Waisbord, 2020). In this context, it has been suggested that some journalists are more likely than others to be targeted. For example, it is suggested that women are more likely to receive abuse, or at least that this abuse is more targeted at them as individuals than is the case with men (Posetti et al., 2021; Sexism's Toll on Journalism, 2021). A comment from a senior female broadcast editor (>100k Twitter/X followers) regarding her experience of social media is illustrative of this:

> 'The abuse I get on it is disgusting. It really makes me angry. And you just have to basically be a punch bag. I mean, I've described it sometimes like a combination of being a lab rat and a punch bag. You know, it's just all awful. It's misogynistic. Sexist. It's classist.

Also, it has been found that journalists covering politics and sports, and more recently also health and science, are more often than others harassed online (Posetti et al., 2021; Waisbord, 2020). There is often increased frustration there when it seems that this harassment is orchestrated and aimed at silencing journalists by discouraging them from doing their jobs. A senior broadcast editor working on political topics (>100 k Twitter/X followers) describes it like this:

> What's frustrating, actually, is when you know very well that some political activists are using it very deliberately just to try to stop you doing your job. Or to try to create an impression. And that's just really frustrating.

And especially... And you just say, 'Oh for God's sake'... And especially when I... I know that some of those people who do that know very well that they don't really have a problem with what we're doing but they know that if they try and create a thing on Twitter... Then, it appears that that is the way, they think that they can sort of advance their own agendas by creating a row on Twitter.

Broadcasters, whose faces and voices are familiar to audiences, as well as those working for national outlets, which have the widest reach, can also be seen to be targeted more frequently than others (Waisbord, 2020). Hence, it does not surprise that many broadcasters interviewed for this book spoke of feelings of sadness and frustration when faced with abuse on social media, as well as feeling powerless to prevent or stop it. A mid-career broadcast editor (10–100k Twitter/X followers) describes the experience of going through a case of 'Twitter storm' like this:

I really didn't like it. I mean, I dealt with it in the sense of responding a little bit to some of the stuff I was sent; just explaining the methodology and saying, 'This is... whatever.' But then it really did bother me. I felt like a real sense of injustice. I thought, 'This is just completely unfair.' But you're very conscious there's nothing you can do about it, so you feel powerless. At a certain point, I literally just... You just switch it off, and you have to stop looking. But you feel crap. You feel crappy.

There may also be feelings of anxiety related to the potential impact that the social media pile-on has on a journalist's reputation and standing at the employer. And while journalists are mainly confident that they would be cleared of charges made on social media should they escalate to an employer or regulator's agenda, there remains a sense of nervousness of being put under the spotlight in such a way and the need to go through the process of defending themselves, which requires additional emotional labour. A senior broadcast correspondent (10-100 k Twitter/X followers) outlines how they felt in a case that seemed could escalate from social media accusations:

Upset. Angry, because it was coming from a couple of people who were misrepresenting a situation from the past. They haven't brought it up with me personally. You know, I'd heard about it through the grapevine, knew they were upset and, you know, that they'd take it to Twitter. It was quite abusive, you know, sort of swear words used, and, you know, threats that conversations I've had with them have been recorded, and they were going to, kind of, you know, sort of embarrass me in public, you know, that sort of thing. So, kind of angry and slightly concerned and nervous about how that might play out if they did decide to try and cause trouble.

Think

As explained in the Introduction chapter, emotional and physical responses to a situation are driven by our beliefs and thoughts through which we interpret that situation. If we are interpreting a situation with negative thoughts, it's more likely that we will perceive it as an inevitable occurrence which we have little or no control over. This can then lead to increased stress. Thinking of the three emotional situations discussed above, Table 7.1 outlines several beliefs and thoughts that might be driving negative emotions.

If you are experiencing negative emotions which you feel you need or want to manage, you can check the beliefs and values, as well as thoughts and expectations that are driving these. In other words, stop and think about what is driving your emotions, how can you update and reframe these with a more positive outlook, and what options you have moving

Table 7.1 Potential beliefs and thoughts that might be driving a negative emotional response to emotional situations associated with work on social media

Pressure to do work with social media	Anticipating negative reactions	Experiencing abuse and harassment
This is part of my job	I made a mistake that others will see and harass me	It's part of the job and I'll be perceived as weak if I have an emotional reaction to it
I must use social media for career advancement	Others will disagree with me	I made a mistake and it's my fault I'm being harassed
I must use social media for work because everyone else is doing it	There will be a pile-on	Audiences do not like and/or respect what I do
	I will be abused and harassed	My work is poor or unappreciated
		This is my problem, and I should deal with it on my own

forward. For example, if you think that you must use social media because it's part of your job—who said it was part of the job? Which social media are you expected to use? How often? Can you negotiate with the editor the use of selected social networks for work, while others can remain private spaces? Can you disconnect from work-related social networks outside of work? The next section outlines these and other strategies that practising journalists apply in updating and upgrading their thoughts, beliefs and expectations in managing their emotions when working with social media. However, it is worth pointing out a few thoughts that you may keep in mind throughout the chapter:

- Abuse is never acceptable, and it is not part of the job.
- Abuse is not about a journalist's ability. Civil and constructive criticism is something else.
- Online abuse is an industry- and society-wide issue. In other words, a global, rather than an individual's problem.
- It is okay not to be okay. Journalists unaffected by online abuse are as rare as white antelopes.

The chapter now turns to emotion management strategies most commonly applied by journalists in dealing with emotional situations related to social media.

CHOOSE: EMOTION MANAGEMENT STRATEGIES

The most commonly mentioned emotion management strategies by British journalists when dealing with emotional situations outlined above are boundary-setting; internal processing in the form of perspective-taking; verbal processing with peers and well-being professionals; and attentional deployment.

Boundary-Setting

One of the most talked about emotion management strategies among journalists when it comes to work with social media is boundary-setting. It involves various practices aimed at setting your own boundaries related to how, why and when you want to use social networks. In the first place, the strategy of strategic use of specific social networks might allow for less pressure to use social media for work and hinder some of the work-related anxiety when using social networks in a private capacity. Specifically, journalists report clearly distinguishing which social networks they use as professionals, and which they use as private individuals. Often Twitter/X, and sometimes Facebook, are mentioned as being used in a professional capacity. On the other hand, Instagram is reportedly frequently used by journalists in a private manner, with these accounts being set to private to filter and secure the content shared there. With these boundaries in place, journalists can ensure that, for example, on days off they can still enjoy social media without the anxiety that they will see work-related content which can cause stress. Also, using only selected platform(s) for work reduces the pressure to perform across various social networks.

Further, many journalists report that they do not have the Twitter/X app on their phone, or they once had it but have deleted it since, in order to manage the frustration with the pressure to use the network. In this way, they only access the network when they choose to do so, giving them agency and power over the choices of when and how they use a particular network. Also, many report using applications such as TweetDeck, which allow them to customise their social media experience. This might alleviate some of the frustration about needing to use social media, as well as anxiety about seeing audiences' reactions. An early career print correspondent (10-100 k Twitter/X followers) explains how they made Twitter/X work for them in terms of newsgathering, but eliminating the frustration and anxiety arising from users' comments or the pressure to engage with them:

> When I'm using TweetDeck, I just move the notifications column, like, off the view of the screen, and I turned off my Twitter notifications. So, it means I can still use what, you know... Service that is very helpful for me to use, but I don't have to interact with anybody that's interacting with me, if that makes sense?

Also, a senior broadcast editor (10–100k Twitter/X followers) suggests that it is possible to avoid some of the pressure to use social media and deal with the anticipation of negative comments by asking another team member to scan social media for reactions to a programme or output, rather than exposing yourself to it directly. They say:

I will, whenever I am done with a broadcast, I will ask somebody else in my team to take a quick look at Twitter, to make sure... Because it is possible... Occasionally, people highlight a genuine mistake that you've made, and one that you need to know about, because it needs to be corrected. Often, they just take issue with what you said, because they disagree with you. But it needs to be watched and managed because it's an early warning system for errors or mistakes that needs to be clarified or corrected. But I now ask other members of my team to take a look at that, because to find one or two pertinent tweets that have a point, you've got to wade through hundreds of... Bile, frankly... Which, although I know is there, it definitely has a much more marked effect on my emotions if I actually read it.

Those who have dealt with emotional situations deriving from experiencing abuse on social media often draw on social media affordances in order to manage their emotions related to anticipation of social media users' reactions. A particularly popular strategy is to turn off notifications, so you do not get notified about engagements with the posts you publish and others' mentioning you in their posts. A senior print editor (>100k Twitter/X followers) tells how they came about switching their notifications off:

I received a huge amount of abuse about [a story], some of it very sort of personal. And I really struggled with that, and I found myself doing the whole sort of, you know, lying in bed at night scrolling through the comments. And then a colleague said to me, a male colleague said to me, and I have several women colleagues on my team, and he said, 'It really angers me that it's the women in the team...' He doesn't get the same grief as the women in the team that get it. So, that made me think, 'Oh, actually, so it's about misogyny as well.' It's not just, sort of, you know, it's not like a personal attack. These people don't know me. And I made a decision then for my own mental health to turn off notifications.

Alongside turning off notifications, another possibility is to turn off replies on Twitter/X or disable commenting on Facebook. While this will inevitably limit the opportunity for audiences to interact with your content and hinder the ability to engage with other users, some journalists, particularly those who regularly experience high volumes of abuse, find this an acceptable trade-off in safeguarding their well-being. A mid-career digital editor (10–100k Twitter/X followers) explains it like this:

There was a moment where I completely, completely changed my relationship with Twitter. […] There was something I did, and I just got sent so much abuse and it's normally about being stupid. The abuse that I get is almost entirely from middle aged men. And I just was getting too upset about it, so I just had to stop really. Some people at work were saying, 'You need to turn off your comments,' or you need to, like, whatever it was… So that was in [year]. umm I changed my settings. […] It's really good that I can't see the comments, that must make me in day-to-day life, like, have a nicer experience.

A shorter-term boundary that can be drawn to manage the anxiety about audiences' reactions to your content is to disconnect from social networks ahead of or shortly after the content is published. In the words of a senior print editor (10–100k Twitter/X followers):

If I was feeling very tired, or if I was kind of anticipating what… For the want of a better phrase 'shit was about to hit the fan'… If I'm anticipating that and knew full well… I might just switch off Twitter and just not look at Twitter for 24 hours or something like that, and I have done that quite often. When… Particularly if you've got something else in your life that you want to get on with, the family thing or something, or you want to go and do something nice, the last thing you want is, you know, 'You're a complete tosser! Why are you such an unreliable, biased person?' You know, you don't want that kind of crap in your life. So, you can just switch off. So, that's how you might prepare for it.

It is possible to experience a new wave of anxiety about being switched off and not knowing what is being said about you and your work on social networks. In this case, the strategy of asking someone else to look and report back might be appropriate. Alternatively, if the anxiety about not knowing is greater than that of knowing, some journalists who do read through and/or engage with social media comments decide to set boundaries regarding whose tweets and replies they wish to engage with. A mid-career broadcast editor (10–100k Twitter/X followers) says their strategy draws on Twitter/X's affordances:

I only tend to read replies from verified accounts now. Because in theory, these are people who are held to some account for what they say, you know, they've got a blue tick so they're probably a public personality or… Or an academic or, you know, somebody with some kind of standing in society so they're less likely to be just purely abusive and more likely to be offering something that might be constructive.

Others who feel anxious about audiences' reactions, and/or have experienced frustration and anger related to received abuse, may decide to set boundaries on who can follow them on social media. In this way, they can, at least to an extent, control who is given access to, and ability to engage with, content they post. While this may not always be possible, especially for high-profile journalists with tens of thousands or millions of followers, a senior print reporter (<10 k Twitter/X followers) shares this strategy:

> If I get someone follow me who's, you know, Davebulldog569355 - I'll look at the followers. I literally do - I look through the followers when they join. I look at them all, every single one that follows me. And if it is someone who's obviously a bot... Bang. Block them. And it saves having a conversation. No skin off my nose. I could probably have [more than a few thousand] followers instead of [few thousand] followers. Doesn't bother me. You know, I'd rather have [few thousand] genuine followers who are interested, and maybe don't agree with me and we'll have a debate about things, than have [more than a few thousand] followers where [few thousand] of them are just bots. Or, you know, someone hiding me on something and wants to, you know, be a troll.

Finally, two other boundary-setting strategies are also often employed by journalists faced with abuse on social media—muting and blocking. The latter means that the user/account which has been blocked cannot follow or contact you, nor see, and consequently, engage with your tweets. Muting involves muting a user or a conversation, meaning that you can no longer see muted account's tweets in your timeline or get notifications about replies to a conversation you've muted. Those muted do not know they've been muted, so many journalists deem this a better strategy than blocking, as it appears less aggressive. In other words, you can eliminate the disturbing content from your view, but others' will not know this is happening.

Internal Processing

Another commonly applied emotion management strategy in this context is internal processing, particularly in a form of perspective-taking. It involves 'dampening the meaning and/or seriousness of the situation' by adopting another perspective on a problematic situation to decrease its emotional impact (Hayward & Tuckey, 2011: 1509). When dealing with anxiety about potential social media responses, one of the ways to do this is to reflect on and acknowledge the process you went through in producing a story and reassuring yourself that you've done what is expected of you. An early career broadcast journalist (<10k Twitter/X followers) explains it like this:

> Have I done this properly? So, you know, did I rush something? Did I cut a corner or not? And telling myself that I haven't. So, knowing that, therefore, if there's an issue, it's something that I can discuss with an editor, but I'm not going to... You know, it's not going to cause a problem because I know that I did X, Y and Z and I can show that I did X, Y and Z. That's quite important for me...

Another early career digital journalist (<10k Twitter/X followers) adds that it is also important to acknowledge and accept that a journalist's job often involves reporting about controversial topics that may invoke strong reactions from audiences:

> You're never going to please everybody; I don't think you should try and please everybody. And a lot of the time you're going to write things that people don't want to read and that's a good thing, you know, it's good to show people information that they don't like. So, it's sort of to be accepted, I think. And I feel like a lot of the time, people are angry about certain topics and... Legitimately angry about certain topics. But then, if you write something that they disagree about that has to do with that topic, they're going to direct the anger at you. When it's not your fault, you know.

Internally processing your own beliefs and values, as well as reflecting on your work, may also alleviate some of the sadness and frustration about received abuse. An early career print journalist (<10k Twitter/X followers) explains their process in this way:

> I've had to do a lot of work, even in counselling and just internally about, you know, 'Okay, what are my values? What am I proud of? And what do I think was true, and, you know, good?' And, so, the more I develop that inside and I look at a piece and say like, 'Do I think I'm being honest

and clear and helpful?' And if the answer is yes... You know, the less I feel punctured by someone else online just being like, 'This is horrible,' you know. So, I think, yeah, definitely, I've worked into, like, looking inward a bit more and being like, 'What do I take pride in?'

Another important perspective that those faced with angry and uncivil social media users take is that the pluralism of ideas and opinions in a society is to be expected, and it is likely that, especially if you share opinions and beliefs, there will be those who will disagree. And who are unlikely to be changing their minds anytime soon. In the words of a senior print editor (10–100k Twitter/X followers):

> If the criticism is about some inaccuracy and that, and you have to deal with that, the best thing to do is just to deal with it and say, 'Look, okay, that figure, we got that wrong.' Just get out there and deal with it. The rest is, you know, opinion, slant, whatever way you want to put it. That's... You can't really deal with that. Because that's your view against theirs.

A perspective-taking related to this may also entail acknowledging and processing the view that there are rarely 'winners' in social media debates. Faced with a high-volume of tweets, replying to all of these and engaging in extensive conversations in which you can pacify or bring the other side to look at a situation from your viewpoint may be an unrealistic task. An early career broadcast journalist (<10k Twitter/X followers) explains the perspective-taking in this regard:

> There's often a value to be had in drafting a tweet, but not necessarily sending it in the heat of the moment. Especially during an argument or something. There's no benefit into getting into an argument with some-body, I found. And you can get so wound down in it. And it's taking that moment, step away and go, What's the point?' And slowing yourself down. So, that's something that I have learned. It's a kind of a coping mechanism. It's, like, realising that you're not going to win an argument. But, you know, you've made your point. They've made their point. End it there without feeling the need to have the last word. And it's difficult. But actually, that can be helpful as well. It's, like, 'Right. I'm done. Moved on.' And it is not always easy to do, but that is something that I think is quite important.

Many of the internal processing strategies employed when faced with social media abuse involve perspective-taking on social media audiences. For example, if experiencing abuse on social media, journalists may stop and think about whether those audiences are their target audiences and whether their voices are representative of those they aim to represent. A senior print editor (>100k Twitter/X followers) puts it like this:

> You know, I think there's important things I try and remember with Twitter is that it's not reflective of the whole country. David Cameron was right in that respect. It's a very particular section of society and a particular political makeup and it tends to be people who are quite active politically as well, so have strong views. So, while it's, you know, a part of what I do, and in my world is quite important part, it by no means... You know, I absolutely rely on the reach of our newspaper, because that really reaches "the real world" and that's really important to me, to be able to do that.

Others may take the perspective that while the abuse is targeted at them, they might not really be those who audiences have a quarrel with. Sometimes it's a 'shoot the messenger' kind of thing. Other times journalists may be attacked because they are seen to represent the organisation audiences perceive as failing in some regard. In the words of a mid-career broadcast editor (10–100k Twitter/X followers):

> You know, it's... It's not personal, is it? That's the thing. They don't see you as a person. You're just... You're just a member of the organisation or a kind of a symbol of something that they're projecting... You know, they project views onto you and stuff like that.

Verbal Processing

The third emotion management strategy that can be employed when dealing with emotional situations on social media is verbal processing with peers and well-being professionals. It entails talking about emotional situations with an aim of achieving emotional release and receiving emotional support. In terms of managing the pressure to perform on social media, there is sometimes a level of uncertainty about what is exactly expected of journalists in this regard. That is, while you may know you're expected to produce a number of stories a day or week, it may not be equally clear if, what and how often you're expected to publish on social media. To manage this, it may be possible to discuss, and perhaps negotiate, specific requirements with the editor or line manager.

Speaking with editors, or perhaps social media specialists if these exist in a newsroom, ahead of publishing content may also alleviate some of the anxiety about posting content. An early career broadcast journalist (<10k Twitter/X followers) explains how this works for them:

> Sometimes if it's something that I'm really not sure about, I'd like to pre-clear it with an editor rather than wait until afterwards. Because then if something does come up about it, I know that I've prepared this with an editor and that helps.

Those who experience social media abuse also report gaining an emotional release and support from colleagues by sharing their experiences with them. This can help rationalise the emotional event and legitimise emotions and their consequences. A mid-career digital editor (10–100k Twitter/X followers) talks about their experience of verbal processing in this way:

> I'm very surprised actually that talking about it again has made me so upset. [It helps talking about it] because I think it legitimises how I feel about the job and sometimes, you know, 'Why am I so sad?' or, 'Why am I so stressed?' Well, actually, maybe that being in the background is just a bit of a negative thing.

Journalists who feel that a particular case of social media abuse is escalating, may also wish to talk to their editors and management. Not everyone who reported doing this said they found a sympathetic ear or were given constructive advice. However, it is worth noting that a company has a duty of care towards their employees, and they can be expected to offer a range of supporting mechanisms, from security in case there are serious threats being made, to facilitating counselling if a journalist prefers to verbally process emotional events with well-being professionals. A positive case of management's reaction following a discussion of social media abuse is described by a senior broadcast correspondent (10–100k Twitter/X followers):

> I discussed it with management, and they were very supportive. There was an offer made at one point, you know, 'Do you want us to kind of get

security people to look at it?' I didn't think it was needed, you know, but they are... On the record, the organisational work was pretty good at that sort of thing.

Attentional Deployment

Finally, perhaps a less mentioned emotion management strategy when dealing with emotional situations on social media, yet still an important one, is attentional deployment in the form of engaging in diversionary activities which aim to balance negative with positive emotions. In other words, do things that make you happy when you're not working. This entails any activity that gives you joy, for example, spending time with family and friends, playing with pets, reading, exercising, meditating, etc. While some journalists spoke about engaging in these activities to take their minds off experienced abuse, others have mentioned it as a strategy to deal with anxiety about anticipating audience reactions to posting content. An early career print correspondent (10–100k Twitter/ X followers) explains their approach:

> So, often, I... I kind of shut things away so, you know... I'm thinking, if I'm worried that I'm going to get angry messages or calls from people, then I just put my phone on airplane mode and sort of give myself 5 or 10 minutes, sometimes longer. If I want to go for a walk as well then maybe like an hour... Before I sort of turn it back on. And I sort of give myself that time to prepare for kind of going into battle a bit more, rather than sort of being caught a bit more off guard.

A hint—spending time in nature has been found to have many positive effects on people's physical and mental health. You don't even have to exercise—sometimes just being outside in natural light and spending time in a green space can help you feel more relaxed, less stressed and even improve your confidence.

Finally, while the emotion management strategies discussed above may assist you in developing resilience in the face of working with social media, you should keep in mind that you are not and should not be alone in this process. Media organisations have a range of support mechanisms to support your work with social media, some of which you may find more useful than others, but it's worth knowing what is on offer. For example, Reach has had an online digital safety editor since 2021 who can be approached on issues discussed in this chapter. More publishers may follow their cue. Also, there is a range of support materials offered online that could be useful in dealing with social media, from Digital Safety Courses to legal advice. Being informed and ready to protect yourself may alleviate some of the stress of working in this field.

In sum, this chapter has covered several emotional situations that are likely to arise when working with social media, namely: the frustration related to pressure to do work on social media; the anxiety and nervousness about posting content given the perceived negativity of social media spaces; and the frustration, sadness, anxiety and anger with received abuse and harassment on these platforms. It has been suggested that key strategies to manage these include boundary-setting, such as applying disconnecting practices; internal processing in form of perspective-taking; verbal processing with peers and well-being professionals; and attentional deployment in the form of engaging in diversionary activities to balance negative with positive emotions.

The UK: Leona O'Neill on Social media abuse

Leona O'Neill has been a journalist in Northern Ireland for over 20 years, working with Irish News, Belfast Telegraph, Al Jazeera, CBC, Vice and others. In 2019 she witnessed the murder of fellow journalist Lyra McKee at a riot and developed PTSD. She's an avid campaigner for better newsroom mental health. O'Neill is head of Undergraduate Journalism at Ulster University.

I have been a journalist in Northern Ireland for 25 years. I was a young journalist when social media was born and it has evolved since then in parallel with my career. Social media is a great journalistic tool for finding sources for stories, to promote your work, to get your brand out there. But there are also many downsides to it. The harassment and abuse journalists face—particularly female journalists—is astounding, and it can have a significant detrimental impact on mental health.

In 2019, I was standing beside my journalistic colleague Lyra McKee when she was shot dead at a riot in Northern Ireland. Following the murder, I was hounded on social media by conspiracy theorists who claimed that, because I had interviewed Nancy Pelosi that day and was beside Lyra that night, that I was 'in the Illuminati' and had had her 'murdered as a sacrifice to Ms Pelosi.' Others claimed it was a false flag and that she wasn't really dead, that we were all actors and were hiding her. Social media was awash with people who believed this nonsense, and more insane ramblings.

While dealing with the trauma of seeing someone being murdered, I had to contend with hundreds of people harassing me on social media, calling for me to be arrested, attacked, hounded out of my city, stabbed, shot, and my children hurt to give me a 'taste of my own medicine.' The experience left me with PTSD.

There is a pressure on journalists to be on social media. Freelancers need it to promote their stories and get work, many outlets demand that their journalists push their work out over their own social media. Journalists need to remain visible so that sources can find them. It's an arena we are expected to navigate daily yet it is often an extremely hostile environment that can damage our mental health.

What I found has helped me navigate this is setting boundaries around time spent on social media. Because we carry our phones around in our pockets, we are basically allowing trolls and abusive people to reach us in our homes and safe havens. I have taken social media apps off my phone so that I'm not getting hateful notifications while I'm at home. It gives me back a sense of control in what can be an environment akin to the Wild West.

I also don't post any pictures or details about my children, I don't disclose where I am, where I socialise or give any indication of my address. Online harassment can often transfer to in-person harassment, and I want control over that.

I always make sure to check in with my journalistic friends and colleagues. We are of one tribe, we face the same challenges, the same harassment, and it's good to talk these things through and rationalise that people online do not know us, know nothing about the kind of people we are and that their opinion doesn't actually matter. Understanding that trolls will target prominent journalists with hate because they want a response—and therefore more exposure for themselves—is also important to put it in context.

And finally, I always make sure to prioritise self-care. Social media can be a horrible cesspit of hate. Leaning into your comforting, beautiful things—pets, walks in nature, favourite films, good food and good company—can remind you that social media isn't the real world and should never be treated as such.

Top Tips

- Distinguish personal and professional social media accounts
- Be aware of what is expected from you on social media and what kind of institutional (and other types of) support is there if you need it
- Consider your online and physical safety when posting on social media
- Gain an understanding of social media affordances and audiences— How do people use a specific network? In what purpose? Who? How to spot bots and trolls?
- Set boundaries that work for you—When are you accessing social media? What information are you sharing? Whose content are you reading/watching? Who are you engaging with?
- Speak to peers to gain emotional release and support, and with well-being professionals if you need further support

Read, Watch and Listen

- Read 'Protecting journalists from online abuse: a guide for news-rooms,' Gideon Sarpong's 2022 report written for the Reuters Institute for the Study of Journalism—https://reutersinstitute.pol itics.ox.ac.uk/protecting-journalists-online-abuse-guide-newsrooms
- Read through Committee to Protect Journalists' 'Resources for protecting against online abuse'—https://cpj.org/resources-for-pro tecting-against-online-abuse/

- Watch Bailey Parnell's TEDx talk 'Is Social Media Hurting Your Mental Health?' outlining key stressors on social media and ways to protect yourself from its potentially harmful effects—https://www.youtube.com/watch?v=Czg_9C7gw0o
- Listen to Behind the Headlines podcast episode featuring BBC's Disinformation and Social Media Correspondent Marianna Spring in which she talks about journalists' online safety and the impact of online abuse on their mental health—https://audioboom.com/posts/8084971-marianna-spring
- Listen to WhoWhatWhy podcast episode 'The Era of Social Media Journalism Is Over' with Ben Smith, co-founder of Semafor and former editor-in-chief of BuzzFeed News—https://whowhatwhy.org/podcast/the-era-of-social-media-journalism-is-over/

Scenario Exercises

Scenario 1

You report from the UN Climate Change Conference. Professor at the Department of Earth Sciences at the University of Cambridge and a Fellow of the Royal Society, with over 30 years of experience researching climate change, makes the following statement in one of the panels: 'If we don't change course, by 2050 the heat exposure and air pollution will be among the leading causes of death in the United Kingdom.' You tweet: '.@Cambridge_Uni @royalsociety Professor warns: "By 2050 the heat exposure and air pollution will be among the leading causes of death in UK."'

There are many reactions to your tweet, ranging from people saying how scary this is, and those who accuse you of scaremongering. One user, who you are unfamiliar with and do not follow, replies: 'Seeing these 'journalists' pushing these lies as facts is why people don't think it's a proper profession anymore. Just call it PR already and stop embarrassing yourself.'

- How does this make you feel?
- What are you going to do? Why?

Scenario 2

You report from Westminster about a political struggle at the top of the government. There is talk that the governing party will try to launch a vote of no confidence in their party leader which would also mean a change of the Prime Minister. You work your sources and one of them, a high-level source from the Cabinet, tells you that everything is in place and the event will play out tomorrow, but asks to remain anonymous. You tweet: 'Cabinet source says leadership no confidence vote on for tomorrow. It seems we might get a new Prime Minister.'

There are many reactions to your tweet, ranging from people saying that the Prime Minister has it coming and praising your investigative work, with others criticising the communication of unconfirmed rumours and the use of anonymous sources. One user, who you know regularly attacks you on Twitter, writes in reply: 'We've had enough of your bias and incompetence! You must be utterly stupid to be these charlatans' spokesperson and just write whatever they tell you.'

- How does this make you feel?
- What are you going to do? Why?

REFERENCES

Bahador, B. (2021). Countering hate speech online. In S. Waisbord & H. Tumber (Eds.), *The Routledge companion to media disinformation and populism* (pp. 507–518). Routledge.

Broersma, M., & Graham, T. (2016). Tipping the balance of power: Social media and the transformation of political journalism. In A. Bruns, G. Enli, E. Skogerbo, A. O. Larsson, & C. Christensen (Eds.), *The routledge companion to social media and politics* (pp. 89–103). Routledge.

Dubois, E., Tenove, C., Wilkinson, S., & Deley, T. (2021). Trolling with the punches: How journalists navigate online harassment. *International Journal of Press/Politics Virtual Conference.*

Gulyas, A. (2017). Hybridity and social media adoption by journalists. *Digital Journalism, 5*(7), 884–902.

Hayward, R. M., & Tuckey, M. R. (2011). Emotions in uniform: How nurses regulate emotion at work via emotional boundaries. *Human Relations, 64*(11), 1501–1523.

Lezard, B. T. (2020). *NUJ survey reveals shocking evidence of abuse and harassment of journalists*. National Union of Journalists. https://www.union-news.co.uk/nuj-survey-reveals-shocking-evidence-of-abuse-and-harassment-of-journalists/

Löfgren Nilsson, M., & Örnebring, H. (2016). Journalism under threat: Intimidation and harassment of Swedish journalists. *Journalism Practice, 10*(7), 880–890.

Muck Rack. (2023). *The state of journalism 2023*. https://info.muckrack.com/state-of-journalism-2023

Newman, N., Fletcher, R., Robertson, C., Eddy, K., & Nielsen, R. (2022). *Digital news report 2022*. Oxford University.

Orgeret, K. S., & Tayeebwa, W. (2020). Introduction: Rethinking safety of journalists. *Media and Communication, 8*(1), 1–4.

Ott, B. L. (2017). The age of Twitter: Donald J. Trump and the politics of debasement. *Critical Studies in Media Communication, 34*(1), 59–68.

Oz, M., Zheng, P., & Chen, G. M. (2018). Twitter versus Facebook: Comparing incivility, impoliteness, and deliberative attributes. *New Media and Society, 20*(9), 3400–3419.

Posetti, J., Shabbir, N., Maynard, D., Bontcheva, K., & Aboulez, N. (2021). *The Chilling: Global trends in online violence against women journalists*.

Rossini, P. (2021). More than just shouting? Distinguishing interpersonal-directed and elite-directed incivility in online political talk. *Social Media and Society, 7*(2), 1–14.

Rowe, I. (2015). Civility 2.0: a comparative analysis of incivility in online political discussion. *Information Communication and Society, 18*(2), 121–138.

Santana, A. D. (2014). Virtuous or vitriolic: The effect of anonymity on civility in online newspaper reader comment boards. *Journalism Practice, 8*(1), 18–33.

Sexism's toll on journalism. (2021). Reporters without Borders. https://rsf.org/sites/default/files/sexisms_toll_on_journalism.pdf

Šimunjak, M. (2022). *Tweeting Brexit: The social media in the aftermath of the EU referendum*. Routledge.

Waisbord, S. (2020). Mob censorship: Online harassment of US journalists in times of digital hate and populism. *Digital Journalism, 8*(8), 1030–1046.

CHAPTER 8

Speed of Process and 24/7 Journalism

One of the most stressful jobs I did in journalism was as a sub-editor for the sports desk in national daily newspapers. I regularly worked the evening shift, which was usually from around 6 pm till midnight, when the last edition went to print. I was usually on my own in the newsroom at this time. The job entailed liaising with reporters, receiving copies, checking stories and editing them, selecting photographs, writing headlines, captions, standfirsts and subheads, and then working with the graphics team to design the story layout within the designated place on the page. We all loved working the evening shift on Mondays and Fridays. Yet, the weekends, and mid-week shifts when Champions League and Europa League were on, were anything but relaxed. There were sometimes only minutes between the time I'd receive a copy and the deadline to send the page to press. Given all the moving parts of the story on the page, I'd lie if I said no mistakes were made. Incorrect caption. Body copy edited with an axe rather than a scalpel. A poor headline as the preferred one did not fit in the designated space and the creative part of the brain stopped collaborating in the countdown. Once it's sent to press, it's done. All my mistakes were very public and I would imagine them being judged in cafes over morning coffees. Rightly so.

It took me a while to find ways to manage this deadline stress and minimise potential mistakes in the process. Once I realised that some of it at least comes from working at a time of day when my ability to

© The Author(s), under exclusive license to Springer Nature Switzerland AG 2023
M. Šimunjak, *Managing Emotions in Journalism*, https://doi.org/10.1007/978-3-031-38631-2_8

focus is way past its prime, as I was a full-time student at the time and would usually come to work after classes, I knew I needed to find ways to compensate for tiredness. I've created a printed checklist of all the things I need to do before I send a story to press and would shamelessly carry it with me and go through the list with the graphics team before clicking 'send.' This prevented many wrong captions, standfirsts and photos being printed. Also, by observing my colleagues in the process, I've learned there are some things I can do even before I get a copy from the reporter, such as check the selected story layout to note all the bits I need to provide, select photos and think of captions, headlines and standfirsts, if possible, etc. This relieved some of the stress from the time pressure. Deadline stress remained there until the last day on the job, but more as a driving rather than incapacitating force. I accepted it as part of work, but knew that I have tools and processes to rely on to meet the deadline and avoid making mistakes.

This chapter deals with the environment in which journalism operates and emotional situations that may develop because of it, examining it through the 'stop, think, choose' model of emotional intelligence. The 'stop' section discusses emotional situations related to this environment. In particular, the speed of process required in daily news reporting, as well as time pressure when working on breaking news and live reporting, can lead to anxiety about meeting deadlines, as well as nervousness near deadlines, which some find to be driving and motivating, but it may hinder others' ability to concentrate and deliver. The other element that the chapter focuses on is the 24/7 environment in which journalism exists, meaning that the news cycle seemingly never ends. This often leads to work outside of regular hours, on days off and on holidays, inducing excitement if it is perceived the story is an important one; but also, frustration with work-life balance; as well as tiredness, weariness and mental exhaustion following continuous exposure to stressors. In the 'think' section, some beliefs and thoughts which may be driving mentioned emotions are outlined. The 'choose' section suggests emotion management strategies informed by interviews with practising journalists. These include internal processing by perspective-taking; boundary-setting, such as setting boundaries in the use of digital technologies; and attentional deployment in forms of concentration on task by stepping, as well as engagement in diversionary activities both during work time and outside of work to relieve exhaustion and improve sense of well-being.

Stop: Emotional Situations

Study of journalism job ads in the US revealed that working under pressure and to tight deadlines has increased in importance as a journalism skill (Wenger et al., 2018). Specifically, the proportion of job ads that listed this as a required skill increased from 28 to 56% from 2010 to 2015. This is indicative of the trends in the industry, which has always been driven by deadlines (Lund, 2012; Usher, 2018), requiring its professionals to deal with the 'deadline stress' (Ternes et al., 2018). Yet, in many media systems, it appears there are nowadays more deadlines to meet, and the need to meet them faster. This seems particularly the case in systems with high and advanced use of digital technologies, as the development of digital technologies and their incorporation in news production processes has contributed to the need to publish more news almost immediately as they happen (Paulussen, 2012; Usher, 2018). This sense of increased workload and time pressure is shared by British journalists interviewed for this book, too. In the words of a senior print editor:

> I look at my 20+ years in journalism and, you know, every journalist is expected to do twice as much as they did. Because there's more to do with digital, than, you know... We're just expected to do more and more for less and less.

A new type of journalism came into being with the normalisation of the use of formats of real-time coverage, such as live blogs, rolling news, news alerts and push notifications, as well as news updates by journalists on social media (Rom & Reich, 2020)—ambient journalism (Hermida, 2010; Sheller, 2015). This had an impact on journalistic deadlines—with some saying they are now 'constant' (Paulussen, 2012) and other claiming they have 'disappeared' (Gonzáles Fernandes & de Mendonça Jorge, 2017), but meaning the same thing—that all journalists in media organisations practising ambient journalism are nowadays on the same deadline—that online (Daum & Scherer, 2018; Usher, 2018).

Deadline Stress

The speed of process in daily newswork, as well as time pressure when working on breaking and/or rolling news, can contribute to **anxiety and stress about meeting deadlines**. Journalists with all levels of experience regularly acknowledge this emotional situation as part of their everyday work, as this senior broadcast correspondent notes:

There's obviously stress associated with deadlines. Nothing terribly unusual about that.

It appears that the anxiety associated with meeting a deadline is accepted as a regular part of the job, and one that is commonly experienced. An early career print correspondent describes it like this:

I'd say that sort of working to tight deadlines can make you anxious, getting stuff in on time... [...] You know, it's not a massive thing; it's usually something... I mean, I'm quite kind of good at getting stuff done on time and... So, it's just something I put on myself really, and once it's done, it's kind of done. And it's not... Although I do feel it, it's not something that's kind of a heavy weight, I guess, I would say, for me.

And while meeting any deadline arguably comes with a 'rush' and a degree of anxiety, the deadline stress can be exacerbated with developments that are perceived as hindering journalist's ability to meet a deadline. In the words of a senior broadcast editor:

You're kind of in that slightly, you know, slightly taut emotional kind of position. And, as you get closer and closer to the deadline... Obviously, if things aren't quite going right, you haven't got the elements assembled, then, you know, that kind of anxiety gets a little bit more acute.

The extensively discussed tension between speed and accuracy in contemporary news production (see, for example, Lewis & Cushion, 2009; Porlezza, 2019) also features in journalists' minds when they are required to publish information fast, such as in breaking news or on live blogs. In this context, working to tight deadlines often involves working with just acquired information that may not have been fully verified. This tension between the need to publish the information quickly, yet ensure its quality, can add to the stress about meeting the deadline. An early career digital journalist describes the situation like this:

Stress is caused by the pace of the news for me. I do a lot of breaking news so... It will be, like, in a moment, you have five minutes to write four paragraphs and there's a pressure because you know that those four paragraphs that you're writing line by line, you have to file within five minutes or are going to be pushed out with a push notification to however many million people. The stress comes, I guess, from the pressure and the gravitas of knowing you've got to get this right.

Interestingly, the **deadline stress is often described by journalists as a positive element, as they say they find it driving and motivating, helping their ability to concentrate and meet deadlines.** Journalists at all levels of seniority spoke of it in this way, indicating that it is a feeling that persists across one's career in the industry. A senior print editor shares their experience of feeling 'adrenaline fuelled excitement' near a deadline:

> I think that there's a degree of underlying stress. But, maybe I should say nervous energy rather than stress because it's less... It sort of helps keep me ticking over and driving me. I don't always regard it as a negative phenomenon, and it's kind of, you know, it sort of, it pushes me and keeps me on my feet, rather than being something that I find difficult to cope with.

The feeling of deadline stress as a positive driving force has been particularly mentioned by journalists who perform live reporting and cover breaking news. An early career digital journalist shares their account of this situation:

> I don't view stress as a bad thing. I actually thrive off of it, I thrive in that situation and quite enjoy it. You get adrenaline... [...] I use it to just focus my mind on exactly what I'm doing and that time. As a person, my mind... When I'm not at work, my mind can sort of wander all over and I'm quite chilled out, but like... When I've got a task to do, my personality type is like... When I've got a task to do, I can do it. And the pressure for me means... Usually when there's pressure, it's because I've got a specific task, and my mind works like that. I can then focus purely on that.

And while deadline pressure is considered a normal aspect of daily work, one that is rarely seen as having serious consequences, there are journalists who consider that working to constant deadlines and feeling constantly under pressure might have some longer-term implications for their well-being, as this mid-career digital reporter who reports on live blogs contemplates:

There is a sort of a feeling, which is sort of pressure, it feels stressful when you're doing it, but I don't necessarily come out of it thinking, 'Oh, that was a terribly stressful shift,' because, I think, as a journalist, especially one that does live reporting for a while, you get sort of used to it. [...] When you're doing live reporting you kind of need that pressure. [...] And, so, it is a useful emotion, pressure and stress. And, so... I guess maybe health-wise it might not be in 20 years' time. A doctor might say, 'Well, it was bad for you.'

24/7 Job

This worry should be taken seriously. Working in an environment of constant deadlines, alongside the now standard requirement to multi-task by reporting across different media, as well as having increasing workloads in 24/7 news environments in which the news cycle never ends, can contribute to exhaustion and burnout. The increased time pressure in everyday work has been noted in technologically advanced media systems in Northern America, Europe, as well as in Australia and New Zealand (Harro-Loit & Josephi, 2020). Also, studies across these systems, such as those carried out in the US, Australia and Belgium (Bossio & Holton, 2021; Paulussen, 2012; Reinardy, 2011) found concerning levels of exhaustion and burnout among journalists. To illustrate, Monteiro and Marques-Pinto's (2017) study of Portuguese reporters revealed that the two key job stressors in daily newswork are task-related stressors, in which meeting deadlines, time pressures and multi-tasking feature prominently, and structural work conditions, that include work schedule and excessive work hours. Portuguese journalists also reported that these stressors contribute to feelings of burnout, including emotional exhaustion, impact their physical and mental health, as well as family relationships through work-life conflicts.

And while this working environment has largely been enabled by the rise of digital technologies, it is the media economics that have been driving it through cost-cutting which created the context in which less journalists are expected to produce more work with less resources to tighter deadlines in a never-ending news cycle (MacDonald et al., 2016; Örnebring, 2010; Paulussen, 2012). As Usher (2015: 130) noted by examining the US media operations, '[t]he desire for the news organisations to be constantly updated creates physical wear and tear on the people producing the content.' A review of research into burnout in the industry revealed that early career reporters working in smaller newsrooms are most at risk from burnout (MacDonald et al., 2016). Yet, British journalists of all levels of seniority and years of experience in the industry spoke of the **tiredness, weariness and exhaustion induced by working in a 24/7 job environment that requires them to be 'always on duty.'** In the words of a mid-career digital editor:

> I think our job is 24/7 now. You know, you can wake up in the middle of the night and see a news alert and you're on duty. You know, you can always be on duty, permanently.

Social media has been frequently mentioned by journalists describing their jobs as being 'always on.' Similar to the feelings of fatigue brought about by constant connectedness and information influx from social media that were observed among journalists in the US and Australia (Bossio & Holton, 2021), British journalists too perceive the pressures on their daily work lives exacerbated by the introduction of this technology into their routines. A senior broadcast editor describes their experience and perceived impact of this unabating news flow from social media in this way:

> If you think about the sort of job of being a journalist sort of decade ago to now, what has changed is that there is a sort of… Social media has fundamentally changed what we do. Not only in terms of the structure of newspapers and kind of the competition and also the business models which has put the press under a lot of pressure. But also, just the relentlessness and intensity of the work, because it never stops. It never switches off. You know, the news never stops coming. The story never stops. It's 24/7 across, you know…

Journalists regularly acknowledge that their jobs are not the regular '9 to 5,' and hadn't been that way even before digital technologies transformed the information flow. They accept that off-diary events can happen at all hours and given both organisational pressure to be available to cover them, and internalised role conceptions telling them they should, in practical terms they feel the need to be constantly available for work. And while the implications of this pressure are not widely acknowledged nor researched, some journalists feel that working in this environment must take its toll. In the words of a senior broadcast editor:

I assume most journalists you speak to work ridiculous hours, and are also on call 24/7, so even when you've got some downtime... You know, the phone might ring at any moment, something could have happened... I think we are probably all, or certainly my generation, very bad at recognizing the emotional toll that takes. [...] I can't plan today because something might drop at any moment. I can't say, 'Between two and four I'm not going to look... I'm not going to even check my email, so I can get this piece of work done.' I'm constantly being dragged in different directions. It's the nature of the work.

Even for journalists who do shift work, so are less likely to be required to be available for work outside of work hours, there may be difficulties in switching off from work, which can contribute to a sense of exhaustion, with consequences for their well-being, job motivation and performance (Day et al., 2010). This seems particularly the case when journalists feel the need to keep on top of new information being released regarding their beats outside of work, to be able to perform their jobs during work hours. For example, an early career print journalist describes how the topics they have covered have contributed to a sense of work requirements imposing on their off-work time:

I feel it can be a very all-encompassing job and quite... And I also think that it's been very different over the last year in that the areas that I've been covering have been [international] politics, which is very volatile, and also the other thing that I've been covering was COVID. So, both of those topics are quite difficult to switch off from, possibly for different reasons, actually. COVID because you're also living through the thing that you're reporting on. And then with [international] politics, actually, because I'm based in London, the time difference meant that often by the time I would finish my shift at two o'clock or three o'clock UK time, there's still like another 12-14 hours of [international] news that can happen. So, it felt like you have to keep checking on the news all the way through the day anyway, so that you wouldn't start the next day without a huge backlog of knowing what happened. So, I feel like it's very, all-encompassing.

The trade-off, protecting one's off-work time so the job does not feel all-encompassing, might come with its own challenges. For example, not keeping updated with new information might make journalists feel anxious about not being up to date and/or feeling that competition is ahead of them. Realising that this might be the outcome of safeguarding your personal time from work can induce further feelings of frustration with the work environment and perceived job requirements. To illustrate, a mid-career digital editor tells of their frustration of starting a working day on Twitter:

> Well, it's just like.... Oh, here we go. Here's 1 million opinions and most of them will be horrible about the world. And from a journalistic point of view, it's about what's happening, feeling that you're not up to date, that you've missed things, that you're not current and.... Often, you know, when I get up, some journalists have already been working like four hours and because they do very early shifts, but that's just the nature of their jobs. And sometimes they're putting stuff on Twitter... And it already makes me feel behind.

Alongside the temporal overload that can be induced by constant news flows, British journalists also speak about the information overload that can be brought about by the sheer volume of information they are exposed to and process on an everyday level. Studies done in journalistic cultures across the world, such as those from Austria, Australia, China, Hong Kong and the US, also report a series of challenges of information overload enabled by the use of digital technologies (Bossio & Holton, 2021; Ninaus et al., 2015; Xu & Gutsche, 2021) as does wider research on experiences of knowledge workers (Day et al., 2010). British early career broadcast journalist describes the situation of being presented with continuous flows of information in this way:

> Sometimes getting too much detail about too many different stories and going ons, and therefore not being able to kind of shut down about things... Sometimes it is tough.

A commonly mentioned consequence of the information overload was again the feeling of exhaustion and burnout, which can affect journalists' mental health, well-being and work-life balance, and can even motivate journalists to consider a different profession, as studies of journalists in the US and Australia have shown (Bossio & Holton, 2018, 2021). The situation doesn't seem much better in Europe, where a 2016 study by the European Federation of Journalists found that over 80% of journalists feel work overload, and in most countries, more than 25% of the workforce has experienced burnout (Brédart, 2017). In the words of a British mid-career broadcast journalist:

It is overwhelming, I think. You know, I do sort of wonder if there's a kind of natural burnout stage that everyone gets to… You know, maybe after 10 years people do question if they really want to be so overwhelmed by information, knowledge, with the time.

Finally, working in a 24/7 job environment can also cause **frustration with work-life balance**. The work-home conflict, which describes the simultaneous pressures of performing work roles and responsibilities of home life, seems common in journalistic contexts in which journalists feel they are 'always on duty' (Lukan & Čehovin Zajc, 2022; Paulussen, 2012). Long and irregular work hours, as well as the constant connectedness through digital technologies, have been identified as some of the key predictors of work-life conflict in several countries, such as the US (Snyder et al., 2021) and India (Kumar & Gowda, 2018). Further, this tension between work demands and personal life has been found to contribute to burnout and depression, and consequently, decreased job performance and increased turnover intentions (Lukan & Čehovin Zajc, 2022). In journalism it seems work often trumps personal life, as Lukan and Čehovin Zajc (2022: 1) observed in Slovenia, reporting that 'work comes first with respect to the work–home balance in journalism.' Many British journalists share this sentiment. Some of them, while recognising the toll this mindset has on their personal lives, speak of it as a conscious choice based on personal values. A mid-career print editor tells of their experience:

> Massive consequences from my career choice, as much as I love it, in my, you know… In my almost [number of] years, as you reminded me, much to my horror… On things like personal relationships, you know, on time spent with family and things like that, even time spent with friends… Because it is one of those jobs that… You know, it is one of those things that you've got to really want to do, because if I… I'll probably leave the office about half past seven tonight. If I get home and halfway through my supper or whatever the phone rings and I start working again at nine… You just have to. And, you know, no one in my HR department would tell me that I would be obliged to do that, but if you don't… Well, it's not a question 'if you don't,' because you want to. You know, you want to be a part of it.

Others may find that they do not have a choice and have to respond to job calls outside of work hours as they perceive their roles demanding it. A mid-career broadcast journalist describes such a situation and its emotional implications:

> But it's the job. I can't not work when certain events happen. For example, bloody Downing Street briefings... So, I have an obligation to monitor those and to watch them and to, you know, react to them. But... I am disappointed and frustrated.

The feeling of personal responsibility to be available for work outside of work hours may be particularly evident in local or smaller newsrooms where there is often only one person covering a beat, meaning that the story might not get covered or might not be reported to the same degree of quality, should the journalist decide to prioritise their personal lives over work. The decision to put the job first and work outside of work hours, whether this is exciting or frustrating, can have an impact on journalists' well-being as the lack of time to recharge and rest can lead to feelings of exhaustion and burnout. A mid-career broadcast editor describes their experience of work in this way:

> Is tiredness an emotion? (laughs) Like... There is... It's endless, I would say. It's not a job where you start at nine o'clock and finish at five o'clock. So, it's kind of constant. So, you can sometimes feel, I suppose, a weariness, because it's perpetual... It's always... On a day off, someone will text you at eight o'clock in the morning and ask you something, and you can't not do it because you're the only one who knows about it or you're the only one who understands it and you're the only point of contact or whatever. [...] And that does sometimes make you feel a bit... Yeah, can make it difficult to switch off and makes you feel a bit tired, I would say, at times.

Writing of experiences of Slovenian journalists, Lukan and Čehovin Zajc (2022) report that by mid-career stage some journalists put more efforts into trying to protect their personal lives from being invaded by work obligations, yet the nature of the job often makes this impossible so those who are keen to establish a work-life balance often move into another field, such as a public relations role. Some of the senior British journalists too spoke of the frustration of working odd and unsociable hours at later stages of their careers, as this senior broadcast editor explains:

As I've got older, I found the stresses and anxieties of your life being thrown upside down by the phone ringing or something happening and, 'Right, they need you there now...' And being... You know, perhaps 20 years ago I would have... Definitely, 20 years ago I would have, you know, sort of bundled into action enthusiastically. Now, like, there's a sort of knot in the pit of my stomach, kind of, 'Oh my God, here we go again...'

THINK

As explained in the Introduction chapter, emotional and physical responses to a situation are driven by our beliefs and thoughts through which we interpret that situation. If we are interpreting a situation with negative thoughts, it's more likely that we will perceive it as an inevitable occurrence which we have little or no control over. This can then lead to increased stress. Thinking of the emotional situations discussed above, Table 8.1 outlines several beliefs and thoughts that might be driving negative emotions.

If you are experiencing negative emotions which you feel you need or want to manage, you can check the beliefs and values, as well as thoughts and expectations that are driving these. In other words, think about what is driving your emotions, how can you update and reframe these with a

Table 8.1 Potential beliefs and thoughts that might be driving a negative emotional response to emotional situations associated with meeting deadlines and working in a 24/7 environment

Anxiety about meeting deadlines	Frustration with work overload	Frustration with work–life conflict
I will miss the deadline	I have to always be up to date with my beat	I have to always be available for work
There isn't enough time to do the story right	My job is 24/7	If I'm not available, story will not be covered
Mistakes will be made in a fast turnaround	I am expected to follow news even outside of work	If I'm not available, story will not be covered well
	I will be seen as weak and lazy if overwork makes me tired	My employer will see me as unreliable if I'm not constantly available
		My bosses/peers will think I'm not a good journalist if I don't prioritise a story

more positive outlook and what options you have moving forward. For example, if you're anxious about meeting a deadline because you believe there isn't enough time to do the story justice, consider what is exactly expected of you in terms of delivering the story? Is it to offer a comprehensive account? Is that even possible? What can you and cannot do in the time allocated for story production? What is reasonable to achieve? If you are frustrated with work overload and you believe you have to be across all information about your beat all the time, consider if this is an expectation you put on yourself or has it been imposed by someone else? Is it something you expect from your peers? How reasonable is that expectation? Do you necessarily need to be plugged into the news agenda all the time to keep up to date? If you are frustrated with work-life conflict and believe a story will not get covered if you don't work outside of work hours, consider how you came to this perception? Is it an internal role conception or was it imposed on you? Whose expectation is it? Whose responsibility is it to ensure a story gets covered? If you are always available to cover a story, what does this signal to your employer about the need for more people to cover the beat? Is it likely that this frustration with work-life balance will ever be eliminated if the same patterns of work and beliefs persist?

The beliefs and values that drive these emotional situations will differ from journalist to journalist, so it's important you try to unpack what exactly is inducing your own emotions in this context. Are they rational? Logical? What evidence do you have to believe what you think is happening? And while, similarly, journalists may decide to manage their emotions in diverse ways, there are some common emotion management strategies that journalists apply when faced with emotional situations tied to meeting deadlines and operating in a 24/7 environment, that the chapter now turns to.

CHOOSE: EMOTION MANAGEMENT STRATEGIES

The most commonly mentioned emotion management strategies by British journalists when dealing with emotional situations outlined above are internal processing, including perspective-taking on personal values; boundary-setting (e.g., deciding/negotiating in which situations you wish to be called outside of working hours; not taking on more work than you can reasonably complete; not checking email on holidays etc.); and attentional deployment in both forms—focusing on practice and routine, and directing the focus on activities that will divert attention to non-work experiences that induce positive emotions.

Internal Processing

Internal processing, particularly in forms of perspective-taking and positive reappraisal, could assist in alleviating some of the anxieties and frustration associated with deadline stress, 'always on' approach to work, and work-life conflict. For example, when faced with deadline stress, it might be helpful to remind yourself of your previous success in meeting deadlines. This can help reinforce the feeling of confidence in your abilities to deliver the story on time and relieve some of the deadline pressure. If helpful, you may try some positive affirmations to remind yourself of your skills and abilities. British journalists interviewed for this book, particularly those with many years of experience in the industry, spoke of the benefit of thinking of past experience of successfully working to tight deadlines as a technique of managing deadline pressures. A senior broadcast correspondent describes it like this:

> I think, when you get to a certain level of experience, you know that you can usually pull it out of the hat. (laughs) However tight the deadline and however bad the situation...

When it comes to the frustration with the workload and work-life conflict, some perspective-taking might be useful. In the first place, it is beneficial to be aware of your personal values (note there are exercises for establishing these in the Introduction chapter) and the extent to which these align with your organisation's values, perceived demands of the job, and your perception of the payoff you get by being constantly available for work. This is important as value dissonance is, alongside workload, a strong predictor of emotional exhaustion (Gascón et al., 2021). For example, if you are driven by ambition and social recognition, you could use positive reappraisal to consider the frustrating situation of being called into work during off time as an opportunity to accomplish your goals and pursue your values. On the other hand, if you value family and friendships most, you might experience value dissonance if your organisation requires you to be constantly available for work and this causes tensions with your desire for spending time with those you value most. In that case, you might experience work-life conflict which can contribute to a feeling of burnout. Possible interventions here include setting clear priorities and considering trying to change your work patterns to deal with the root cause of frustration and burnout (Hatch, 2021; Valcour, 2016). The latter is often easier said than done, particularly if there is pushback from the employer. However, it is important you are aware of your values and how these feature in your experiences of work, so you can consider what the best ways forward for you might be.

In doing so, it is also important that you are able to recognise the ways in which the 'always on' work patterns impact you, including knowing the symptoms of burnout as well as your own limits. Kim Brice, the co-founder of The Self-Investigation—foundation aimed at improving media workers' well-being—emphasises that journalists 'need to take the time to learn about their own mental limits, especially knowing the difference between feeling challenged and feeling overwhelmed' (Hatch, 2021). If you recognise that you are feeling exhausted, cynical and/or unproductive at work, which are key symptoms of burnout, it may be helpful to consider different perspectives on your work, such as what you can and cannot change, what are and are not your work priorities, what is and isn't expected of you, what you can do to gain more control over your workload and what kind of support you can access in changing your work patterns to those that are better aligned with your values and safeguard your well-being (Lukan & Čehovin Zajc, 2022; Valcour, 2016).

Boundary-Setting

Next, one of the most frequently mentioned strategies for managing workload and expectations of constant availability, and by extension, preventing burnout, is boundary-setting, which often refers to ways in which digital technologies are managed. Indeed, advice to journalists on how to recover from and/or prevent burnout regularly contains suggestions for disconnecting from digital technologies for a set amount of time, or, in other words, setting boundaries in the use of digital technologies, and in particular smartphones and social media (Bélair-Gagnon et al., 2022; Bossio & Holton, 2021; Hatch, 2021; Huang, 2012; Lukan & Čehovin Zajc, 2022; Snyder et al., 2021). Similar to strategies reported by journalists in the US and Australia (Bossio & Holton, 2018, 2021), British journalists spoke of techniques they employ on social media, such as turning off notifications, as well as muting and blocking certain conversations and accounts, in order to manage the information flows from social media (for more on this see chapter 7). In order to manage temporal and information overload from social media, some British journalists also managed their use of smartphones. On the one hand, some journalists report deleting the social media apps from smartphones, to control the amount of information they are exposed to and its impact on their work and personal lives, as this mid-career digital editor explains:

> Just recently I've deleted it [Twitter/X app] from my phone, which is weird because literally my thumb is still going to that app all the time, to open it. It's like it's in built and... So, I'm just going to see how that works out. It's not really practical right now, not to have the app on my phone, but more seeing Twitter as something I log into for work and then can come out of it, otherwise you will be on it all the time.

On the other hand, some journalists create boundaries between personal and work lives by managing their use of digital objects, in particular smartphones, as was observed in Slovenia as well (Lukan & Čehovin Zajc, 2022). The practice is employed by those who have work phones, which they physically distance from in off-work periods, in order to create separation between work and home life, and minimise opportunities for work impeding on home life. Yet, this can cause anxieties for journalists who feel the need to be constantly available. In which case, journalists report the need to process and reflect on their decisions to disconnect, and consciously acknowledge their priorities and values. In the words of a mid-career broadcast editor:

> I'll often... I have two phones... So, I'll often... My work phone, which has my work email and stuff on it, I will often plug that in next to the bed and leave it there when I'm off. [...] But it is hard to separate the two. It's kind of always... It's kind of always there. And again, that comes down to that idea of the personal responsibility. So, if I don't look, if I haven't picked up on the message or whatever, nobody else is going to. So, you sort of have to take personal responsibility for that. To ignore something, you have to kind of tell everyone, 'I'm going to be incommunicado for two weeks and I'm not, you know...' But you have to kind of reconcile with that and be like, 'Okay, this is what I'm doing.'

Consciously employing strategies that create divisions between work and personal lives has been particularly emphasised by more senior journalists with many years of experience in the industry. They appeared aware of the strain of working in 24/7 environments and the importance of setting boundaries that would allow them to recharge, relax and enjoy their personal lives. Alongside managing work devices, some referred to managing their off-work time spent on social media, to achieve this. A senior broadcast editor describes their strategy in this way:

> I've got quite a strict separation between, you know, like very strict separation between my professional life and my personal life, so I become... Because it's been, you know, such a kind of crazy busy few years, I've become quite strict. Like, if I'm not working, I'm not sitting, looking, glued at Twitter. You know, I work enough hours as it is, there are enough hours when I have to be at work, and I work very long hours and that's fine. But when I'm not working... Like, if somebody really needs me, they will call me. I don't have to sit staring at social media all day. I have quite a strict separation and I think that's a bit of a survival mechanism in a way, you know.

Setting boundaries in terms of work hours in order to manage workload and achieve work-life balance has also been mentioned as one of the key ways to prevent burnout and protect personal lives from being taken over by work. In the words of a mid-career broadcast journalist:

> At the risk of sounding like a cliché, potentially, I'm very sort of strict with my hours and about overwhelming myself. I'm very, very strict about sort of having downtime, having appropriate time on the weekends...

Attentional Deployment

The third key strategy for managing emotions arising from deadlines and working in 24/7 environments is attentional deployment. On the one hand, the strategy of focusing attention on professional routines and practices can help alleviate some of the deadline stress, particularly in the form of 'stepping,' that is, breaking down the process into smaller, more manageable steps, in order to create a workable pathway to the outcome and relieve the feeling of being overwhelmed by the task. For example, Stupart (2022) found that noting down pieces of information and/or creating checklists, as well as using habitual routines of professional practice that allow completion of tasks without too much conscious effort, can assist journalists in meeting deadlines under pressure. This kind of self-organisation can also assist with setting priorities, making multitasking easier and identifying areas in which extra support might be needed (Lund, 2012). To illustrate, an early career digital journalist shares their technique for alleviating deadline pressure:

> I try... In a short time, I would take some deep breaths and try and write down a plan of everything that I need to do, so it's not all stuck in my head.

On the other hand, attentional deployment in the form of focusing attention on non-work activities can help prevent and/or recover from burnout. For example, it is emphasised that taking regular breaks during work time is important in ensuring that the workload does not become overwhelming, and work exhausting (Hatch, 2021). An early career digital journalist shares their technique:

> I have a good routine as well, so I'm not always constantly sat down looking at a computer, but I'll make sure I get up at least once an hour and get out of the house as well, go for a walk. If it's really bad, if I'm really stressed, then I'll get out the house and go and walk around the block for 10, 15 minutes or so.

Outside of work hours, it is suggested that journalists can distance themselves from work-related thoughts, eliminate stress hormones from the body and increase their sense of work-life balance, by engaging in non-work related endorphin-inducing activities, i.e., those that make them happy. For example, Huang (2012) suggests investing time and effort into hobbies, developing passion(s) for non-work related activities, and travelling to unfamiliar places that are likely to occupy body and mind. The range of activities that are endorphin-inducing will be different from person to person, but it is the conscious effort into scheduling these and pursuing them that matters in allowing the body to recover, recharge and maintain important social relationships (Snyder et al., 2021). And while burnout is often discussed as something experienced after many years in the industry, among the British journalists interviewed for this book it was actually the emerging professionals who most frequently spoke of consciously planning and engaging in diversionary activities in order to safeguard their well-being. An early career broadcast journalist described their approach to fighting burnout:

It's watching... You know, it's watching movies, finding other ways to unwind. Holidays... In fact, it's the thing.... Taking time off... It's... It's really noticeable that you don't think that you need a holiday until you get the holiday. Until you take a week or two off it, and you realise that you really... Like, you were struggling. Sometimes that's only... Either you think you're just in a bad mood, but actually, it's a build-up of things. You just needed a break. So, you know, making sure that you're taking that time off and time away from it is helpful.

As this quote illustrates, alongside making sure to relax and de-stress in between work hours, taking regular holidays as a prolonged period in which temporal and information overload can be eased and work-life balance restored has been mentioned as really important in preventing and managing burnout. Sometimes it is precisely in this period that signs of burnout before the break are actually acknowledged and reflected upon. The benefit of taking regular holidays is emphasised by this early career broadcast journalist:

But actually, the thing more recently that I have... In the past I would only have done like long weekends and things like that. Whereas now I'm definitely seeing the value of taking the week off and actually having a proper break. And that does help. That definitely helps.

Finally, the literature on stress and burnout management indicates that investing time and energy in enhancing well-being can mitigate some of the negative consequences of work-related stress. Specifically, studies have found that aerobic exercise can reduce exhaustion, cynicism and inefficacy, which are the symptoms of burnout (Oberste et al., 2021; Rosales-Ricardo & Ferreira, 2022). Making sure that you are eating well and having good quality of sleep are also mentioned as well-being enhancing activities that can help the worker be better prepared to endure working under pressure and to manage stressors in the workplace (Firth et al., 2020; Newsom & Rehman, 2023; Sano et al., 2015). A mid-career broadcast editor shares their experience:

I try to exercise in the morning, which then makes me a little bit more resilient, I find, heading into the day. It makes... it sets me up for a positive mindset so I'm kind of attacking obstacles and challenges and things, coming from a more optimistic mindset than if, maybe, you know, other times if I've not had exercise or been taking care of myself and maybe I'm a bit tired and then I'm going into the day feeling a bit more negative and those challenges around deadlines and the general exhaustion of the job can... Can create a far more kind of negative form of anxiety.

In sum, this chapter has covered several emotional situations that are likely to arise in the process of meeting deadlines and working in a 24/ 7 environment, namely: anxiety related to meeting deadlines; exhaustion caused by the need to be 'always on;' and frustration with work-life conflict caused by overwork. It has been suggested that key strategies to manage these emotions include internal processing by perspective-taking; boundary-setting, such as setting boundaries in the use of digital technologies; and attentional deployment in forms of concentration on task by stepping, as well as engagement in diversionary activities both during work time and outside of work to relieve exhaustion and improve sense of well-being.

The US: Alden Bentley on 24/7 journalism

Alden Bentley is the Breaking News Editor (Finance & Markets, Americas) at Reuters. He joined Reuters in 1996 after a career as a foreign exchange dealer in New York. Bentley has held senior editor roles focused on capital markets, economics, exchanges, the Fed and commodities, and spent six years as a copy chief. Alden lives in New Jersey, has two adult children, and is an avid reader and history buff, an outdoorsman and sailor.

I have been a wire-service journalist and editor for 27 years. This is my second career. Others say I don't look it, but I'm in my sixties and probably at least a decade older than most of my colleagues and higher ups. I am trying to accept that I don't have youthful energy and reflexes, even as I strive to keep up with the 24/7 news flow, new ways of delivering stories and, of course, expectations that rise every year. Plus, aging is something you really can't talk about at work. I began my professional life in the pre-internet trading world on Wall Street in the mid '80s. I loved to write and the transition to journalism, and leadership, came naturally. Newsroom stresses and trading room stresses were similar, requiring snap judgements, longer-term thinking and smart resource deployment—to cover a breaking story or to move blocks of money fast.

My workday runs from 5:30 a.m. until after 5 p.m. When news breaks or social media starts buzzing about something potentially newsy, it's my job to help mobilize a global reporting team on verification, publishing alerts, covers and updates, while making sure my market reporters are prepping to send instant headlines and updates if stocks, bonds or currencies react. It's a lot: directing traffic, editing copy, getting correspondents to call investors, juggling virtual meetings, fielding calls from reporters and editors, assigning trunk writing and sending around coverage plans... Pretty much simultaneously.

Losing a daily in-person interface with my team in 2020 was a seismic professional misery. Working from home during the pandemic we had to rely, like many other companies, on a desktop platform limited to audio, video, phone and messaging. Using a virtual collaboration tool, and monitoring multiple conversations when markets are volatile, slowed reaction times. Plus, all the toggling between them requires extra manual dexterity, which I am losing not gaining.

Twenty-seven years ago we measured wins and losses in minutes, sometimes hours. Now, timings are tracked to the millisecond. I've kept up with the need for speed, but my curve has flattened in the last couple of years. My training and market experience compensated for physically slowing... But not completely. That widening imbalance increased my stress levels. I'm delegating some responsibilities to others, out of necessity. I mentally turn devices off at the end of the day. Of course, I will take an important call, or edit on a deadline into the evening. But I deactivate notifications. I am duty editor several weekends a year, but otherwise reserve Saturday and Sunday for myself, friends and family. I exercise regularly, see my doctors (and therapists) as needed and take every vacation day I am entitled to. These strategies keep me as sharp and refreshed as I can be. Overall, I feel good, if exhausted, much of the time. A positive, and philosophical, attitude helps a lot. Tempus Fugit!

Australia: Rachael Dexter on 'always on'

Rachael Dexter is a City reporter for Australian daily newspaper The Age, covering local government, planning and life in Melbourne. She specializes in audio and video journalism and has produced the 'Wrong Skin' podcast, which won the Australian Podcast of the Year award. Rachael previously worked with Australian Broadcasting Corporation and Al Jazeera Media Network.

One of the questions that loom most large for me, and a lot of the working journalists here, is that separation; when do you turn off if you are always expected to be 'on' and if a story can always be updated? When do you stop? That was something that particularly came up during the pandemic. During lockdowns when we all worked from home for a few years, and had this functioning system where we were putting a newspaper together every day completely remotely, it embedded this sort of culture of always being available, always being on screens... This constant 'standby mode.' It wasn't until we all started coming back to the newsroom, that we started to realize how much had been asked of us. How much our jobs had asked of us. And when we talked about it, we started to realize, 'Oh it's not cool to still be taking calls at 8.30 pm at night.'

During the pandemic, I went out of my way to get a second phone. That was firstly, for mental health reasons, but then it was for safety reasons as well. I reported on anti-lockdown protests and really dug into who was leading those, as well as some of the people who were in the freedom movement' (anti-lockdown movement in Australia) and the more conspiratorial elements of that movement. It became clear to me pretty early on that there were elements of safety that I needed to be thinking about. During the pandemic, addresses of politicians were found and circulated on Telegram. They pulled out Daniel Andrew's (State Premier of Victoria) mother's home address and it was circulating on Telegram. That's when it became clear to me that there were lots of different people caught up in this anti-vaccination movement, and you only need one person who works in a government agency to do the wrong thing and leak something. It was not a big stretch of the imagination to think that maybe my home address could be put out into the world. So, I went about getting a second mobile phone. I surrendered my phone number that I was already using to the world and accepted that that was probably floating around already, but made sure that it was registered to my work address. I then got a personal number that only five of my closest family and friends have—and accessed it on a completely different phone.

It came from a security concern, but it also became one of my very few tools for coping mentally with this job—having the work phone that I can turn off or just put away and not look at. If there's a day that I'm not filing, I try to not look at that phone at all. I'll turn it off until I'm back on the clock the next day. That's good for days I'm not filing, or a story has been filed and I know there's no more queries with it. But the days where you do have a story in the paper it's not uncommon that I'll leave the office and then it goes through subs, and then it goes through a second level of subs, and then the lawyer might have a query, then there might be late, breaking news on it, with changes at the top of the story altogether. It's not uncommon that those nights you can't switch off. I still need to take calls. But I still try to cultivate a bit of a culture where we can switch off sometimes. I try to convince younger colleagues to do it. I have a few younger colleagues who I've convinced to get a second phone to deal with this. Because whether its work asking you to, or it's our compulsion, we still need that separation.

Top Tips

- Consider your values and abilities—acknowledge what you value, reflect on your strengths and weaknesses and recognise the signs of burnout
- Use 'stepping' towards a deadline—breaking the task into steps towards the goal can alleviate the anxiety about hitting the deadline
- Take regular breaks during work hours to give your body and mind respite from stress and prevent burnout
- Set boundaries in the use of digital technologies to manage information and temporal overload, and help separate work from personal life

- Consider adjusting work patterns by discussing your work experience and its impact on your well-being with peers and bosses
- Engage in well-being enhancing activities and practices, such as doing exercise, eating healthily and having good quality sleep, which can help you de-stress and better manage work-related stress

READ, WATCH AND LISTEN

- Read 'Creating A Healthy Work/Life Balance As A Freelancer' by Karen Edwards on Journo Resources—https://www.journoresour ces.org.uk/advice-healthy-work-life-balance-freelancer-journalist/
- Read the article 'Connected and content: Managing healthy technology use' by American Psychological Association—https://www.apa.org/topics/social-media-internet/healthy-technology-use
- Watch the video 'Burnout: Symptoms & Strategies' created by McMaster University students in collaboration with the McMaster Demystifying Medicine Program—https://www.youtube.com/watch?v=3FMVECPf5is
- Watch TED talk by psychologist Guy Winch 'How to turn off work thoughts during your free time' - https://www.youtube.com/watch?v=fc3c3OrpKSI
- Listen to The Takeaway podcast episode 'Journalists are burning out' with Bruce Shapiro, executive director of the Dart Center for Journalism and Trauma—https://www.wnycstudios.org/podcasts/takeaway/segments/journalists-are-burning-out

SCENARIO EXERCISES

Scenario 1

You work as a senior finance reporter for a regional digital media outlet. You have a background in economics and have been covering finance and business for over 10 years. In this time, you've covered several budget announcements. Yet, this is the first time you're covering it for your current employer, and you don't yet feel fully familiar with the region you're now reporting about.

The new budget has just been published by the Finance Minister in a document with several hundred pages. Trial balloons and budget rumours have been swirling in the past few days, but none have been confirmed by the government ahead of the publication of the budget. The editor is asking for a breaking news item to be pushed out in 5 minutes, a news piece on the highlights of the budget to be published in 20 minutes, and a news story on what the new budget means for the region in an hour.

- How does this make you feel?
- What are you going to do? Why?

Scenario 2

You are an early career crime reporter for a local newspaper. You have been in the job for a few years, covering all sorts of crime stories, including those about robberies, assaults, cybercrimes and murders. You are interested in continuing your career as a politics reporter, and you see the current job as a stepping stone towards your preferred specialism. You are the only crime reporter in the newsroom and are often called into work at odd hours and on days off to cover a story. You have already been called into work after your shift ended twice in the past week.

It's your day off and you're preparing to go out to meet friends for dinner. The editor calls you to say that the local police has issued an alert relating to an unnamed incident near one of the local shopping centres. They are asking for citizens to stay away from the area. The editor wants you to head there and cover the story.

- How does this make you feel?
- What are you going to do? Why?

REFERENCES

Bélair-Gagnon, V., Bossio, D., Holton, A. E., & Molyneux, L. (2022). Disconnection: How measured separations from journalistic norms and labor can help sustain journalism. *Social Media + Society.* https://doi.org/10.1177/20563051221077217

Bossio, D., & Holton, A. E. (2018). The identity dilemma: Identity drivers and social media fatigue among journalists. *Popular Communication, 16*(4), 248–262.

Bossio, D., & Holton, A. E. (2021). Burning out and turning off: Journalists' disconnection strategies on social media. *Journalism, 22*(10), 2475–2492.

Brédart, H. (2017). Burnout among journalists, a symptom of discontent in newsrooms. *HesaMag,* 12–16.

Daum, E., & Scherer, J. (2018). Changing work routines and labour practices of sports journalists in the digital era: A case study of postmedia. *Media, Culture and Society, 40*(4), 551–566.

Day, A., Scott, N., & Kelloway, E. K. (2010). Information and communication technology: Implications for job stress and employee well-being. In D. C. Ganster & P. L. Perrewé (Eds.), *New developments in theoretical and conceptual approaches to job stress* (pp. 317–350). Emerald Publishing.

Firth, J., Solmi, M., Wootton, R. E., Vancampfort, D., Schuch, F. B., Hoare, E., Gilbody, S., Torous, J., Teasdale, S. B., Jackson, S. E., Smith, L., Eaton, M., Jacka, F. N., Veronese, N., Marx, W., Ashdown-Franks, G., Siskind, D., Sarris, J., Rosenbaum, S., ... Stubbs, B. (2020). A meta-review of "lifestyle psychiatry": The role of exercise, smoking, diet and sleep in the prevention and treatment of mental disorders. *World Psychiatry, 19*(3), 360–380.

Gascón, S., Fueyo-Díaz, R., Borao, L., Leiter, M. P., Fanlo-Zarazaga, Á., Oliván-Blázquez, B., & Aguilar-Latorre, A. (2021). Value conflict, lack of rewards, and sense of community as psychosocial risk factors of burnout in communication professionals (Press, radio, and television). *International Journal of Environmental Research and Public Health, 18*(2), 1–12.

Gonzáles, S., & de Mendonça Jorge, T. (2017). Routines in web journalism: Multitasking and time pressure on web journalists. *Brazilian Journalism Research, 13*(1), 20–37.

Harro-Loit, H., & Josephi, B. (2020). Journalists' Perception of time pressure: A global perspective. *Journalism Practice, 14*(4), 395–411.

Hatch, B. (2021). *Creating 'sustainable journalists': Six steps you can take to prevent burnout*. Ground Truth. https://thegroundtruthproject.org/creating-sustainable-journalists-six-steps-you-can-take-to-prevent-burnout

Hermida, A. (2010). Twittering the news: The emergence of ambient journalism. *Journalism Practice, 4*(3), 297–308.

Huang, T. (2012). *5 ways journalists can strike a better work-life balance*. Poynter. https://www.poynter.org/reporting-editing/2012/5-ways-journalists-can-strike-a-better-work-life-balance

Kumar, S., & Gowda, S. (2018). A study of work-life balance of journalists. *International Journal of Management, 8*(3), 77–93.

Lewis, J., & Cushion, S. (2009). The thirst to be first: An analysis of breaking news stories and their impact on the quality of 24-hour news coverage in the UK. *Journalism Practice, 3*(3), 304–318.

Lukan, T., & Čehovin, J. (2022). "If you don't agree to be available 24/7, then you have nothing to do in journalism": The boundary work tactics of precarious journalists. *Community, Work and Family*. https://doi.org/10.1080/13668803.2022.2050356

Lund, M. K. (2012). More news for less: How the professional values of 24/7 journalism reshaped norway's TV2 newsroom. *Journalism Practice*, 6(2), 201–216.

MacDonald, J. B., Saliba, A. J., Hodgins, G., & Ovington, L. A. (2016). Burnout in journalists: A systematic literature review. *Burnout Research*, 3(2), 34–44.

Monteiro, S., & Marques-Pinto, A. (2017). Journalists' occupational stress: A comparative study between reporting critical events and domestic news. *Spanish Journal of Psychology*, 20(34), 1–17.

Newsom, R., & Rehman, A. (2023). *The relationship between diet, exercise, and sleep*. Sleep Foundation. https://www.sleepfoundation.org/physical-health/diet-exercise-sleep

Ninaus, K., Diehl, S., Terlutter, R., Chan, K., Huang, A., & Erlandsson, S. (2015). Benefits and stressors—Perceived effects of ICT use on employee health and work stress: An exploratory study from Austria and Hong Kong. *International Journal of Qualitative Studies on Health and Well-Being*, 10(1), 1–15.

Oberste, M., de Waal, P., Joisten, N., Walzik, D., Egbringhoff, M., Javelle, F., Bloch, W., & Zimmer, P. (2021). Acute aerobic exercise to recover from mental exhaustion—A randomized controlled trial. *Physiology and Behavior*, 241. https://doi.org/10.1016/j.physbeh.2021.113588

Örnebring, H. (2010). Technology and journalism-as-labour: Historical perspectives. *Journalism*, 11(1), 57–74.

Paulussen, S. (2012). Technology and the transformation of news work: Are labor conditions in (online) journalism changing? In E. Siapera & A. Veglis (Eds.), *The handbook of global online journalism* (pp. 192–208). Wiley-Blackwell.

Porlezza, C. (2019). From participatory culture to participatory fatigue: The problem with the public. *Social Media and Society*. https://doi.org/10.1177/2056305119856684

Reinardy, S. (2011). Newspaper journalism in crisis: Burnout on the rise, eroding young journalists' career commitment. *Journalism*, 12(1), 33–50.

Rom, S., & Reich, Z. (2020). Between the technological hare and the journalistic tortoise: Minimization of knowledge claims in online news flashes. *Journalism*, 21(1), 54–72.

Rosales-Ricardo, Y., & Ferreira, J. P. (2022). Effects of physical exercise on burnout syndrome in university students. *MEDICC Review*, 24(1), 36–39.

Sano, A., Johns, P., & Czerwinski, M. (2015). HealthAware: An advice system for stress, sleep, diet and exercise. *International Conference on Affective Computing and Intelligent Interaction,* 546–552.

Sheller, M. (2015). News Now: Interface, ambience, flow, and the disruptive spatio-temporalities of mobile news media. *Journalism Studies, 16*(1), 12–26.

Snyder, I., Johnson, K., & Kozimor-King, M. L. (2021). Work–life balance in media newsrooms. *Journalism, 22*(8), 2001–2018.

Stupart, R. (2022). Anger and the investigative journalist. *Journalism,* 1–18. https://doi.org/10.1177/14648849221125980

Ternes, B., Peterlin, L. J., & Reinardy, S. (2018). Newsroom Workers' job satisfaction contingent on position and adaptation to digital disruption. *Journalism Practice, 12*(4), 497–508.

Usher, N. (2015). The late great International Herald Tribune and the New York Times: Global media, space, time, print, and online coordination in a 24/7 networked world. *Journalism, 16*(1), 119–133.

Usher, N. (2018). Breaking news production processes in US metropolitan newspapers: Immediacy and journalistic authority. *Journalism, 19*(1), 21–36.

Valcour, M. (2016, November). Beating burnout. *Harvard Business Review,* 98–101.

Wenger, D. H., Owens, L. C., & Cain, J. (2018). Help wanted: Realigning journalism education to meet the needs of top U.S. news companies. *Journalism and Mass Communication Educator, 73*(1), 18–36.

Xu, N., & Gutsche, R. E. (2021). "Going offline": Social media, source verification, and Chinese investigative journalism during "information overload." *Journalism Practice, 15*(8), 1146–1162.

CHAPTER 9

The Joy of Journalism

My last full-time job in journalism was with a national broadcaster where I worked as a news anchor and editor. It was full on. It was hectic. It was 24/7. Days off were few and far between. And yet, it was one of the happiest work experiences I've had. I was happy then, and I remember that period now with much fondness. It was a great team of lovely people I worked with. I was covering what I loved most—sports. Every day I was meeting new and fascinating people, and I would get excited by the passion they had for what they do. And by the time I've managed to control the anxiety of going on air, the work in front of the camera became enjoyable too. There was a sense of personal satisfaction after a broadcast well done.

This chapter, rather than offering a conclusion, adds a final layer to the discussion of emotions in journalists' work. It is based on British journalists' answers to the question: 'What makes you happy in journalism?' Because, while it was established in the book that journalism is an emotional job and a profession with high levels of emotional labour, in which some journalists may be negotiating and managing challenging emotions on a daily basis, it also seems to be seen as a fulfilling and satisfying job by those working in it. There are plentiful studies of job satisfaction in journalism, primarily from the US, but in recent years also much wider, with case studies of journalistic cultures in Asia and Africa getting much scholarly attention (for a systematic review of these studies

© The Author(s), under exclusive license to Springer Nature   207
Switzerland AG 2023
M. Šimunjak, *Managing Emotions in Journalism*,
https://doi.org/10.1007/978-3-031-38631-2_9

by mid-2010s see Thomas & Nelliyullathil, 2015). These studies regularly emphasise the importance of working conditions (workload, pay, job security, etc.) and organisational and social support for journalists' job satisfaction (Kwode et al., 2019; Liu & Lo, 2018; Reinardy, 2013; Song & Jung, 2022; Viererbl & Koch, 2021). And while issues related to work conditions and support motivate a (significant) section of journalists to consider changing professions (Rick, 2023), there is still much joy to be found in doing journalism and being a journalist (Gottfried et al., 2022; Hughes et al., 2021; Perreault, 2023). Because, while journalism is a challenging profession that, among other things, requires effective emotion management to enhance and sustain much needed resilience, it is also one that has much to offer in terms of personal fulfilment.

What follows are testimonials of journalists who report feeling proud of their work which makes a real difference in the world; satisfied when they feel they've helped people make choices about their lives; excited by learning new things and uncovering untold stories; content in producing a copy that offers an impartial narrative which audiences can use to make up their own minds on important issues; pleasure when their stories do well and so on. These are grouped under three themes that signpost key origins of happiness in journalism according to interviewed British journalists: everyday work, fulfilment of journalistic roles and a sense of personal accomplishment.

THE JOB

Various positive emotions arising from different aspects of journalists' everyday work have been mentioned throughout this book, such as the excitement of finding or being tasked with covering a good story, the thrill of the chase in putting the story together, joy at landing a good interviewee or finding an important piece of information in research, the elation of going live and so on. And while these are important on a granular level, when British journalists spoke of the things about being journalists that make them happy, they regularly spoke of the nature of the job itself. Interestingly, some of the key elements of the job mentioned in this context, such as it being varied, dynamic and people-focused, are also among key motivations that journalism trainees in the UK (Jackson et al., 2020), as well as in the US (Coleman et al., 2018), have for pursuing this career. It seems, then, that the job delivers on these expectations which contributes to a sense of happiness about being a journalist.

In the first place, journalists love that their jobs grant them **access to people and places** they wouldn't ordinarily have the opportunity to engage with. Journalists' 'right' to approach people and ask questions brings much joy to those in this profession and is often mentioned as a 'privilege,' particularly by those relatively new to the job. In their own words:

Early career print journalist:

> You know, speaking to people... [...] Being able to call up someone at random, and just be like, 'Hey, tell me about your life.' (laughs) Be curious and sort of put their story out in the world. Like, I love that part of my job.

Early career digital journalist:

> Being able to talk to really interesting people about the most interesting stuff that's going on, is... It feels like a privilege, I think, to have the access to just be able to ring up an interesting person and say, 'Can you tell me about this interesting thing you do,' is really exciting and yeah, feels like a privilege in many ways.

Early career digital reporter:

> I feel very privileged to be able to hear people's stories, particularly people who have not ever been able to tell their stories before. And feeling like you're sort of that person that has to put that story out there and communicate it in the right way and tell people about it. I think that's what I always get most excited about being a journalist. I feel like I am very lucky to be able to hear so many people's stories and I hope I will continue to do so.

Early career print journalist:

> The social, human interaction side of journalism I just think is really nice. Being able to talk to people when they've achieved really big things or if they're sort of at the lowest ebb, you can, kind of, talk them through it and try and do what you can to help them. Yeah, because I do see journalism as a privilege; that you can talk to people in their biggest moments, and also at the, sort of, most desperate. You can help them when, you know, things are hard, and also celebrate when things are great.

Also, the opportunity to be in spaces where something interesting and/or important is happening, and have access to people with perceived influence, is also mentioned as exciting and rewarding. For example, many journalists covering Queen Elizabeth's death and/or King Charles' coronation took to social media to share the feeling of 'privilege' to bear witness to these historical events. One of my former students, a BBC producer at the time of King Charles III's coronation, Ella Cotton, shared on LinkedIn following the event: 'Growing up and watching the news, I used to dream of being at the scene of the big stories. To be part of the BBC Radio London team covering the historic #Coronation is a huge dream come true.' Similarly, a senior print correspondent describes it like this:

> I have a slightly shallow enjoyment of the kind of, you know, more super-ficially glamorous parts of the job. So, you know, for example, on occasion you have to go on trips with senior politicians, when you're on the same plane as them and stuff like that. And, to an extent mixing with them. And it's that whole thing that anyone has of this proximity to power, and I guess, you know, glamour in one sense of the word, that's really exciting.

Secondly, the nature of the job enables and indeed requires, journalists to **constantly learn new things**, contributing to their job satisfaction. The fact that those with substantial number of years on the job mentioned this suggests that the novelty of stories and knowledge does not wear off and that it helps keep the job seem fresh and persistently interesting, as these accounts illustrate:

Mid-career broadcast editor:

> Learning about different things... I think I'm like a lot of journalists, I'm probably a bit of a chameleon... Yeah, you're, kind of, constantly learning about something new, and fitting into a new situation, and you become an expert in like half an hour, so you can talk with great conviction on the [main] news. (laughs) But um yeah, I personally enjoy that... You know, I like learning about something, trying to understand it and explaining it to other people. I really enjoy that.

Mid-career print reporter:

> I do enjoy just the day to day variety of journalism. That's the thing I always say to kind of people who are interested in it... [...] I would say

just the variety is... And because of the variety you're learning new stuff and that, you know, keeps you interested really.

The joy of learning new things can be seen to go hand in hand with another happiness-inducing aspect of the job—its **diversity and variety**. For many journalists no two days in the week are the same, and the unpredictability of what might happen and will need covering brings excitement and thrill to the job. A mid-career print editor reflects on this aspect in this way:

> I have relished the experience. I've loved every minute of it. Well, that's not quite true... Not every minute. But I've, as a whole, I'm very pleased at my career choice. And, you know, every morning coming into office, I think, 'What could happen today?' And there, you know... There are days, especially recently, where you wouldn't have thought that that thing would have... You couldn't have possibly even predicted that that thing was going to happen. So, to have the ability to take that information and... um Get it out there to as wide an audience as possible, has always given me great pleasure. And I find it even now, when I'm so long in the tooth... Find it terribly exciting. So, yeah, I get a real buzz from it.

Some journalists go into this job because they have a passion for a particular specialism or topic, such as sports, fashion, travel, politics and many others. They speak of how gratifying it is to do a job in which you are **engaged with topics that are of personal interest**. The following accounts illustrate the happiness that comes from doing such a job:

Early career digital journalist:

> Sometimes I feel like I'm not really working because the things I'm doing just interest me and it's nice to read about them and then write about them.

Senior print editor:

> I find incredibly satisfying what I do. I think I feel lucky every day that I have managed to pursue a career path that I, you know, that I always wanted to. And, you know, I sort of feel very blessed that I can, you know, write about subjects that I think are both interesting and important.

THE ROLE

The second key aspect that brings joy to journalists in their work is when they perceive that they are reporting in line with the journalistic role they value and strive to perform. Research of journalistic cultures across the world (including 67 countries) revealed that most highly valued journalistic role is *monitorial* which refers to the 'watchdog' function of journalism—primarily holding powerful to account and providing citizens with information they need to be able to make informed decisions about their lives (Hanitzsch et al., 2019). The monitorial role is key to journalists' identity in developed democracies across the world, including the UK. Also, this 'social purpose' of the job has been found as one of the key motivations for pursuing a career in journalism in the UK (Jackson et al., 2020). It then, perhaps, does not come as a surprise that fulfilling this role, that is, reporting information that is perceived as important to citizens and **revealing misuse of power**, brings much joy to journalists, as these two senior print editors explain:

Senior print editor:

Just to feel that you're not, that you are... That you have not allowed, say, in my world politicians, to get away with something, is immensely satisfying and that's what we should be doing all the time and that's what a lot of people who go into journalism don't really realise that that's what it's actually about.

Senior print editor:

I think I've got the most interesting job in the world. Every day is different and I love the fact that you can be a witness on history. And that you have the capacity to, you know... I think it's so important to be able to hold governments to account and it feels like such a privilege that I can do that. I think it's... Yeah, it's interesting... I find it often exciting, I feel a real sense of responsibility. And I think that journalism is absolutely one of the fundamental tenets of democracy, and I feel very strongly that that needs to be preserved.

The informational function of the monitorial role, based on the understanding of journalists as information disseminators whose job is to **keep audiences informed about issues that affect their lives** (Hanitzsch & Örnebring, 2019), seems to resonate strongly with interviewed British journalists as well, as was found in the US too (Perreault, 2023). Indeed, many of them, of all levels of experience in the industry, speak of the happiness that follows when they feel they realised this aspect of their role, as the following accounts illustrate:

Early career digital reporter:

> I think it's a combination of knowing you're doing something meaningful because you're communicating information to people that they may not otherwise have known, or may give them a reason to think about something differently.

Senior broadcast editor:

> I feel huge satisfaction when I am able to take the complexities of the world, and without compromising on that complexity, I'm able to provide people with a sort of roadmap that they can use to sort of navigate the world around them and help their understanding, change the.... Or add to the public conversation, in a way that makes it of a higher quality, a more informed conversation. If I can do that, I feel huge satisfaction.

Mid-career digital editor:

> I think it's probably pride, and it sounds probably quite cheesy, but I think... We do what we do, and we do it really well, under growing pressure, less resources, and, you know, we have a... I firmly believe we have a job to do in democracy, and that is getting information out to people, and I think doing that is something still to be really proud of.

Finally, while research found that British journalists find *accommodative* role, which depicts journalists as providers of entertainment, relaxation and, in general, stories that interest largest audiences, more important than *interventionist* role, which includes setting agendas and advocating for social change (Hanitzsch et al., 2019), it appears that performing the latter brings more happiness in work. Specifically, interviewed British journalists spoke of the joy they feel when they perceive their **reporting has an impact**, whether that is raising an underreported issue on the agenda, contributing to changes of policy or helping any one person lead a better life. In their own words:

Early career digital journalist:

You know, the most important thing that I find most satisfying is either doing a big story or reporting on a topic that I think is really important and underreported. So, I do a lot of environment and politics stuff, and there are aspects within that I think are underreported and I think... You know, I can play a small role in increasing awareness about certain aspects of those topics.

Mid-career broadcast editor:

What makes me happy in journalism is... Is when you've really helped somebody tell their story, and in doing so you've helped alter policy in a way that potentially improves life a little bit for some people.

Mid-career print editor:

You know, I've worked on national newspapers and regional... We actually get to... Believe it or not, we actually get to do more of that impactful stuff to our community on regionals than you do on national newspapers. And you see the impact of things, you know? You see local decision makers changing their mind on something because of something you've dug out or something you've fought for. There is a sense of civic pride that goes along with that, as well. And that's, you know, that's... That can be a very emotional thing as well; when you see something... You've made a difference in your community, even in a small way.

THE SUCCESS

In the last place, but maybe no less important for some, is the happiness derived from the personal satisfaction and public recognition for doing a good job. **Personal satisfaction** that follows the evaluation that a job has been done well is hardly unique to journalism. Yet, it can be seen as an important motivation both for those who are producing daily journalism, and hence, may feel that they need to prove themselves each day, as well as journalists working on longer-term projects who may feel the pressure to justify the time and effort that have gone into the production of a story. A senior broadcast editor describes the sense of personal satisfaction induced by a successful piece of work like this:

I get excited and gratified by presenting a program or doing a good live interview. I mean, that's the kind of... Live political interviews are a sport, really. And if you feel you have performed well on any particular occasion, you can go home both proud of yourself, and, you know, quite jazzed up really. It's an adrenaline fuelled, exciting environment. And so, when it goes well, that can be great, but there is jeopardy in it can go badly and that can leave you feeling terrible. But yeah, those are the rules you choose to engage with.

The value of **public recognition** isn't surprising as, on the one hand, the importance of social prestige of journalism work has been found as one of the important motivations for pursuing a career in journalism among journalism students in the UK (Jackson et al., 2020) and the US (Carpenter et al., 2018; Coleman et al., 2018). On the other hand, given the publicness of journalists' work, both their successes and failures are public, and it is reasonable to expect that the public recognition of their work would bring them joy. This may particularly be the case in highly competitive media markets and those in which there is much attention paid to metrics by newsroom bosses in evaluating journalists' performance (see, e.g., Ferrucci, 2020; Usher, 2013). In the words of British journalists:
Mid-career print reporter:

I think when I, you know... When I've done a story I'm proud of, that's got sort of good reception and I feel it's an important issue... That makes me happy.

Early career broadcast journalist:

Just putting something out there that you have, kind of, made, and seeing it, kind of, do well, and is shared... Like, even if it was like, say, just a little piece on how you can work abroad... Then just seeing that kind of being referenced and doing well and just like... There's a buzz to that.

It would appear that the old journalism ideals of 'being the first' and 'bringing exclusives' are also very important and can induce happiness to those who feel they've delivered on them. Breaking big stories, seeing them being picked up by colleagues in other outlets and setting agendas is a particularly rewarding aspect of public recognition that has been mentioned by several British journalists, as these accounts illustrate:

Early career print correspondent:

> I think I'm very driven by sort of success and making, you know… So, what makes me happy is getting exclusive, original stories that are impactful and well-read and picked up by other journalists and news organisations.

Senior print editor:

> Well, to be ahead of others on a story is very, very rewarding. And to see other people following up what you've done, where you've led the way… It's very satisfying.

Finally, despite the rise of digital media and its importance in media systems and audiences' media consumption habits, it appears that appearing on television still carries significant value and a sense of accomplishment and joy to those who feel they've performed well in this context. This is in line with the finding that among journalism trainees in the US, those who value the social prestige of the job most are usually those interested in broadcast (Carpenter et al., 2018). Yet, it appears that this is an important aspect of personal satisfaction and public recognition even for those who do not normally work in broadcast. A mid-career digital editor explains the happiness induced by invited media appearances on television programmes:

> Me and a friend were recently saying that the times we often felt best is… Sometimes when we do broadcast or do TV and, you know, people ask us our opinions and we feel like we gave a good account of what's going on politically and… We felt that doing that on broadcast, which is actually not our job, it's just something that we get asked to do sometimes, actually gave us like a lot of self-worth and we felt really good about that.

In sum, the dynamic and people-focused aspects of the job, its importance in the society and social prestige, are among the key features of working in journalism that bring its professionals a sense of happiness and gratification. Rather than summarising these, I'll leave you with a senior broadcast editor's wise yet succinct reflection on the job:

> There's an immediacy about it, be that criticism or praise; be that a success or a failure; it interacts with you all the time, every day. So, it takes you on quite an emotional journey between, you know… You can have a day

where someone else gets a scoop and you feel wretched, and then you land a great interview, and you feel great and then, you know, and then something astonishing happens and you just feel mesmerised. So, it just... It takes you through all these emotions. It makes you feel very alive.

REFERENCES

Carpenter, S., Hoag, A., & Grant, A. E. (2018). An examination of print and broadcast journalism students' personality traits. *Journalism and Mass Communication Educator, 73*(2), 147–166.

Coleman, R., Lee, J. Y., Yaschur, C., Meader, A. P., & McElroy, K. (2018). Why be a journalist? US students' motivations and role conceptions in the new age of journalism. *Journalism, 19*(6), 800–819.

Ferrucci, P. (2020). It is in the numbers: How market orientation impacts journalists' use of news metrics. *Journalism, 21*(2), 244–261.

Gottfried, J., Mitchell, A., Jurkowitz, M., & Liedke, J. (2022). *Journalists sense turmoil in their industry amid continued passion for their work.*

Hanitzsch, T., Hanusch, F., Ramaprasad, J., & De Beer, A. S. (Eds.). (2019). *Worlds of journalism: Journalistic cultures around the globe.* Columbia University Press.

Hanitzsch, T., & Örnebring, H. (2019). Professionalism, professional identity, and journalistic roles. In K. Wahl-Jorgensen & T. Hanitzsch (Eds.), *The handbook of journalism studies* (pp. 105–122). Taylor & Francis Group.

Hughes, S., Iesue, L., de Ortega Bárcenas, H. F., Sandoval, J. C., & Lozano, J. C. (2021). Coping with occupational stress in journalism: professional identities and advocacy as resources. *Journalism Studies, 22*(8), 971–991.

Jackson, D., Thorsen, E., & Reardon, S. (2020). Fantasy, pragmatism and journalistic socialisation: UK journalism students' aspirations and motivations. *Journalism Practice, 14*(1), 104–124.

Kwode, P. A. K., Adam, B. Y., & Benjamin, A. (2019). Journalists, job satisfaction and performance: The perspectives of journalists in tamale metropolis of Ghana. *International Journal or Research and Scientific Innovation, 6*(12), 54–61.

Liu, H. L., & Lo, V. H. (2018). An integrated model of workload, autonomy, burnout, job satisfaction, and turnover intention among Taiwanese reporters. *Asian Journal of Communication, 28*(2), 153–169.

Perreault, G. (2023). Finding joy as journalists motivations for newswork. In V. Bélair-Gagnon, A. E. Holton, M. Deuze, & C. Mellado (Eds.), *Happiness in journalism.* Routledge.

Reinardy, S. (2013). Depleted resources causing burnout for layoff survivors. *Newspaper Research Journal, 34*(3), 6–21.

Rick, J. (2023). Journalists considering an exit. In V. Bélair-Gagnon, A. E. Holton, M. Deuze, & C. Mellado (Eds.), *Happiness in journalism*. Routledge.

Song, H., & Jung, J. (2022). Factors affecting turnover and turnaway intention of journalists in South Korea. *Journalism and Mass Communication Quarterly, 99*(4), 1072–1098.

Thomas, M., & Nelliyullathil, M. (2015). Journalists' job sasfacon: A systemac review of theories, determinants and measurements. *Communication & Journalism Research, 4*(1–2), 25–40.

Usher, N. (2013). Al Jazeera English online: Understanding web metrics and news production when a quantified audience is not a commodified audience. *Digital Journalism, 1*(3), 335–351.

Viererbl, B., & Koch, T. (2021). Once a journalist, not always a journalist? Causes and consequences of job changes from journalism to public relations. *Journalism, 22*(8), 1947–1963.

INDEX

© The Editor(s) (if applicable) and The Author(s), under exclusive licence to Springer Nature Switzerland AG 2023
M. Šimunjak, *Managing Emotions in Journalism*,
https://doi.org/10.1007/978-3-031-38631-2

The manufacturer's authorised representative in the EU is Springer
Nature Customer Service Centre GmbH, Europaplatz 3, 69115 Heidelberg,
Germany. If you have any concerns regarding our products, please
contact ProductSafety@springernature.com

Printed and bound by CPI Group (UK) Ltd, Croydon, CR0 4YY

24/04/2026
02096315-0003